Mastering the Merger

Mastering the Merger

FOUR CRITICAL DECISIONS THAT MAKE OR BREAK THE DEAL

David Harding
Sam Rovit

with Katie Smith Milway and Catherine Lemire
Bain & Company, Inc.

HARVARD BUSINESS SCHOOL PRESS
Boston, Massachusetts

Printed in the United States of America

08 07 06 05 04 5 4 3 2 1

Library of Congress Cataloging-in-Publication Data

Harding, David, 1958–

Mastering the merger : four critical decisions that make or break the deal / David Harding and Sam Rovit with Katie Smith Milway & Catherine Lemire.

p. cm.

Includes bibliographical references and index.

ISBN 1-59139-438-4

1. Consolidation and merger of corporations. I. Rovit, Sam. II. Title.

HG4028.M4H37 2004

658.1'62—dc22

2004002472

The paper used in this publication meets the minimum requirements of the American National Standard for Information Sciences—Permanence of Paper for Printed Library Materials, ANSI Z39.48-1992.

To my wife, Jan, whose penetrating insights on people, personalities, and relationships have helped me understand the nuances of merger mastery; and to Bryan and Christopher, my sons, whose endless spirit and enthusiasm keep me facile enough to tackle projects like this book.

—DRH

This book is dedicated to my wife, Abigail, and to my children, Nathaniel, Emma, and Eli, with love and appreciation for their understanding that I am tied to "the call of the deal," even though it usually comes on Fridays.

—SR

Contents

Introduction

Mastering the Merger is about making four key decisions in the complex, fast-moving, and sometimes highly rewarding arena of corporate deal making.

By *deal making,* we mean to refer to the whole spectrum of activities that result in a business combination of one kind or another. Let's acknowledge early on that there are all kinds of deals. The terms *merger, acquisition,* and *transaction* all refer to business combinations, and all have different meanings to the accountant, the lawyer, the investment banker, and other specialized professionals. But we are writing for a particular audience—the practitioners who actually make these combinations happen, or will do so in the future—and we think the phrase *business combinations* is just too dry an umbrella.

In this book, we strive to write about mergers, acquisitions, transactions, and deals in ways that are useful and interesting to executives. We will use these terms more or less interchangeably to refer to the acquisition—by cash or stock or some combination thereof—of one business by another, resulting in a business combination, and assume that you will fine-tune our definitions as necessary.

WHAT YOU CAN EXPECT FROM THIS BOOK

Mastering the Merger is structured around the numerous decisions that an executive faces as he or she originates and completes a deal. This path is usually difficult, characterized by unforeseen twists and turns, and in many cases is overgrown with managerial thickets. Staying at a level of generality, hopefully without oversimplifying, we intend to cut a swath through all this complexity by focusing on the four decisions that matter most. You can think of them as the how, which, where, and what of deal making. Make these choices carefully and well, and the odds of deal success move in your favor. Fail to do so, and chances increase that the scene will turn ugly.

Collectively, these decisions span the life cycle of a typical deal. They involve the following key questions:

1. How should you pick your deal targets? Will they advance your core business?

2. Which deals should you close? Have you assessed deal candidates by asking and answering the big questions? That is, why will this deal make your enterprise more valuable?

3. Where do you really need to integrate? Is your integration plan consistent with your deal's investment thesis and the challenges of ownership?

4. What should you do when the deal goes off track? How will you cope with the inevitable problems that arise when things don't work as planned?

Chapter 1 provides an overview of the deal-making process and introduces these four decisions. Each of the next four chapters then digs down into one of these four decisions, explaining and prescribing. In each case, we bring empirical research to bear on the tasks and decisions at hand and cite relevant case histories to reinforce our points.

In chapter 6, we discuss the practice-makes-perfect aspect of merger mastery. It turns out that experience is the best teacher for disciplining deal decisions, and yet many companies are only episodic deal makers. This means that their corporate deal teams are necessarily inexperienced. To be good at deal making, companies need to do a lot of deals—preferably smaller ones—to build a sustainable expertise in business combinations. As with many complex activities, there is a learning curve in mastering mergers, and each deal provides useful lessons that can make the next transaction better.

Emphatically, this is not a technical book. In the following pages, you will not learn the latest valuation techniques or be given a step-by-step checklist for conducting postmerger integration. There are lots of references that already serve these ground-level purposes, and serve them well. (We will steer you toward the best of these resources as we go along.) The reason is simple: We believe that a focus on technical razzle-dazzle or inch-by-inch integration techniques can actually distract a deal maker from focusing on the key decisions, and then making those decisions correctly. This book helps you to keep your eye on the forest; other books can help you tend to individual trees.

So this book is written for decision makers in corporations, especially those who have not had a lot of experience with all aspects of the deal cycle, but may quickly need to gain it. We focus on the entire deal cycle, beginning with the juncture where the logic of the corporate strategy seems to call for a deal all the way through to the integration of the acquired business.

WHY IS IT SO TOUGH?

Most senior executives we have met and worked with over the years think they are pretty good decision makers. After all, they reached the higher rungs on the corporate ladder because they had a strong track record: a history of making and executing sound decisions. But when it comes to making decisions about deals, it turns out, standards sometimes change. For many executives, deal making proves to be something pretty different from the day-to-day running of the business. Deal making can quickly take an executive out of his or her comfort zone. Merger mechanics can, and usually do, require a new kind of mastery.

Think for a moment about the myriad factors in the deal environment that are different from business-as-usual activities. First, of course, there is the intensive involvement of all those outsiders (bankers, lawyers, consultants), many of whom are strangers to the organization. Deal making is greatly complicated by the fact that all these outside players are working on their own agendas. As recent media coverage has amply demonstrated, the investment bankers often have incentives to get the deal done, even when it becomes clear that the deal should be scuttled. But they're not alone in pursuing their own agendas. Lawyers and accountants worry (and should worry!) about meeting external standards and avoiding liability. Plus, they are generally paid to complete deals, not to derail them. Advisors, as a rule, are self-interested agents.

Meanwhile, figuring out what you are really buying often proves more difficult than expected. Perhaps due diligence takes place in a constrained time frame. Maybe the target company has buffed itself up for the sale in ways that require extra effort to decode and discount. If so, senior executives stop doing their real jobs, and start throwing all their effort into managing this critical part of the deal.

Meanwhile, employees worry about losing their jobs, or at the very least, having to deal with new reporting relationships. Executives expend a lot of time and energy explaining the proposed deal internally—or, conversely, incur considerable stress by keeping secrets from constituencies in which they normally confide. All too often, mutual trust is the first casualty.

Once a deal closes, the real work begins, especially when companies discover that their planning for ownership is behind schedule and behind plan. The company's balance sheet and risk profile shift. In many cases, communications come up short, requiring executives to leave their posts and explain the deal yet again. Operational snafus can infuriate new and old customers alike. When results don't materialize, stakeholders, shareholders, analysts, and ratings agencies complain loudly. (Some even go to court.) The challenge of post-merger integration suddenly seems more daunting than expected. Belatedly, the architects of the merger recognize that integration planning should have started far earlier and been far more comprehensive in scope.

A tough picture? Admittedly, we've loaded it up on the negative side of the ledger.

But we're not alone in arguing that more attention needs to be paid to mastering the merger. According to a growing and credible body of research, only about three out of ten large-scale corporate mergers actually create value. As we'll see in subsequent chapters, many complexities and nuances are concealed in this single alarming statistic. But if more than seven out of ten big deals are going bad—

despite all the time, energy, and money that have been poured into them—then something must be wrong. This statistic suggests that a lot of bad decision making is taking place. There must be considerable nonmastery at work.

We wrote this book because we have been to the ultimate merger school—in the middle of the deals themselves—and have learned some useful things about the art of making executive decisions in the deal environment. We have had the privilege of working hand in hand with literally hundreds of executives as they have grappled with the merger process. We have witnessed firsthand how difficult deal-related decisions can be. Many of our clients have made and executed great decisions. (Some, unfortunately, have not.) By sharing our insights, we hope to help the next generation of corporate executives—future stars, waiting in the wings—to avoid pitfalls, and become masters of the merger.

We believe that there are important lessons to be learned from the case histories of executives who have been out there on the front lines, under fire, making deal decisions. So we have included a large number of such stories in this book, accompanied by our own interpretations. Some of the subjects of these case histories have made headlines, good and bad; others have labored in relative obscurity. As much as possible, we tell the tales of real people and explore real professional triumphs and miseries.

Finally, we are well aware that others have gone before us, and that good merger-related ideas are already waiting to be taken up. We have surveyed much of the relevant literature, and in the following pages will encourage our readers to look to some of these other sources.

For example, Harvard Business School professor Joseph Bower's findings in "Not All M&As Are Alike—and That Matters" *(Harvard Business Review)* define a spectrum of deal rationales that we found useful as we tested the implications of a deal's investment thesis for integration planning. Bruce Wasserstein's book *Big Deal: The Battle for Control of America's Leading Corporations* provides a comprehensive overview of deal decisions, which we found helpful as we focused on our own small, but critical, subset. Mark Sirower hits the nail on the head in *The Synergy Trap* when he describes the long odds against merger success, especially against realizing the elusive synergies of mergers:

> Investors around the world have already valued the future expected performance of the target firm. So synergy must translate into gains beyond those already expected. Simply put, achieving synergy means competing better. But in current, hyper-competitive markets, it is a difficult challenge just to achieve expected performance that is already built into existing share prices—at a zero premium.[1]

We have consulted and borrowed ideas from many other sources. We have tried hard to ascribe all the ideas we have found elsewhere to their original authors—including the very bright people at the firms against whom our own company traditionally competes. We apologize in advance if we have overlooked any such contributors.

REAL-LIFE AND STATISTICAL UNDERPINNINGS

This book's authors and contributors are partners of Bain & Company, Inc., a global consulting firm that helps many of the world's great companies develop corporate strategy. Collectively, we have been involved in thousands of deal discussions and analyses, across the full range of industries. Because of our firm's strategic orientation, we are often involved in deals at the very earliest stages, when executives are asking the kinds of strategic questions raised earlier: Why? What kind? Is there an alternative? It's an act of creation that few outsiders get to witness, let alone participate in.

While our experience serves as a strong guide, we have supplemented it with systematic analysis of the relevant data. For example, we began with a database of the largest public companies in the United States, the United Kingdom, France, Germany, Italy, and Japan—seventeen hundred companies in all—and examined the last fifteen years' worth of data. We asked the obvious questions: Is there a defining set of characteristics that distinguish companies that make good deals from those that do poor deals? If so, what are they?

A number of insights emerged from this analysis. One is that companies that do a lot of deals outperform those that do few. Despite the rush to merger mania in irrationally exuberant times, the best performers continue to make deals throughout all market conditions, boom and bust. And, despite the hype around megadeals, the average size of deal for the best acquirers is small. Already, you can begin to see the limits on the conventional wisdom that "only three in ten deals are successful."

We supplemented our research with in-depth interviews of executives that we thought we could learn from, both as best examples, and—phrasing it gently—as testimonies to future learning. These managers were very generous with their time and contributed to many of the case examples we discuss in the text. We appreciate their help, candor, and willingness to be teachers to the next generation of executives.

We also spent a great deal of time with the private equity community. Why? Because this is a group of highly skilled people who buy and sell businesses for a living, and because we have always been impressed by the ability of top-tier private equity players to earn outsized returns in an efficient capital market. By all rights, a strategic buyer of an asset should always be willing to pay more for an asset, and reap a greater benefit from that asset, than a stand-alone financial buyer. But that simply doesn't happen. So how do the private equity firms do it? Among other things, we learned that top-tier private equity buyers are extremely well disciplined at imperatives one and two: picking their targets and deciding which deals merit closing by asking the big questions about a target's potential.

To supplement these two kinds of qualitative, in-depth interviews, we also surveyed corporate managers more generally. We conducted a survey of more than two hundred fifty executives active in deal making around the globe, asking them which decisions their companies got right, and which ones they got wrong and why, as they navigated the deal-making experience.[2]

We also conducted several niche studies aimed at exploring particular deal-decision rules. There are many such rules out there, and we think that these rules—which short-circuit a more rigorous analysis—often lead executives astray. For example, many managers state as a matter of policy that they will not do deals that dilute earnings per share. Making this pronouncement has an obvious appeal. Shareholders and analysts tend to applaud the forceful articulation of this position. But it turns out that this particular decision rule may cause companies to avoid deals they should do.

Similarly, companies have become sensitive to the cultural aspects of merger integration. Yet our niche research around cultural integration shows empirically that cultural differences matter more in some types of mergers than others.

And finally, circling back to where we started, we weighed all of this statistical analysis against our own experience—in developing corporate strategy, screening deals, conducting due diligence on thousands of targets, and then helping to integrate mergers. Did the conclusions suggested by the data square with reality?

In short, they did. And based on these multiple inputs and analyses, we are convinced that there is a right way and a wrong way to go about managing the deal-making process. It is possible to master the merger by responding effectively to the four critical questions. Unfortunately, the only alternative is to be mastered by the merger.

So let's begin our journey.

1

Four Critical Decisions That Make or Break the Deal

Ultimately, the success or failure of a merger grows out of the decisions made by executives at critical junctures throughout the transaction. The better these people are at handling the four imperatives of a business combination, the more successful that merger is likely to be.

Note our emphasis on people. Mergers (like all other key business transactions) reflect the decisions of fallible human beings. Accordingly, we have chosen to start each chapter with the story of a deal maker and the decisions he faced. We will use this example to lead into a broader discussion of our four imperatives or "critical decisions."

So let's start with our first case study. The company is Kellogg, and our main decision maker is the company's chief executive officer, Carlos Gutierrez.

BIG CALLS

The Kellogg board promoted Gutierrez, a lifetime company manager, to the top job in 1999. Both the board members and Gutierrez knew that he was stepping into a tough situation. During the stock market boom of the '90s, when many companies were growing like weeds, industry-leading Kellogg had disappointed shareholders for three straight years. The industry's number-three competitor, Post, was warring on price. The historic second fiddle, General Mills, was out-innovating Kellogg and gaining market share.

Consumers, meanwhile, no longer seemed to be buying the premise that breakfast was the most important meal of the day. And retailers—tired of Kellogg taking more of the profit pool in the cereal business than they did—thought this was a good time to emphasize new private-label offerings. In short, Kellogg was in trouble.

So Gutierrez set about revising the firm's strategy. As he studied the situation, his priorities became clear. Yes, there were specific things Kellogg had to do to get back into shape and regain its momentum in the marketplace. But Gutierrez's most important realization was this: Kellogg wasn't going to be able to solve its problems by itself. To accelerate profitable growth, Kellogg needed to do a deal. This was one of several big things—perhaps the biggest of those big things—that Kellogg had to get right. As Gutierrez told us, "We weren't going to fix the business by focusing on the small things and hoping the future would get better. So I knew when I took the job that it demanded some pretty big calls."[1]

Nevertheless, the decision to do a deal was not an easy one. Kellogg's recent history with deal making had been unhappy, marked by the troubled acquisition of Lender's Bagels. Furthermore, there were competing demands for resources within the company, including requests for more marketing money, more new-product development support, and additional sales resources. Finally, Gutierrez was well aware of the conventional wisdom about deals: that they often lead to shareholder value destruction, rather than value creation.

So the overarching question that Gutierrez asked himself was, simply put, What do we have to do to make the right deal, and to do it right? We believe that the answer lay in getting four critical decisions right: How should he pick his targets? Which deal should he close? Where did he really need to integrate? What should he do if and when the deal got off track?

In a few pages, we will return to assessing the decisions that Gutierrez actually made. But first, let's take a step back and ask, Why should executives do deals at all?

THE PARADOX OF DEAL MAKING

Success at deal making turns out to be no small feat. Dozens of studies have indicated that the odds of success for the classic, big-company acquisition of another big company are no more than about 30 percent. Yet most great companies today are the result of a deal-making past. (The vast majority of companies in the *Fortune* 500, for example, are the product of multiple deals.) So unless something fundamental has changed in the realm of deal making—and there's no evidence to suggest that's true—this indicates that at least some deals are very good indeed.

The essential paradox of deal making is this: Academic studies demonstrate that something on the order of 70 percent of all deals fail to create meaningful shareholder value, and yet empirical observation suggests that it is extremely hard to grow a world-class company through organic growth alone.[2] The conundrum is a classic damned-if-you-do, damned-if-you-don't setup: Mergers go bad more often than they don't—but mergers are indispensable. So how does the forward-looking executive reconcile the low probability of deal success with the need to build acquisitions into a company's growth strategy?

The answer is, be disciplined in your decision making and focus on the four imperatives outlined in this book. Why? Because our research indicates that deal success is not random. Rather, the very best deal makers employ very specific behaviors and tactics. Executives who embrace these behaviors and tactics improve their odds. They make better business decisions systematically, testing and learning as they go. As a result, they deepen their deal expertise and create a virtuous circle. Success breeds success.

Conversely, those executives who ignore our four imperatives decrease their odds of success. In the card game of blackjack, there are certain betting protocols that heighten a shrewd player's ability to win. The goal of the game, simply put, is to get a total card count that's closer to 21 than the dealer's, without breaking 21. Good betting strategy says that you never ask for another card when you are at a hard 18. (You "stand.") Let's suppose that you ignore this rule, ask for a card, and win. Does that mean you made a good decision?

No. It means that you were lucky, and beat the odds. But the longer you stay at the table, the more respectful you have to be of those odds. What we are documenting in this book are the decision strategies that will allow you to stay in the game, keep the odds in your favor, and win most of the time.

As we began this project, we studied the deal history of seventeen hundred large public companies in six industrialized nations (our Global Learning Curve Study), spanning the time period from 1986 to 2001.[3] What we found is that mastering mergers is an outgrowth of experience with mergers. The frequency with which a company does deals correlates strongly with how successful that company is in earning shareholder returns. Those companies that make deal making a core capability outperform those that do deals episodically. It's not like riding a bike, where once you learn you'll always know how to do it. Deal making is more like playing a musical instrument: The less you do it, the less likely you are to be good at it. Mastery rarely grows out of episodic involvement.

So one central focus of this book is to tease out those things that the most practiced deal makers do as a matter of course. For example, the most successful practitioners cut their teeth on small deals and graduate to larger deals, successively branching into areas related to their core business. They standardize their approach as they go. This was true of the 724 companies we studied in the United States, the 293 firms we evaluated in Europe, and the 676 companies we analyzed in Japan. (See appendix, figures A-4 and A-5.)

Conversely, our research strongly suggested that the worst performers tend to be those companies that engage in one-shot megadeals. These are precisely the kind of deals that attract lots of media attention. They also tend to be overrepresented in survey reports. Why? Because unlike the little deals that form the bulk of merger activity, these blockbuster deals are relatively easy to follow and to make extrapolations from. Is this a problem? In some cases, yes. If executives use the track record of the poorest deal makers to draw conclusions about the potential of deal making for enhancing shareholder value, they are making a serious mistake. Deal making done right offers an essential tool for prosperous growth. Deal making done right demands discipline around four critical decisions:

1. How should you pick your deal targets?
2. Which deals should you close?
3. Where do you really need to integrate?
4. What should you do when the deal goes off track?

HOW DO YOU KNOW WHEN A DEAL IS A SUCCESS?

We've been talking about transactions as being more or less successful. The time has come to look a little more closely at the meaning of that word. What constitutes "success"?

In 1999, the accounting firm KPMG International set out to measure the success rate of corporate mergers.[4] Looking at shareholder returns relative to the overall trend in the relevant industry segment one year after the deal was announced, they found that 83 percent of mergers failed to unlock value. (This one-year-return methodology is commonly used to judge deal success.) Next, KPMG sat with the managers of acquiring companies and asked them to grade their own acquisitions. Fully 82 percent of those interviewed were convinced that their acquisitions were successful!

Were those executives simply misinformed or inclined to see the world through rose-colored glasses? Not likely. Rather, they were probably using a different yardstick of success. And herein lies a problem: Depending on which yardstick is used—which methodology, time frame, and scope—the conclusions about whether a particular deal has created value can be all over the map.

There are only two objectively rational ways to quantify deal-making success—and both have flaws. You can assess individual "events" or you can compare the relative returns of companies with different levels of deal-making activity.

With big deals, it is possible to track the business and stock price performance of the acquirer after the event of the deal has been announced or closed. For example, we can compare an acquirer's shareholder return to that of its peers over a specified period of time—say, twelve months—following a deal's announcement. We call the difference between what the acquiring company returned and what everyone else returned *excess return*.

A commonly accepted benchmark of a successful merger is one that generates an excess return of 10 percent or more. You may or may not consider this to be a particularly high standard, but let's take it as a starting point. Seventy percent of all deals fail to meet even this modest target.

You can also argue that one year is both too long to wait to take a deal's pulse and too soon to judge its possible success. Yet it is interesting to note that the stock market is in fact a pretty quick study. Research by Mark Sirower, for example, suggests that the initial reaction of the stock market to a deal's announcement serves as an excellent predictor of share-price performance one and even five years out.[5]

However, event-study methodologies have one overriding limitation: They focus on a relatively narrow subset of all deals. They include only publicly traded acquirers and transactions that are easy to study: ones in which the transaction value is publicly disclosed, significant (typically more than $1 billion), and meaningful to the acquirer (typically at least 10 percent of the acquirer's market capitalization).

But a succession of small transactions can be just as significant as one large one. The reality is that almost 75 percent of all mergers in the United States from 1999 to 2003 had transaction values of $100 million or less—and this figure doesn't even include the deals for which the transaction value was not disclosed.[6] This latter group is more than 60 percent of all deals. So typical event studies, by their very nature, first exclude more than half of all transactions, and then exclude most of the rest. Not a comprehensive measure, by any standard!

For several reasons, we argue that the risks of big deals are greater than those of small deals.

Why? There are two main reasons. First, big deals are inherently harder to implement than small deals, and second, companies that resort to big deals are generally in tougher shape strategically than those doing small deals. As a result, studies that look only at big deals are unduly pessimistic.

The second major way to assess a company's acquisition track record is to quantify its ability to earn excess returns to capital. This means total shareholder return minus the acquirer's cost of equity (measured using the capital asset pricing model, or CAPM). This second methodology is the one we primarily rely upon in this book.

Relatively few inquiries have used this methodology, which obviously focuses on acquirers rather than deals. McKinsey & Company, notably, adopted this approach in its "Trading the Corporate Portfolio" study, which measured abnormal returns of two hundred companies between 1990 and 2000; the results were consistent with what we report in this book.[7] More recently, Marakon has used this methodology with similar results.[8]

Throughout this book, we will report on our findings regarding the ability of companies to generate large positive excess returns through a disciplined deal-making process. The overall results of this work are summarized in the appendix. But as we shall see in the coming chapters, the overall conclusion is a hopeful one: Companies that are active participants in the deal market outperform those that are not.

In sum, there is no perfect methodology. The next time someone quotes numbers to you on merger success rates, ask politely what standard he or she is using to measure success. More important, keep in mind that it's how you measure success that's most important. Maybe you will scrutinize your transaction using one of the two methodologies described above. Maybe you will use some other nonfinancial standard.

In the box The Standards of Success, we stress that you can't measure success without knowing the goal. We raise this point here not only to foreshadow an important prescription that grows out of our research—know why you're doing the deal—but also to help explain the seeming discrepancy in the KPMG study cited earlier: Four-fifths of all tracked mergers don't succeed, at least according to

THE STANDARDS OF SUCCESS

Joseph Bower, in a landmark *Harvard Business Review* article entitled "Not All M&As Are Alike—and That Matters,"* articulated five reasons why a company might want to do a deal:

1. As a tool to reduce industry capacity
2. As a tool to consolidate a fragmented industry
3. As a means of gaining product or market extensions
4. As a means of acquiring R&D
5. As a tool to build a new industry

This list could obviously be expanded. A company also could do a deal to facilitate an investor buyout or to enter a new business, or for purely financial motivations. Multiple factors could be at play in a single transaction. A company's ranking of these goals could, and most likely would, change over time. The point is, before you can assess a particular deal's "success," you have to identify the strategic goal it is intended to help advance.

*Joseph L. Bower, "Not All M&As Are Alike—and That Matters," *Harvard Business Review,* March 2001.

key financial measures, and yet four-fifths of all acquiring executives think that their own mergers have succeeded. These executives believe that the deal accomplished their objective—and in many cases, they're absolutely right.[9]

THE FOUR IMPERATIVES OF MERGER SUCCESS

Experience is the best teacher, and the most experienced practitioners tend to respond effectively to the imperatives. The following sections provide some illuminating examples of each of the four critical decisions.

How Should You Pick Your Targets?

Successful acquirers begin with what we call an *investment thesis,* which is no more or less than a statement of how a particular deal will create value for the merged company. The most compelling investment thesis is the one that explains why and how a new investment stands to improve the existing core business. As Prussian general and military strategist Karl von Clausewitz once asserted, "War is regarded as nothing but the continuation of state policy with other means." Likewise, deal making is an extension of a company's business policy, or strategy. Before a company can form a valid opinion of a potential deal, it needs to assess whether an acquisition will further its growth strategy. The decision to acquire must demonstrate that it will strengthen the firm's overall business portfolio.

Maybe this sounds straightforward, even elementary. If so, good for you; you're ahead of the game. When we surveyed two hundred fifty senior executives who had done major deals, almost half confessed that they did not have a strong (let alone bulletproof) investment thesis behind those transactions.

Making mergers work is inseparable from strategy. You need to have an investment thesis in order to make a strong acquisition. But before you can develop a strong investment thesis, you need to know how your company makes money today, and how it's likely to make money in the future. In short, your corporate strategy must begin to guide your acquisitions long before they fully take shape.

Which Deals Should You Close?

The most successful investors attend to the trees by taking care of the forest. Knowing whether to go through with a deal after conducting due diligence is an acquired skill requiring tremendous decision discipline. In mergers, as in many things in business, what's crucial is not how much you know; rather, it's knowing what you *don't* know.

Based on our experience, we believe that the best practitioners of due diligence are the professional buyers in private equity firms. Their approach to diligence is fundamentally different from the practices we observe in the corporate marketplace. The big difference? They do deals for a living. They take a critical outsider's view of a company and do not take for granted anything about its future prospects. Instead, they get the information they need first-hand to determine if the proposed acquisition can really deliver against the investment thesis. They have little use for the kinds of "check-the-box" diligence exercises that collect reams of data, but fail to tell the decision makers what they need to know in order to decide whether or not to consummate the deal. We will compare the typical corporate approach to diligence—which all too often involves sending in an army of analysts to gather and crunch every number within reach—with the laserlike approach taken by the private equity firms.

Bain Capital (not legally related to our employer Bain & Company) is a top-tier private equity firm that is generally acknowledged to be one of the best in the industry at due diligence. Bain Capital's "secret" is focus. As managing director John Connaughton told us:

> I think there is some value in having a focused team that is trying not only to see the detail, but also the integrated picture. Whenever we have competed against strategic buyers, we always chuckle when we hear that they have sent in fifty people to the data room and thirty-five people to the presentation, and they all try to go back to their offices and write memos and then try to reintegrate at some high level. It's probably more a distraction than it is a cohesive integration of the diligence side.[10]

Connaughton's experience is borne out by our research. In our survey of two hundred fifty executives involved in recent mergers, half of the respondents acknowledged that their due-diligence efforts had failed to uncover critical issues. And in our global study, the top-quartile performers that we interviewed reported that they focused single-mindedly on the big questions during due diligence. They codified their questions and they quantified their answers, establishing a walk-away price—a hard stop—based on a deal's actual value. In short, the best acquirers discipline the decision to close the deal by making sure that they ask big questions and get big answers, with the ultimate goal of enhancing shareholder value.

It's worth underscoring this point about value. Blair Effron, vice chairman of investment banking for UBS Warburg, has done $125 billion in deals over the course of his career. He says, flatly, that no deal is worth doing if it doesn't serve the acquiring company's stakeholders. "When companies focus solely on the strategy," he told us, "too often they lose [sight of] shareholder value."[11] Effective due diligence, driven by big questions, is the best possible inoculation against that loss of focus.

Where Do You Really Need to Integrate?

The best acquirers begin working on the challenges of integration as an adjunct of their diligence activities. Their experience teaches us two key lessons: Plan for ownership early, and focus on getting the few most important facets of integration absolutely right.

Tomes have been written on the cultural and systems challenges inherent in merger integration. Many of these books take a very holistic, work plan–centric view of this task. That approach is understandable—everyone wants to tackle problems in comprehensive ways—but it contains a major pitfall. The truth is, only a few integration activities really matter in determining the success of a deal. If taking a "holistic" approach makes you take your eye off those few key activities, it can be a recipe for trouble.

Mergers aimed at creating economies of scale require near-seamless integration—up, down, and sideways—to achieve savings and improve asset utilization. (In other words, the holistic approach has validity in such cases.) But mergers aimed at extending product, customer, or geographic scope require only selective integration around areas of business or operational overlap.

In other words, prioritize, and prioritize early. Making integration decisions according to a deal's thesis allows companies to focus and move quickly on the few things that matter. And—not unimportantly—it lets the rest of the company's talent stay focused on the base business.

What Should You Do When the Deal Goes Off Track?

Harrison Salisbury, the distinguished *New York Times* reporter and pundit, once was asked what he'd learned from history. "Expect the unexpected," he replied.

Salisbury's advice is also the mantra of best-in-class deal makers. The fact is, no deal goes off exactly as planned. (Few even come close.) Assumptions are proven wrong. People quit. Competitors take advantage of the situation. Customers get upset. What sets world-class acquirers apart from the pack is the way they prepare for and respond to contingencies. The final make-or-break discipline that we will discuss in this book consists of all the tough calls an executive needs to make when his or her master plan goes awry.

The challenge starts with distinguishing between the inevitable, day-to-day, postmerger problems that complicate almost every transaction and those that hint at big troubles down the road—perhaps even around the next bend. It's like discovering an oil spill on a property you've just purchased. Is this an isolated, localized problem? Or is the whole property contaminated? The two circumstances call for very different responses.

The inevitable everyday problems growing out of a merger, such as supply-chain jams or customer-service breakdowns, correspond to the localized spill. They must be treated aggressively. The discipline you'll need here is a commitment to early-warning systems. You'll want to test the strength of your investment thesis against the reality of day-to-day business and stay close to certain customer, supplier, employee, and financial data. Assuming the investment thesis holds, your warning data will tell you when to intervene quickly to address inevitable blips in things like service levels, costs, and employee retention during integration.

But what if the whole property is contaminated? One of the benefits of installing early-warning systems and proactively looking for areas that are underperforming your deal plan is that you develop an enhanced ability to distinguish between a situation that is slightly off track and one where the fundamental investment thesis should be questioned. The sooner you figure out that more fundamental problems are at play, the better chance you have of recovering your investment. To assess these more fundamental problems, you'll want to revisit the steps leading to the deal. If markets have shifted but your investment thesis still holds, then a skilled and concerted turnaround can succeed. If not, it's time to cut your losses.

With these principles in mind, let's go back to the story of Kellogg and Carlos Gutierrez.

THE RIGHT WAY TO GAIN WEIGHT: KELLOGG CONSUMES KEEBLER

In the food business, more than many other industries, acquisitions are an indispensable contributor to growth, and even survival. Every multinational food company with sales greater than $5 billion is the product of extensive acquisitions. Deal making is an essential element of strategy in the food industry: New products are essential to growth, and it's cheaper to buy than to develop a new sandwich spread or snack. At the turn of the millennium, there was a rash of acquisitions by the large food companies: Kraft bought Nabisco, Nestlé bought Ralston Purina, Sara Lee bought Earthgrains, General Mills bought Pillsbury, and Kellogg bought Keebler.

Although each of these transactions came with challenges, all look as if they are going to be successful in the long run. One of these deals—Kellogg–Keebler—worked particularly well, and it is helpful for our purposes to understand why.

We've already introduced some of the particulars of the Kellogg story. Over the course of a century, Michigan-based Kellogg emerged as one of the most successful brands ever. Its products were well regarded. For most of the later years of the twentieth century, the company was very profitable, with top-tier (17.5 percent) operating margins and a leading share of the ready-to-eat cereal category.[12] Despite its leading position, the company was still growing, and it enjoyed the enviable position of being able to raise prices just enough to generate the upside profit surprises that shareholders love.

Just to recap what we have learned: By the mid-1990s, Kellogg's once-crisp universe was growing soggy. Post, the number-three competitor—owned by Kraft—initiated a fierce price war that called for an aggressive response from Kellogg. General Mills, the traditional number two in the category, took the market-share lead. At the same time, retailers tired of Kellogg's seemingly high-handed ways began to step up their offerings of store-brand products. Companies like Ralston Foods happily supplied these goods at lower prices. And consumers increasingly turned their backs on cereal: That bowl of Frosted Flakes, once considered the obligatory way to start the day, now seemed like a luxury—or worse, a hassle—in a time-constrained world.[13]

As a result of all these pressures, Kellogg sagged. From 1996 to 2000 its stock dropped by almost 20 percent, in an otherwise booming market.

This was the situation that Carlos Gutierrez inherited when he took the reins in 1999. As he studied the situation, three priorities became clear. First, he had to make Kellogg's traditional products more appealing. Second, he could not pin all his growth prospects on ready-to-eat cereals consumed at breakfast. Third, Kellogg would have to change its culture—the way it did business—if it was to respond to the times.

Kellogg still had many strengths, of course. Take the issue of changing consumer preferences: Even if people were shunning breakfast, they still liked to snack on cereal-based products during the day. The company had products, notably its Nutri-Grain Bars and Rice Krispies Treats, that lent themselves to snacking. And the snacking game was attractive: Between 1996 and 2001, consumption of snack products grew at more than 8 percent per year, versus a 5 percent decline for traditional ready-to-eat cereals.[14] But if Kellogg was going to play in this game, it needed to build a stronger in-store presence. Big K needed to get into new store aisles and add new merchandising and display capabilities.

The executives studied their options very carefully, in the snack realm and others, paying particular attention to the kinds of capabilities it would need to succeed in a transformed marketplace. Kellogg had three big holes to fill: new-product development, broader distribution, and a culture skilled at executing business plans in a much faster-paced world.

With its newfound insight into what it needed to do, management started building the capabilities to get the job done. It became clear that much of the upgrading could be done in-house—by training people differently, by redirecting spending on capital and R&D projects, and by sharpening communications with customers, suppliers, employees, and vendors. Kellogg's leaders launched initiatives in each of these directions.

At the same time, it became clear that the company lacked certain key capabilities that would be inordinately expensive to build from scratch. This is where Keebler Brands, of Elmhurst, Illinois, came in.

Keebler was the number-two cookie-and-cracker maker in the United States, behind Nabisco. But it wasn't Keebler's cookie-making prowess that excited Kellogg; rather, it was how Keebler took its snacks to market, and to whom it sold those products.

Keebler employs a direct-store-delivery (DSD) system. This means that rather than shipping products to a retailer's warehouse and expecting the retailer to pull product as necessary and put it on the shelf, Keebler sends out a fleet of panel trucks every day to deliver fresh snacks directly from the bakery to the store aisles. This delivery system tends to generate the highest inventory turnover and is an optimal way to deliver snacks.

Most breads, milk products, and carbonated beverages go through a DSD system. (Other kinds of products tend to go the warehouse route.) So when it comes to using DSD, Keebler is in good company. For example, PepsiCo's Frito-Lay unit has long been applauded for the competitive advantage it derives from its immense DSD operation. A 55,000-person sales force pushes everything from snacks to beverages directly to more than 2 million retail customers.

Are there downsides to DSD? Definitely. For one thing, most retailers don't particularly like manufacturer DSD systems, mainly because they diminish the retailer's control over store inventory. And from the supplier's standpoint, DSD is expensive, especially in the start-up phase. In fact, the combination of retailer and cost pressures make it next to impossible for companies like Kellogg—under tremendous investor pressure to improve earnings—to set up a self-sustaining DSD system today. The result? Smart companies seek to take advantage of existing DSD operations. Some co-venture to acquire this capacity. After years of trying to set up a DSD system from scratch, for instance, Procter & Gamble joined forces with DSD veteran Coca-Cola to move P&G potato chips and snack beverages straight to grocery-store shelves.[15] Others seek to buy their way into DSD.

KELLOGG RESPONDS—MOSTLY—TO THE FOUR IMPERATIVES

That was the backdrop as Kellogg started eyeing Keebler. Let's track the acquisition using our four imperatives—picking the right targets according to a sound investment thesis; determining which deal to close after testing that thesis; identifying where you really need to integrate based on the type of deal; and planning for failure, or what you'll need to do when the deal inevitably strays—and relive the deal much as Kellogg experienced it.

How Should You Pick Your Targets?

We've already laid out the fundamentals of the investment thesis. As noted, Kellogg's core business was ready-to-eat cereal, but snacks constituted an adjacent business. In addition, Kellogg had an established position in other breakfast options: Eggo waffles, Pop-Tarts, and Nutri-Grain cereal bars. But to fully exploit the snack-food potential of its products, Kellogg would need access to a DSD channel like Keebler's. From this perspective, at least, the deal fit. Kellogg's investment thesis said the deal would add one to two points of top-line growth to the company by moving Kellogg into a high-growth distribution channel and filling that channel with an expanded product line in snacks.

How did the outside world respond to this investment thesis? Analysts pointed out that the deal would dilute earnings per share—usually an unwelcome development, and often a bad omen.[16] Brokerage reports estimated that postmerger, Kellogg's estimated earnings per share in the first year would fall from $1.75 to $1.30. Moreover, the merged company would add $4.6 billion in debt.[17] (On top of that, at about the same time, Kellogg took a more realistic look at its long-term profit targets and adjusted them downward.)

But—and this is a fascinating "but"—the stock market liked this deal.[18] Between the date of the deal's announcement and a year after the merger was complete, Kellogg's stock rose 26 percent, outperforming its peers by 11 percent.[19] Although other things were certainly going on, it appears that the analysts and investment community bought into Kellogg's investment thesis. In other words, the upside of building on Kellogg's core in the cereal business offset the downside of dilution.

Which Deals Should You Close?

Even before the deal, Kellogg and Keebler were far from strangers. As one analyst put it at the time, "Keebler and Kellogg know each other well, and have had a long history of working together."[20] Keebler copacked several items for Kellogg, and the senior executives of the two firms knew and respected each other. This seemed to portend a smooth and effective diligence process. And on many levels, in fact, the biggest diligence questions were well understood and well researched by Kellogg.

The two big operational questions were pretty clear from the start. First, could Kellogg seamlessly and cost effectively move its snack products into the Keebler distribution system? Due diligence suggested that it could.

Second, could Kellogg achieve significant cost savings through the deal—large enough to help offset the cost of the acquisition, and thereby help justify the deal? By measuring potential cost savings carefully, Gutierrez was able to better judge the value of the deal to Kellogg. "We came up with an accurate cost-savings target," he told us, "[and] did our own projections of what we felt [Keebler's] value was if we owned them, and what their intrinsic value was. On the basis of that, we developed our walk-away price."

Gutierrez understood the challenge, and also the importance, of establishing and sticking to a walk-away price:

> Even though this was a deal that I desperately wanted, I had conditioned myself mentally that I might not have it, that I might lose it. That helped me stand firm on a price. We closed the deal Thursday morning in New York. [But] on Tuesday, I had walked out of a meeting room having said, "I've got $42 a share. That is all I've got. If you can get more, go get it." Then I went to a Yankees-Mets game to just forget about the whole thing.[21]

In our eyes, that is more or less the definition of discipline. Keebler accepted the offer of $42 per share, and Gutierrez had his deal.

The price that Kellogg paid for Keebler was not exorbitant, at least compared with other food-company deals.[22] Due diligence had determined that the deal had a margin of safety based on $170 million in cost synergies by year three. Analysts forecast the combined entity to have a cost structure of $8.5 billion, so these synergies were less than 2 percent of cost—in other words, a conservative number. (As you might expect, it's always a good idea to err in the direction of conservatism when it comes to estimating potential synergies!) As it turned out, Kellogg beat these synergy projections by a wide margin, making the deal even more valuable than projected.

Where Do You Need to Integrate?

The original investment thesis posited that Kellogg would use its expanded distribution capabilities to grow its snack business. Given this objective, due diligence held that the most important aspect of integration was to integrate Kellogg's snack businesses seamlessly into Keebler's sales-and-distribution system.

As noted, Keebler already copacked several Kellogg products, which helped to smooth the integration process. In many respects, this was a reverse merger: Kellogg needed to move its snacking business into Keebler's, rather than the other way around. Fortunately, Kellogg trusted Keebler's number two, David Vermylen—president of Keebler Brands—and contracted to keep him on board for three years after the deal closed. And this was only part of a bigger strategy of integration, launched well before the ink on the agreement was dry. Kellogg knew it was getting into new lines and methods of business that it didn't understand well, and so it made a concerted effort to retain and empower specific individuals within Keebler for two to three years postmerger to make sure that integration was successful.

One advantage that Kellogg brought to the integration challenge actually resided on the other side of the table. Keebler already was an experienced integrator. It had made several acquisitions itself over the previous few years, and had integrated them smoothly.[23] So although integrating with a giant like Kellogg represented a far more complicated task, and although Keebler was now playing the role of acquired rather than acquirer, its executives were in a position to anticipate and head off certain kinds of problems.

But while both companies were experienced acquirers, they nearly did a belly flop when it came to melding their cultures. Keebler's leader, Sam Reed, was a dynamic executive who had built up the company through a series of strong acquisitions. Eric Katzman, the analyst who covered Kellogg for Deutsche Bank, at one point turned in a report that highlighted a real risk associated with the Kellogg–Keebler deal. Under the heading "culture shock," Katzman wrote:

> Every company brings its own culture to the field of competition. We characterize Keebler as being entrepreneurial and cost focused with an LBO mentality. We would not describe Kellogg as being entrepreneurial or, at least historically, a highly cost efficient operator. . . . We believe it will take every effort on Kellogg's management part to retain the talent just hired.[24]

Katzman's crystal ball was in top working order that day. In fact, Sam Reed and several other top Keebler managers left Kellogg within a year after the deal closed. One Kellogg executive who left the company after the merger commented on the rocky marriage of Battle Creek and Elmhurst, referring in passing to the trademark Keebler elf:

> Keebler was really only successful after Sam Reed [Keebler's CEO] came in, because of the culture he created. Keebler's employees were all happy elves working . . . in their hollow tree in Elmhurst. Then Kellogg came in and burned down the hollow tree and killed the chief elf. . . . All of a sudden people don't feel so happy.[25]

By most accounts, Kellogg's initial handling of the cultural issues had serious shortcomings. It could have done more to prevent Reed's departure, or to mitigate for that departure if it was truly inevitable. That being said, most observers also concluded that the company's leaders did an outstanding job of searching out solutions to this significant cultural problem—finding ways to make the elves happy and productive once again—and putting it behind them. And this is where they had to learn to grapple with the unexpected.

What Should You Do When the Deal Goes Off Track?

Carlos Gutierrez and the rest of his management team understood their limitations as they began seeking ways to capitalize on Keebler's advantages, and they therefore put strong Keebler managers in charge of expanding the combined company's snack business. In other words, they hedged against failure by limiting their own initial involvement in running the expanded business. This policy caused an initial wave of frustration among Kellogg executives. "Kellogg people were a little, I don't want to say resentful, but there was some tension," Gutierrez recalls. "The question around here was, 'Who bought whom?'"

But this particular problem proved short-lived, as a wave of Keebler executives left the merged company. David Vermylen, for example, left with a year and a half outstanding on his contract. Kellogg had to work its way through DSD without his help, and the visible Keebler turnover did some damage to Kellogg's reputation. It also led to a second wave of cultural problems. Kellogg people replaced the departing Keebler executives, and this time, the remaining Keebler troops felt frustrated and threatened.

Here it's worth underscoring the fact that even the most successful deal—one that substantially increases shareholder value—is likely to include its share of setbacks and headaches. As suggested earlier, the merged company went through several waves of cultural frustrations. In the end, Kellogg found itself compelled to plow one culture—its culture—through the merged company in order to capture all the benefits. This outcome is consistent with the findings of studies that we have conducted at Bain & Company, which suggest that scale deals like Kellogg–Keebler require the assimilation of the acquired companies—up to and including cultural assimilation.

Gutierrez believed that the best way to address the challenge of blending two very different companies was to focus on the key driver of his investment thesis: getting the benefits of DSD for Kellogg. He therefore put John Bryant, then the thirty-six-year-old CFO of Kellogg USA, directly in charge of the integration, and charged him with that task. Gutierrez also set up an integration steering committee, and named himself its chair. Bryant and others with integration responsibilities reported to the new committee, which included senior executives from both Kellogg and Keebler.

Bryant's first priority, the group agreed, was to get Kellogg's snacks moving through Keebler's DSD system as quickly as possible. Bryant's team developed a strategy that was blessed by the steering committee, and then went to work implementing that strategy. The implementation proceeded nearly flawlessly. "I can tell you that back when we were planning," Gutierrez recalls, "June 18th was the date we set to transfer our snacks to DSD, and that was exactly the date we did it. So there was a lot of very good execution and very good planning."

After getting past these bumps in the road, the company began to gel. The model was clear: Kellogg would change somewhat, and Keebler would conform to the new Kellogg. As Gutierrez explains:

> The trust level has been building. We developed a new set of values with Keebler folks, so that there would be new values for the Kellogg Company that Keebler people also believed in. We transferred many of the Battle Creek people to the Elmhurst campus, and we transferred many of the Elmhurst employees to Battle Creek.[26]

Culture wasn't the only challenge in the wake of the merger. It turned out that Kellogg underestimated the importance in the differences between the two companies' historic approaches to growth. Keebler, as noted, had achieved much of its growth through acquisitions. "They had been buying smaller companies consistently," said the former executive we spoke with, "getting rid of some of the products, and growing the other ones." Kellogg, on the other hand, had a long history of organic growth. And although Kellogg fully expected to learn things from Keebler, that did not mean that Kellogg was going to abandon its own traditions. Gutierrez explains:

> We went into this thing believing that we were going to pick up more from Keebler than we could add. That was the mindset of Kellogg at the time, because we were still trying to turn

> this company around. Keebler had been on a real roll. The press was against the Kellogg part, because we were seen as the "gang that couldn't shoot straight," and Keebler was seen as guys who built a lot of value. Over time, we realized that there is a huge difference between running a company for the long haul and being an LBO [leveraged buyout] manager, which is really what Keebler was. So we are changing Keebler's strategy from roll-up acquisitions to organic growth. And that requires different skills than what they had before.

Based on the track record summarized in the previous pages, we argue that Kellogg's acquisition of Keebler is a good example of solid deal management. Yes, there were decisions that Kellogg could have made better. But the decisions it got right included targeting a deal that fundamentally helped their core business; identifying how to get maximum value out of the resources acquired, from an operational point of view; planning a complex logistical move; and responding reasonably well when things went awry.

We chose to include the Kellogg–Keebler interaction not because it was the most flawless merger out there. (It was not.) Instead, we chose it because we can learn a lot from it. In summary, it featured a good investment thesis and good operational diligence—but also a potentially fatal error on cultural issues, a slow start on integration, and a belated embrace of the unexpected.

So this is reality, in the context of a transaction that is better than most. Now let's look at one that destroyed serious shareholder value.

A TOUGH CHEW: NEWELL BITES OFF RUBBERMAID

As we look at Newell and Rubbermaid, we'll ask and answer the same kinds of questions that we raised in the context of Kellogg–Keebler. As you will see, this second case is a far less inspiring example.

By most estimates at the time, the Newell Corporation's 1999 acquisition of the Rubbermaid Corporation was supposed to be a big success—maybe even a home run. But Rubbermaid was unlike any deal that Newell had ever consummated. And this story serves as a caution: Even experienced acquirers can fall off the learning curve when their desire to do a deal overcomes decision discipline.

In 1995, Rubbermaid was (according to *Fortune* magazine) the "most admired company in America."[27] It was very profitable and was growing quickly. It made a range of low-tech plastic items that anyone could relate to: from laundry baskets and janitor's buckets to Little Tikes toys. It had a business model that relied on innovation, smart brand marketing, and a strong, small-town corporate culture. Yet beneath the positive facade, things were starting to go bad. Sales growth was slowing and cost pressures rising. Quietly, the Rubbermaid board began looking for a buyer.

Enter Newell Corporation. Newell was, and still is, a conglomerate that sold everyday items through discount retail channels. Its portfolio included curtain rods, cookware, fasteners, and combs. Newell was a highly respected company with a strong track record of growth and consistent value creation. In the ten years running up to the Rubbermaid acquisition, Newell had achieved a compound sales-growth rate of 14 percent, an earnings-per-share growth rate of 16 percent, and an average annual return on shareholder equity of 21 percent. These results were consistent with Newell's formal goals of achieving earnings-per-share growth of 15 percent per year and maintaining a return on beginning equity of 20 percent or higher.[28]

Daniel Ferguson, who served as the company's CEO and then its chairman from 1965 to 1997, and also structured the Rubbermaid deal before stepping down, articulated Newell's corporate strategy in a 1998 company profile in *Harvard Business Review*. "Newell defines its basic business," he explained, "as that of manufacturing and distributing volume merchandise lines to the volume merchandisers."[29] By all accounts, Ferguson was a smart guy. He realized very early on that the emerging discount retailers (Wal-Mart, Kmart, and Target) would be the winners in the retail sector, and that one could build a very good business by supplying low-cost, high-volume products to these fast-growing companies.

Since at least the mid-1960s, Newell has been a very aggressive acquirer. Between 1967 and early 1999, when the Rubbermaid acquisition closed, Newell made more than seventy-five acquisitions.[30]

(This puts Newell into the top 10 percent of all corporations in terms of acquisition activity.) For a quarter of a century, Newell saw the acquisition and integration of a large number of small companies as a tremendous source of competitive advantage. Throughout this book, we argue that being a disciplined, frequent acquirer that gradually scales deal size is generally the best approach to mergers (absent any significant complicating factors). Newell, historically, embodied this approach. The company was neither blinded by glamour nor bowled over by big deals. "What we did in M&A back in my early days was 99 percent strategy," Ferguson told us. "I waited, and I took advantage of someone who was down and out a bit. We were a business that understood low-cost value."[31]

In Newell's early years Ferguson himself targeted, vetted, and integrated the company's acquisitions. As he recalls:

> When we started out, I would walk the aisles at Woolworth's and Wal-Mart. If it sold at Wal-Mart and was large volume and low cost, it was a fit, and we were disciplined about buying it. I used to go to the big department stores and look for the things they were selling that I could make and sell to Wal-Mart a lot cheaper.

And Newell had discipline. By all accounts, including Ferguson's, the company was a tough negotiator, and a bargainer that rarely overpaid for an asset. Traditionally, the senior management (which in the early years consisted of Ferguson and an associate) did proper diligence, and knew exactly what they were buying. They were also accomplished operators. Ferguson was so confident of Newell's operational skills, in fact, that he frequently sought out underperforming companies to buy, because he knew Newell had the resources and management processes to turn them around. "When we bought a business," he recalls, "I would go in there for some months and run it myself until we had it on track."

So in 1999, Newell, a disciplined, expert acquirer, was presented with the prospect of uniting with Rubbermaid, one of the world's most admired companies. What could be better?

The answer, it turns out, was almost anything. The Newell–Rubbermaid marriage has been viewed almost universally as a disaster. *BusinessWeek* dubbed it the "merger from hell."[32] Newell shareholders lost 50 percent of their value in the two years after the sale, and Rubbermaid shareholders lost about 35 percent, relative to the pretransaction trading price. How could this be?

We put this question to Ferguson. He responded as follows:

> We had no organic growth. We had to buy companies if we were to grow. Listen, I would rather have five companies with a billion dollars in sales than twenty companies at $250 million. So we had been knocking on doors of big companies. We had talked to Black & Decker as well as Rubbermaid. When Rubbermaid said that they would be interested in a deal, we went for it.

At the time, the analyst community loved the merger, even though the market discounted Newell on the first day of trading by 12 percent. (You will recall that this is Mark Sirower's red-flag warning that shareholders may be in for a drubbing.) Consider this fairly typical assessment of the deal from Bear Stearns analysts Constance Maneaty and Parinaz Pahlavi:

> The merger with Rubbermaid forms a powerful household products company that melds the best attributes of both companies, in our opinion. It will increase Newell's visibility, as Rubbermaid is one of the most recognized brands in the U.S., and, over time, Rubbermaid's skill in developing new products may increase Newell's internal sales growth rate. Newell will turn Rubbermaid's businesses into the lean, flexible, and market-sensitive units that define Newell's operations, and that have made Newell one of the most profitable companies in the personal care and household products world.[33]

Or consider this forecast from Prudential Securities analyst Carol Warner Wilke:

> I think, once the dust settles, that the stock will perform well because this really is a very big opportunity. . . . If you look at the end company, Newell has got great brands, and Rubbermaid, one would argue, is one of the most recognized

> brand names around . . . with good products and great market share. . . . This will be a very, very strong company when it's all done.[34]

Why this chorus of approval? At first blush, the advantages of the deal seemed clear. Both companies sold household products through essentially the same sales channels; therefore, they had very complementary skills. In addition, there appeared to be terrific cost synergies to be had from combining two companies in the same business. In theory, at least, Newell could operate Rubbermaid—a great branded marketer with traditionally high-margin products—as a stand-alone division, maintaining its positive characteristics while fixing a number of known weaknesses in Rubbermaid's supply-chain management. Finally, Rubbermaid would help Newell expand its geographic scope, providing a launch pad for overseas expansion. In short, the analysts (like the executives at Newell before them) saw all the makings of a terrific deal.

A FLIGHT FROM DISCIPLINE

So, a fairy-tale wedding turns into the marriage from hell. Once again, let's track this acquisition using our four imperatives—how to pick your target, which deals to close, where to integrate, and what to do when things stray off track—and figure out how Newell fell into some decision traps in the Rubbermaid deal.

How Not to Pick a Target

Newell believed strongly in growth through acquisition. Although acquisitions in the past had been small (and manageable), the company's leaders now believed they needed to think bigger. They thought Newell could rapidly build scale and gain brand identity through the Rubbermaid deal, which is exactly what the company needed in order to go toe-to-toe with the big discount chains. Says Ferguson, "The growth was in putting together a package that let you look Wal-Mart in the eye."

But the deal did not fit the thesis. The fault line ran thus: Yes, Rubbermaid and Newell were both selling a lot of household basics to the same customers. But the two companies had fundamentally different bases of competition. Rubbermaid competed on the basis of brand strength, whereas Newell competed on the basis of low-cost production. Their production processes and costs were different; their value propositions were different. They were actually in very different businesses, and Rubbermaid's strategy simply wasn't going to work in the markets that Newell relied upon.

Which Deals Smell Bad?

What problems did Newell face in diligence? First of all, as noted, Rubbermaid was no ordinary acquisition for Newell. Newell was comfortable swallowing minnows and goldfish; Rubbermaid was a whale—fully ten times the size of any deal that Newell had ever done.[35] Second, Rubbermaid succeeded in making its business look a whole lot prettier than it really was. Within legal bounds, companies commonly work hard in advance of a potential sale to put the best possible face on their financial records. Rubbermaid smelled good—first to all those outside observers, and then to Newell—but it was really what might be called a "perfumed pig."

And there wasn't much time to sniff out the sorry truth: Rubbermaid permitted only three weeks of diligence. Thus, Newell failed to ask and answer the critical questions about the health of Rubbermaid's business, and as a result, Newell overpaid dramatically for this new property. In 2002, it finally wrote off $500 million of goodwill. "We should have paid $31 a share," admits Ferguson, "but we paid $38. We paid too much."

We would phrase it slightly differently. In our terminology, Newell left behind its traditional deal discipline, and paid dearly for that lapse.

A Case of Overintegration?

The Newell management team, accustomed to integrating small, "tuck-in" acquisitions, sorely underestimated the challenge of choreographing a "merger of equals" in the Rubbermaid transaction. More troubling still, Newell failed to focus on the kinds of overarching issues that might have made the difference between success and failure.

And finally, Newell failed to heed the logic of its own investment thesis when it came time to integrate its enormous acquisition into the Newell fold. That thesis—to broaden Newell's scope in branded products—called for a selective integration. Instead, Newell attempted to "Newellize" Rubbermaid, and in so doing, squeezed out what little talent was left in the upper levels of the acquired company.

The financial results tell the story. Newell predicted $300 million in cost savings and $50 million in increased revenues during the first two years after the Rubbermaid merger. But when the dust settled in 2001, Rubbermaid had delivered no new sales and only $230 million in cost savings—most of which were wiped out by increases in the cost of polymer resins.

What Did Newell Forget to Do When the Deal Strayed?

Newell, a low-cost producer of largely unbranded housewares, had to learn how to leverage a high-margin brand when it bought Rubbermaid. Again, Newell sorely underestimated this challenge. The company's warning system should have set off alarm bells as synergies failed to materialize and gaps in know-how began to emerge. "We had to replace a lot of people," admits Ferguson. "The guys now running Newell understand brand power and how to market it. That's a revolution. It takes a different mind-set, a different group of people."

Unexpectedly, in other words, Ferguson needed to move the company into turnaround mode. But it took a while for Ferguson to find the right person to lead the charge. He started by looking inside his company. He had retired as chairman of the board in 1997 and made his CEO, William Sovey, chairman, and promoted insider John McDonough to CEO. Less than three years later, though, McDonough was gone and Sovey was serving as interim CEO. In 2001, Ferguson—still a company director—began looking for help outside Newell's walls. He persuaded his board to hire Joseph Galli, a veteran of Black & Decker, as Newell's new CEO. As we shall see in chapter 5, Galli is working to get the company back on track. But already, two painful years had passed, and a lot of damage had been done to the company.

Let's remind ourselves that, at this point, Newell is far from alone in running up on the merger reefs. Deal discipline lapses more often than it holds firm. In a world where the line managers responsible for integrating a merger and capturing its synergies are often not involved in the up-front assessment of a deal's benefits, it's easy to see why those lapses occur. And in a world where most advisors get paid based on the closing of any transaction—rather than the closing of a strategically sound, reasonably priced transaction—one can see why discipline leaves the system entirely, resulting in stock-price fiascoes.

The case of Newell and Rubbermaid illustrates the hard fact that merger reefs await even the most experienced of acquirers. Newell's investment thesis was incomplete, and its due-diligence process failed to detect this. The two businesses' fundamentally different processes and cost positions made integration difficult. Management, insufficiently mindful of its own shortcomings, exacerbated its own woes and reacted too slowly when problems surfaced.

Was any one decision the killer? No. Executives make poor decisions all the time, and most such mistakes are reversible. But the cumulative effect of a string of bad decisions, each building upon and compounded by its predecessors, can be devastating. This was the case with Newell, and we believe it is a common pattern.

In fairness, we should note that Daniel Ferguson still maintains that the Rubbermaid acquisition was a great deal:

> The investment thesis was right, but we overpaid and had lots of technical problems. . . . They've given us a hard time for four and a half years. But we're a hundred years old! What's four and a half years?

He attributes the unhappy aftermath of the acquisition to Newell's lack of experience with consumer-brand marketing and to managerial problems at Rubbermaid. (Curiously, he also cites the exodus of Rubbermaid executives, who presumably shared some of the responsibility for their company's premerger problems.) And we fully understand his impulse to pick a new time frame for measuring the success of the deal. This restates a point that we made earlier in this chapter: "Success" is in part a measure of the particular moment when you choose to take a deal's pulse. Finally, we give Ferguson credit for admitting that errors were made and taking the painful steps needed to get the company back on track.

We will return to the Newell–Rubbermaid story in chapter 5. As a case study, it captures many of the most important lessons that would-be acquirers should learn, well in advance of entering the merger fray. Also in chapter 5, we will train our attention on current Newell CEO Joseph Galli, a roll-up-your-sleeves type of executive who is pushing hard to make the initial vision of this deal work.

FINDING A WAY TO WIN

What can we learn from studying cases like Kellogg and Newell? For one thing, we can learn that in the final analysis, decision discipline and leadership converge, and become synonymous. The CEO who has a well-articulated strategy and a business system that performs effectively is far less likely to pursue a value-destroying deal than a CEO who is in strategic trouble. Our analysis shows that a CEO is more than twice as likely to lose his job when he engages in a large deal that destroys value. Of course, that is scant consolation to shareholders who have lost their money.

Companies that know who they are and where they want to go make the best deal decisions. The sad, shocking truth is that such companies are the exception, not the rule. Most senior deal-making executives cite the perceived need to "do something." Like Daniel Ferguson, they look to grab growth to get their company back on track. They don't talk much about the need for a disciplined, constant pursuit of businesses that strategically fit their company. In fact, many admit that their passions get the better of them. In our poll of two hundred fifty senior executives around the world, half of survey respondents cited "allowing politics or emotions to interfere with the decision-making process" as a major reason for due diligence—and therefore deal—failure. (For more, see the box Why Good Executives Make Bad Deal Decisions.)

We argue that *Mastering the Merger* is all about disciplined decision making. And at the risk of confusing some of our international

WHY GOOD EXECUTIVES MAKE BAD DEAL DECISIONS

Why is decision making in the merger environment so hard? We have already identified a number of factors that work against good merger outcomes, including the presence of third parties who are invested in completing the deal, the turmoil that deals cause within an organization, and the ugly truth that sellers always know more about an asset than buyers.

The industry that has grown up to support corporate deal making is already huge, and continues to grow rapidly. This growth is fueled in large part by the profits involved, which are enormous. On deals greater than $1 billion, companies on each side of a transaction typically pay their investment banks around 0.9 percent, so approximately 1.8 percent of a large deal's price goes to investment bankers. For deals at the $100 million–plus mark, the fees can go as high as 2.5 percent for each side.

So: $2.5 million in fees to our investment bankers for their help on that $100 million deal, and we haven't yet gotten the bills from our lawyers and accountants. At these prices, companies are very reluctant to incur high fees for busted deals. Many therefore make compensation contingent on deal completion. It's a risky approach, since it puts deal discipline at odds with deal incentives. All those advisors working on contingencies are very likely to spot the upside inherent in every transaction, and overlook the downside.

And there may be additional, more subtle eroders of discipline at work. In our experience, many CEOs simply don't believe they can maintain the level of performance that is priced into their stock without "growth injections" from outside. In many cases, they're absolutely right. The truth is that organic growth is hard to achieve—very hard. A study by Mercer across eleven major industries found that after stripping away factors that can mask growth (such as acquisitions, aggressive price increases, and international expansion) from an industry's 1995–2000 compound annual revenue expansion, the largest company in each industry enjoyed only modest core

(continued)

(continued)

growth—if it enjoyed any growth at all. In fact, four of these eleven companies experienced either flat or negative core growth.*

So in some cases, the announcement of a deal is the most palatable way for management to deliver some unwelcome news to shareholders: "We're out of other options for growth." The recent merger of Hewlett-Packard and Compaq Computer Corporation provides a case in point. In advertisements to convince shareholders to support the merger, HP argued that it could not prosper without the deal.

Sellers always know more than buyers, and sellers always have unstated reasons for parting with an asset. When buyers come down with deal fever, they often lose sight of this fundamental truth. The experienced deal makers refrain from falling in love with a particular transaction. They seek instead to understand the real reasons why a seller is moving an asset.

Finally, it is all too easy to get caught up in the hunt. For many executives, a big deal may be the most exciting thing they do in their career. This phenomenon was documented by Bryan Burrough and John Helyar in their entertaining (and sometimes devastating) *Barbarians at the Gate,* which chronicled the sale of RJR Nabisco.

*Adrian J. Slywotzky and Richard Wise, "The Growth Crisis—and How to Escape It," *Harvard Business Review,* July 2002.

readers, let us end this chapter with a reference to the American game of baseball.

Throughout the course of a season, baseball players make thousands and thousands of small decisions: when to swing, where to stand in the field, when to steal a base, what pitch to throw next. What researchers have discovered about baseball is that an application of disciplined decision rules to the game can significantly improve a team's chances of success over the long course of a season.

Sure, when it comes to any particular decision, fate may be fickle and outcomes cruel. As a pitcher, on any given Saturday afternoon, you may make the perfect pitch—and watch that pitch sail into the seats in deep center field. But over the course of the season, if you make really smart pitching choices in a disciplined way, you are likely to come out ahead.[36]

In this book, we are trying to help management teams make the right decisions most of the time in the merger arena. Next, in chapter 2, we will focus on the first critical decision: How should you pick your targets? In chapter 3, we'll look at which deals you should actually close, and in chapter 4, where you really need to integrate, depending on the type of deal you have closed. Not all decisions will work out as planned, hence our emphasis (and our final critical decision) in chapter 5 on what you should you do when the deal goes off track. But if you make the highest probability decisions consistently, you put your company in a position to win—the subject of our closing chapter. And that, we believe, is a pretty good definition of managerial excellence.

2

How Should You Pick Your Targets?

This chapter focuses on the first of our four key decisions: the all-important process of picking your targets. Determining what you want to buy should be deeply rooted in understanding your current business: selecting your targets is all about reinforcing your core.

One helpful way to introduce this subject is to look at how *not* to select candidates for acquisition. All too often, the early stages of corporate mergers and acquisitions follow an ad hoc, unsystematic, nonstrategic process, which goes more or less as follows.

An investment banker calls with a target for sale and a deal book that provides background material. Usually, he or she has thought of a positive reason for you to do the deal. For example: "This is your chance to be the industry leader." Or, "Your core is stagnant, and you need to look elsewhere for growth."

In response to this overture, your corporate development staff run a quick screen, based on a cursory review of the deal book and a superficial industry overview. If they discover that the banker is bending the truth or that the company is in a lot of trouble, they'll almost certainly balk. But for deals that continue to look interesting—however that may be defined—the acquisition team members launch a more exhaustive process. They build a valuation model, calculating year-one accretion or dilution. They interview the management team. Eventually, they conduct financial and legal due diligence.

Over the course of what usually amounts to a few weeks, the team members build a case to support the deal. Then they dive into hundreds of hours of negotiating, presentations, and board discussions—all aimed, more or less consciously, at naming a price that will fly and getting a green light from the board.

Hopefully, none of this sounds familiar to you. We say "hopefully" because the odds against picking an appropriate target based on this kind of process are overwhelming. If the acquisition team's efforts aren't grounded in a sound portfolio strategy—and if the investigators are reacting, rather than acting—they are likely to mistake a bad deal for a good one. They are likely to pursue nonstrategic, plain-vanilla deals with prices below the valuation model, or apparent year-one accretion. As a result, too many deals get made that have a limited upside, and an almost unlimited downside. Meanwhile, they turn down deals that appear to be too expensive, but actually aren't in terms of long-term strategic benefit. And finally, they fail to uncover the kinds of opportunities that they might be turning up on their own if they were following a strategic road map.

In the last chapter, we focused on the fundamental paradox of deal making: Something like 70 percent of all deals fail to create meaningful value, and yet it is virtually impossible to build a world-class company through organic growth alone. Most firms have to grow at a healthy pace; most firms can't get there without acquisitions. The inescapable conclusion: Most firms should engage in selective, strategy-driven deal making, which usually translates into both selling and buying. In short, you need to do deals—but do them in a disciplined way.

So how do you get started? What should you buy (or sell)? How will this help your shareholders?

No two firms are alike, and therefore no two firms should answer these complicated questions in exactly the same way. In the following pages, we'll help you think systematically about the sequence of successful deal-targeting.

First, though, let's look at the story of a Texas family that, over the course of three decades, built a world-class broadcast empire by mastering the art of the merger.

CLEAR SAILING AT CLEAR CHANNEL

In 1972, investment banker Lowry Mays accidentally found himself in the broadcast business. A friend for whom he had provided debt financing backed out of a radio-station deal, and Mays was left holding the property.[1]

This turns out to have been a happy accident, indeed. Over the next twenty-three years, Mays and his two sons, Mark (COO) and Randall (CFO), became accomplished deal makers in the broadcast field. Their San Antonio, Texas–based company, Clear Channel Communications, vaulted to number six in radio-broadcast revenues, close behind Infinity, Evergreen, Walt Disney Company, Chancellor, and Cox Radio.

By 1995, however, the Mayses had hit a ceiling. Federal law limited broadcasters to two stations per market and forty nationwide, and Clear Channel was bumping up against these limits.

The story might have ended there, but for the fact that Congress deregulated the industry in 1996, raising the per-market ownership caps to eight and eliminating the nationwide limits entirely. From that day forward, the radio world divided itself two categories: those who would buy, and those who would be bought.

The Mayses intended to be buyers. They jumped out of the gate, and in a surprisingly short period of time, left their competitors far behind them. By the end of 2003, Clear Channel owned about 1,200 radio and nearly 40 television stations in the United States, and had equity interests in more than 240 radio stations internationally. (By way of comparison, that's five times as many radio stations as number two–ranked Viacom.[2]) And that's not the end of the story. In 1997, perceiving cross-selling and bundling opportunities for local advertising, Clear Channel diversified into the billboard business by acquiring a succession of small companies. Then, in 2000, it became the leading live-concert promoter through the acquisition of SFX.

The financial results of the Mayses' acquisition-driven growth strategy have been exceptional. Between 1986 and 2001, company revenues grew by 46 percent annually. The company generated a 36 percent average annual shareholder return, which was 21 percent higher than their cost of equity.

Clear Channel entered its race with several key advantages. First, of course, was the skill and perseverance of the founding family. (In business, as in life, it's wise to pick your parents well.) In addition, by the time the race heated up in 1996, the Mayses were already experienced deal makers. They had acquired stations one by one over many years, thereby exercising their acquisitive muscles. When the opportunity arose to accelerate their pace of acquisition, they were well prepared to do so.

And finally, the Mayses well understood the scale benefits that could be achieved by consolidation in the radio field, and were determined to go after those economies in a systematic way.

STEPS TOWARD THE RIGHT TARGETS

We will return to the Mayses after we work our way through the steps that you should take to identify appropriate targets and define deals that make sense for your organization. Among other things, you will need to:

- Determine your basis of competition
- Rationalize the core
- Identify potential targets
- Develop a sound investment thesis for each target
- Develop good relationships with your targets
- Focus on the right size and the right frequency

Determine Your Basis of Competition

The Mayses knew how they made their money, and they structured deals that reinforced their ability to transact profitably more tried-and-true business. That's the essential starting point for systematic deal making. Every good company has a successful business formula that defines its base set of competencies—a clear picture of how it makes money and how it competes to win. We'll call this essence of the company the "core." When a company has a well-defined core that it is willing to invest in and defend, it is more likely to earn superior returns.

Two of our partners at Bain, Chris Zook and James Allen, recently coauthored a book entitled *Profit from the Core*. Their preliminary research pointed to a startling conclusion: Only 13 percent of publicly held companies achieve profitable growth over a sustained period.[3] Intrigued, they dug deeper, probing into how this small fraction of firms succeeded. Their ultimate conclusion: Companies with the best track records of profitable and sustainable growth religiously invested in their core businesses and/or expanded into highly related businesses that reinforced the core. Conversely, companies that strayed from their core sooner or later turned into underperformers, a topic Chris Zook expands on in his sequel, *Beyond the Core*.

The high-performing companies understand the fundamental basis of competition within their core businesses, and focus rigorously on what they're good at. They drive their businesses to achieve full market share and profit potential before taking on something new. When they do branch out from their core for growth, they take incremental steps—pursuing closely related products, customers, or geographies—and follow opportunities only where they can see a clear path to a leadership position.

In figure 2-1, we lay out the five different bases on which most companies compete: cost position, brand power, consumer loyalty, real asset advantage, and government protection. No company is a pure play; in fact, most companies pursue most of these competitive advantages to varying degrees. But our work with clients suggests that often only one or two of these bases of competition make a significant difference in a company's earning power.

Let's look again at Clear Channel Communications. This is a company that was built around a well-defined core: the operation of radio stations. For years, the basis of competition in radio lay in securing exclusive licenses granted by government regulators in particular geographies. But when the government changed its policy, the relative basis of competition changed to cost, which argued for operating on a national scale. The Mayses understood this better than anyone, and used a combination of acquisition strategy and innovative new

FIGURE 2-1

Five Bases for Achieving Industry Leadership

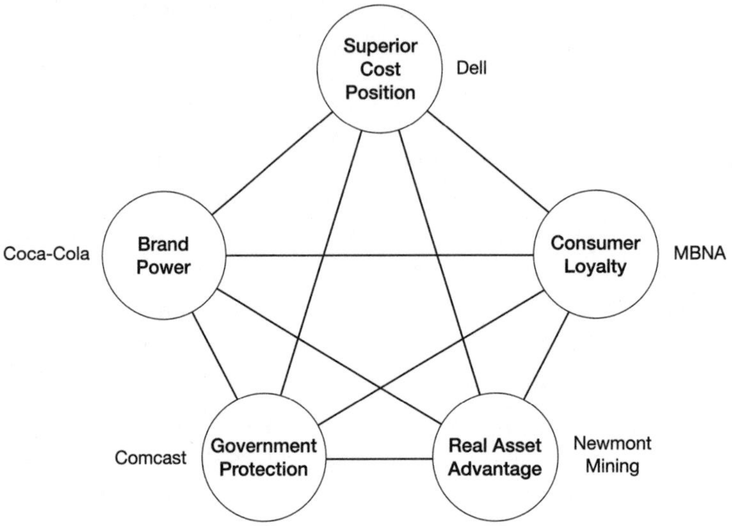

operating practices (such as using the same "local" weatherman to report on cities as far away from each other as Tampa and San Diego) to redefine the industry.[4]

Once Clear Channel had achieved the necessary expansion of its core, it moved into two adjacent markets: outdoor advertising and concert promotion. These moves made good use of many competencies the company had developed over the years: management of distributed local businesses, knowledge of and connections to the recording industry, and strength in bundling the sale of local and national advertising. In addition, the Mayses saw the potential to use the strengths and capabilities of the three businesses to promote and advance each other. And just as they had achieved a leadership position in their core broadcast business, so, too, did they seek to lead in each new business they entered.

This issue of market leadership warrants some scrutiny. For years, business schools have taught students that leadership is a function of market-share position. But is this conventional wisdom correct? Yes and no: The thesis certainly applies in some industries, particularly capital-intensive ones. But there are too many examples of non-market-share leaders that make very attractive returns (think Southwest Airlines), and too many examples of share leaders that make low or no returns (think American Airlines).

Some B-school theorists might argue that the airline business is the classic example of a structurally lousy industry: high fixed costs, low pricing power, numerous competitors, low barriers to entry, and significant government regulation. We would respond that this only makes the success of the Southwests and JetBlues all the more interesting. If size is no virtue in a particular industry, then virtue must lie somewhere else.

What it takes to be a leader varies significantly, industry by industry. As you develop your corporate strategy, you need to define what leadership means in your industry, and translate that insight into superior returns over an extended period of time. If you can do that, you may be in a position to run a great business even in a traditionally low-margin industry, such as air transport or papermaking.

To flesh out this point, let's run through a series of industries with different bases of competition, and look briefly at deals that benefited from an understanding of the basis of competition (or were hurt by the lack of that understanding).

In the consumer-products industry, for example, we have found a direct correlation between a company's brand power and its overall earnings capability. But brand power does not always derive from market share. Instead, the most profitable brands derive their strength from their ability to command the largest price premiums over private label.[5] Brands have power if we consumers are willing to pay more for the branded product even when the retailer puts a cheaper alternative right in front of us.

Take, for example, the ice cream business. For years, ice cream was a commodity category. The local dairy supplied the grocery store with half-gallon tubs of vanilla, chocolate, and strawberry. (Occasionally, for variety, they would put all three in the same tub!) Along came Ben & Jerry's and Häagen-Dazs, who put higher-quality ice cream in lots of different flavors in small containers, for which they charged a premium. Together, they redefined a small but highly profitable sector of an otherwise low-margin market. Ben & Jerry's and Häagen-Dazs never came close to selling the most ice cream, nor were they ever the low-cost producers. But they earned far and away the highest returns in their industry, and as a result are both now owned by international food companies that recognized their value.

In the financial-services industry, the highest returns go to those companies that capture the largest share of wallet from their best customers. In *The Loyalty Effect,* Frederick Reichheld demonstrates that in financial services, the cost of acquiring new customers is so high that the best strategy is to invest heavily in retention programs and so cater to the loyalty of those customers you already serve.[6] Witness mutual fund company Vanguard, whose focus on customer loyalty has helped it to keep costs down, undercutting giant rival Fidelity Investments without sacrificing profits.

What does Vanguard do differently? Three things: First, it educates its consumers in its philosophy on fund management ("buy and hold" is better than active trading; use indexing versus superstar fund managers). Second, it has built an operating model that is inherently low cost. Third, it discourages low-loyalty investors from coming into Vanguard funds in the first place. Vanguard prefers to do more business with a subset of ideal customers than to do minimal business with the many. It is a winning formula, and—given its current rate of growth—Vanguard should one day overtake Fidelity.

Not understanding the basis of competition within your core can lead to disaster. Vivendi Universal is a case in point. Vivendi's former CEO, Jean-Marie Messier, attempted to transform his plodding-but-competent water utility into a high-flying media conglomerate. But running a utility—where success comes largely from managing the relationships with the government agencies that determine how much money a utility is permitted to make—could not be more different from running a media empire. Messier pointed Vivendi squarely against the current, and the pursuit of media glory nearly led to Vivendi's collapse.

Unfortunately, Messier is not one of a kind. Too many executives plunge more or less blindly into businesses that appear more attractive than their own, without understanding the basis of competition in the new business. If they're lucky, there will be enough overlap between the acquirer's skills and the acquisition's deficits to make the deal work after the fact. If they're not lucky, there won't be.

So far we have looked at companies with a basis of competition in cost (Clear Channel), brand power (Ben & Jerry's), loyalty (Vanguard), and government protection (Vivendi and Clear Channel, in their early days). How about what might be called "asset advantage"?

Asset advantage comes from owning something that is rare, or even unique. Obviously, this includes extractive industries, such as mining, oil and gas development, and wood pulp. But less obviously, it includes industries like retailing and lodging. Sometimes, even the players within these industries misunderstand their asset advantage. One example in the lodging sector is Starwood Hotels & Resorts. Starwood—which then managed 30,000 hotel rooms (including the Westin chain, which it had just bought)—purchased ITT Corporation, a hospitality and gaming company that operated Sheraton, Four Points, St. Regis, and Caesars Palace, in 1998. The goal of the merger was to create the largest lodging operator in the world.

If the lodging industry were a cost-driven industry, with standardized operating practices, then being the largest (or at least, "huge enough") would have strategic merit. But the business model that Starwood actually used—that is, operating chains that ran the gamut from the Four Point Hotels (which cater to the budget conscious) to the premium St. Regis collection of properties—meant that there were few economies of scale to be realized. Each chain had its own brand elements, processes, and procedures. Even the bedspreads and their washing facilities differed substantially between, say, the "W" in New York City and a Sheraton franchise just across the Hudson in New Jersey.

Starwood's acquisition of ITT was based on a fundamental misunderstanding of the business in which Starwood actually competed. Within a year, the deal was, by most reckonings, a disaster. Starwood's shares lost nearly half their value in the twelve months following the deal, and the chain continued to underperform its industry benchmark for two and a half years following the deal.[7]

Rather than end this section on a gloomy note, let's cite an example of another company that used its clear understanding of its basis of competition to its advantage—and also to the advantage of an entire industry.

The example comes out of a sector that most of us would probably think of as slow-moving and low-opportunity: cardboard-box manufacturing. Michael Smurfit—CEO of the company then known as Jefferson Smurfit, which was a leading player in the corrugated containers and containerboard industry—made a series of highly successful acquisitions of other packaging companies through the 1980s and 1990s, and these deals steadily improved the company's cost position in its core business.

Smurfit knew that in commodity manufacturing, the fundamental basis of competition is cost. By extension, he knew that investing at the bottom of the market cycle—both to drive costs down and get good deals—would contribute mightily to success. In 1998, Smurfit merged with Stone Container to form Smurfit-Stone Container Corporation. The new company catapulted to market leadership in the United States. This in itself didn't immediately confer value. But Smurfit recognized that for the first time, a company—his company—had a large enough share of industry containerboard capacity that closing mills to reduce capacity (heresy in a capital-intensive industry!) would benefit not only the industry, but—disproportionately—his own company.

He also understood that there was substantial upside to be gained in cutting costs, leveraging purchasing scale, and transferring best practices between the mills and box plants of the two companies. The result? The combined company survived plummeting market prices by dramatically cutting costs and reducing industry excess capacity—dramatic steps, for which Michael Smurfit won the paper industry's CEO of the Year award.

Rationalize the Core

Once you have properly defined the basis of competition within each of your businesses and honestly assessed your company's competitive position and core competencies, it is time to think about reallocating resources. Although this book is primarily focused on acquisitions, the same principles apply to decisions regarding divestitures.

In many cases, the right way to start strengthening a multibusiness portfolio is to strategically disinvest. Why? Because over time, most corporate portfolios come to include mistakes, accidents, and afterthoughts. They include businesses that may have seemed like a good idea at the time of acquisition, but which have turned out to be misfits with the parent company's basis of competition. Such units tend to bleed off resources and—by definition—don't reinforce the core. It is not unusual to find management teams taking one of their most valuable and scarce resources—their own time—and sinking it heavily into attempts to fix problem children, rather than building on their strengths.

An example of a company that has remade itself by exiting businesses where it could not see a long-term winning business case is information publishing giant The Thomson Corporation. From 1997 to 2002, Thomson transformed itself from a traditional conglomerate encompassing newspapers, travel services, and professional publications into a focused provider of integrated electronic information to specialty markets.

How? Starting in 1997, Thomson focused on the small number of businesses in its portfolio that it understood better than anyone else. As the company's leaders saw it, its basis of competition centered on building scale in its key markets and developing proprietary technologies that transformed the way information was delivered and integrated into its customers' workplace. Exploiting this technological potential became the core of the Thomson investment thesis.

Thomson divested its vast newspaper and travel businesses and used the proceeds to invest heavily and continue to build positions in its core markets—educational, legal, tax, accounting, scientific, health care, and financial information publishing. Thomson coordinated the sale of approximately $6 billion in assets and used the proceeds to acquire nearly $7 billion in new businesses between 1997 and 2002. More than 60 companies and 130 newspapers were divested and over 200 other businesses acquired during this period.

Today, the company is a leader in its markets, where the ability to control the flow of information allows the company to earn superior returns. Over the course of this transformation, Thomson has improved its operating margin by 6 percent.[8]

We should note, at this point, that the strategic decision to divest a business can have practical implications that make carrying out the plan uncomfortable. (Taking medicine isn't always pleasant.) These can include, for example, cash-flow hiccups, earnings dilution, balance-sheet woes, public relations woes, and unfavorable valuations. One of the ironies of portfolio management is that assets with poor strategic fit and/or growth prospects often provide corporations with stable cash flow and earnings. Thus, the decision to sell may require resetting earnings expectations, absorbing reduced earnings per share, cutting dividends, and/or restructuring the debt on the balance sheet. Not surprisingly, many CEOs—upon reviewing this kind of math—decide that divestiture isn't worth the bother.

But that's short-term thinking, and CEOs are paid (or should be paid!) to think long term. The path to long-term success is clear: First, develop a superior business system that gives you a core competency along some basis of competition, and make this a part of your long-term strategy. Next, evaluate each business in your portfolio through this lens. Then, if a business does not fit with your long-term strategy, get on with life—dispose of that asset!

If you need arguments in favor of getting on with life, here are three good ones:

- As noted, candidates for divestiture command a disproportionate share of management's attention. Divesting noncore assets permits management to focus its attention on its core business, rather than its "problem children."

- The perceived risks of earnings dilution and cash flow are generally less than the actual risks. Our client histories include numerous examples of companies that have divested assets and seen a significant rise in their postdivestiture stock price. Take General Dynamics, for example: Between October 1990—when it began divesting noncore assets—and the end of 1996, the company's stock price rose more than 1,200 percent, while the rest of the defense industry struggled through a structural decline. Thomson, too, saw significant stock-price appreciation while it made extensive divestitures. (We will revisit this issue later, in a section on the dilution/accretion debate.)

- Finally, the decision to restructure the portfolio creates a good opportunity to reshape the company's message to investors, employees, and other interested stakeholders. A divestiture can act as a catalytic and even a cathartic event. It positions management to take an overdue action, such as cutting overhead, reinvesting in core businesses, establishing a new earnings baseline—or making a strong acquisition.

Identify Appropriate Targets

So far, we have focused on the need to understand and rationalize your core business, looked at through the lens of your basis of competition. Our partners, Zook and Allen, argue forcefully that the best acquisition strategies are ones that reinforce the core. You can do this by buying businesses within the core—for example, more radio stations—or by moving into closely related adjacencies, such as outdoor advertising and concert promotion. But how, exactly, do you act on this kind of laudable but general principle?

The first part of our answer is: Do your homework, which comprises three related activities in the following sequence: (1) Create a list of potential targets, (2) screen all targets, and (3) develop detailed profiles.

Create a list of potential targets. As you'd expect, the first step toward effecting successful mergers is to create a comprehensive list of potential targets. If you're planning a scale-building move in an industry you understand, the target list is probably short, and the task of setting priorities is likely to be relatively straightforward. On the other hand, if you're considering a series of smaller "tuck-in" moves to fill a capability gap, or you plan to enter an adjacent market, then you may need more time to engage a broad base of people in the search process. This means deploying the troops—your field organization—and bringing in outside help—your suppliers, business brokers, investment bankers, and consultants. All can be valuable resources for uncovering small, below-the-radar firms, including privately held prospects.

The companies that we consider to be world-class at screening deals—for example, Clear Channel, Nestlé, and Citigroup—all rely on a combination of the corporate team and the individual line organizations to generate deal ideas that will help them grow their businesses. As the preceding discussion implies, line managers in these companies intuitively understand the basis of competition in their businesses, and therefore understand how it can best be exploited through selective acquisitions. Corporate takes in all these good ideas, prioritizes them, and puts the company in a position to respond when an opportunity arises.

Screen all targets. Next, you need to perform an initial screen of potential targets, using criteria dictated by your basis of competition. Use this screen to discard targets that are a poor fit and then to rank the rest. Consider the case of Cintas Corporation, a successful acquirer that we will profile more extensively in chapter 6. This uniform supplier's deal team generates a list of all potential targets—about seven hundred fifty companies were on their radar screen in the fall of 2002—and assists in their qualification and ranking. The team rates each of the targets on a scale of one to four in terms of desirability.

Develop detailed profiles. Next, you need to build your fact base so that you can develop a profile of each target company. Well before a deal prospect becomes available, the best acquirers already well understand that target company's industry; they know its competitive position, recent performance, and current management team.

Let's return to Clear Channel and look in more detail at how it finds and screens its targets.

Clear Channel has the great luxury of being a cash generator, which means that for the most part, it is able to fund its growth internally. This is an enviable position, and one that the Mayses are loath to give up. As a result, their strategy has a distinctive jumping-off point: finding businesses that will give them operating leverage while also reinforcing cash returns. With this cash-as-king mentality firmly rooted in every operating manager's brain, the Mayses then ask for deal ideas from the operating divisions. These proposed deals are vetted at the corporate level.

From Clear Channel's point of view, what is the ideal acquisition? One that:

- reinforces cash returns (cash is king!),
- is close to the existing core (radio, outdoor advertising, and live entertainment), and
- is underperforming.

The ability to put these last two points together—investing in related businesses that are underperforming—turns out to be a hallmark of many of the best acquirers. Their investment thesis addresses not only why this is a good business, but also how improvement to the business will justify the acquisition premium.

You will recall that as Clear Channel saw it, outdoor advertising was attractive because it was fragmented and undercapitalized. In other words—as Randall Mays explains—it was an inefficient business system in which Clear Channel was convinced that it could invest its capital gainfully: "Clear Channel had a lot of cash that it wasn't putting into radio at the time, so we moved it to outdoor billboards, where it would get the best return. Each time we acquired billboards, we were able to tear out costs (by closing a plant) and drive cash flow."[9]

Mays explains that in these cases, they "could double or triple cash flow, so we can approach buyers and pay a very good price . . . and that puts them in a situation where we could pay a higher price than they could ever generate on their own." As time went on, of course, this got more difficult. By that point, however, Clear Channel's scale advantage and potential for synergies were such that competitors had a hard time outbidding Clear Channel.

Clear Channel's strategy reflects both market opportunities and the company's ready access to cash. When structural market opportunities arise—for example, as the result of dislocations in markets—the company has engaged in concentrated acquisition programs. Such dislocations have been caused by external factors such as deregulation (radio) and industry-specific factors such as insufficient access to capital (outdoor billboard). "A lot of it has to do with underlying changes in the industry," reports Randall Mays. "We were significantly more proactive when changes created benefits to consolidating assets." The radio market provides one example of a targeted strategy. Post-deregulation, Mays recalls, he and his colleagues "pulled out our list of every market" to screen for stations that would make sense to acquire.

Even when there is no clear strategic acquisition in sight, Mays adds, Clear Channel is "always opportunistic." For example, the company will pounce on an asset in a market that it has long sought to break into; similarly, it will move quickly when a privately held target corporation becomes available—provided, of course, that these deals are consistent with the company's overall strategy and basis of competition. Mays admits that Clear Channel is more opportunistic today than in the past, but suggests that this change could be related to where the company is in its overall life cycle. In the early days, the company was "a lot more proactive." But this relates again to the availability of cash. "With access to cash at attractive rates," he says, "we become more proactive."

To sum up: Merger masters plan for opportunity by being proactive, involving line management in generating, assessing, and thoughtfully prioritizing opportunities. They also prepare to move quickly when an opportunity arises—which involves not just effective screening, but also cultivating targets that grow out of that screening process.

Develop a Sound Investment Thesis

We have structured this chapter around the sequence of tasks that you're likely to take up in the early stages of deal making. If instead we had structured the chapter around the importance of those tasks, we would have opened it by talking about the investment thesis: a critically important tool.

Every deal your company proposes to do—big or small, strategic or tactical—should start with a clear statement how that particular deal would create value for your company. We call this the *investment thesis*. The investment thesis is no more or less than a definitive statement, based on a clear understanding of how money is made in your business, that outlines how adding this particular business to your portfolio will make your company more valuable. Many of the best acquirers write out their investment theses in black and white. Joe

Trustey, managing partner of private equity and venture capital firm Summit Partners, describes the tool in one short sentence: "It tells me why I would want to own this business."[10]

Perhaps you're rolling your eyes and saying to yourself, "Well, of course our company uses an investment thesis!" But unless you're in the private equity business—which in our experience is more disciplined in crafting investment theses than are corporate buyers—the odds aren't with you. For example, our survey of two hundred fifty senior executives across all industries revealed that only 29 percent of acquiring executives started out with an investment thesis (defined in that survey as a "sound reason for buying a company") that stood the test of time. More than 40 percent had no investment thesis whatsoever(!). Of those who did, fully half discovered within three years of closing the deal that their thesis was wrong.

Studies conducted by other firms support the conclusion that most companies are terrifyingly unclear about why they spend their shareholders' capital on acquisitions. A 2002 Accenture study, for example, found that 83 percent of executives surveyed admitted they were unable to distinguish between the value levers of M&A deals.[11] In Booz Allen Hamilton's 1999 review of thirty-four frequent acquirers, which focused chiefly on integration, unsuccessful acquirers admitted that they fished in uncharted waters.[12] They ranked "learning about new (and potentially related) business areas" as a top reason for making an acquisition. (Surely companies should know whether a business area is related to their core before they decide to buy into it!) Successful acquirers, by contrast, were more likely to cite "leading or responding to industry restructuring" as a reason for making an acquisition, suggesting that these companies had at least thought through the strategic implications of their moves.

Not that tipping one's hat to strategy is a cure-all. In our work with companies that are thinking about doing a deal, we often hear that the acquisition is intended for "strategic" reasons. That's simply not good enough. A credible investment thesis should describe a concrete benefit, rather than a vaguely stated strategic value.

This point needs underscoring. Justifying a deal as being "strategic" ex post facto is, in most cases, an invitation to inferior returns. Given how frequently we have heard weak "strategic" justifications after a deal has closed, it's worth passing along a warning from Craig Tall, vice chair of corporate development and strategic planning at Washington Mutual. In recent years, Tall's bank has made acquisitions a key part of a stunningly successful growth record. "When I see an expensive deal," Tall told us, "and they say it was a 'strategic' deal, it's a code for me that somebody paid too much."[13]

And although sometimes the best offense is a good defense, this axiom does not really stand in for a valid investment thesis. On more than a few occasions, we have been witness to deals that were initiated because an investment banker uttered the Eight Magic Words: If you don't buy it, your competitors will.

Well, so be it. If a potential acquisition is not compelling to you on its own merits, let it go. Let your competitors put their good money down, and prove that their investment theses are strong.

Let's look at a case in point: the Mayses' decision to move from radios into outdoor advertising (billboards, to most of us). Based on our conversations with Randall Mays, we summarize their investment thesis for buying into the billboard business as follows:

> Clear Channel's expansion into outdoor advertising leverages the company's core competencies in two ways: First, the local market sales force that is already in place to sell radio ads can now sell outdoor ads to many of the same buyers, and Clear Channel is uniquely positioned to sell both local and national advertisements. Second, similar to the radio industry twenty years ago, the outdoor advertising industry is fragmented and undercapitalized. Clear Channel has the capital needed to "roll up" a significant fraction of this industry, as well as the cash flow and management systems needed to reduce operating expenses across a consolidated business.

Note that in Clear Channel's investment thesis (at least as we've stated it), the benefits would be derived from three sources:

1. Leveraging an existing sales force more extensively
2. Using the balance sheet to roll up and fund an undercapitalized business
3. Applying operating skills learned in the radio trade

Note also the emphasis on tangible and quantifiable results, which can be easily communicated and tested. All stakeholders, including investors, employees, debtors, and vendors, should understand why a deal will make their company stronger. Does the investment thesis make sense only to those who know the company best? If so, that's probably a bad sign. Is senior management arguing that a deal's inherent genius is too complex to be understood by all stakeholders, or simply asserting that the deal is "strategic"? These, too, are probably bad signs.

Most of the best acquirers we've studied try to get the thesis down on paper as soon as possible. Getting it down in black and white—wrapping specific words around the ideas—allows them to circulate the thesis internally and to generate reactions early and often.

The perils of the "transformational" deal. Some readers may be wondering whether there isn't a less tangible, but equally credible, rationale for an investment thesis: the transformational deal. Such transactions, which became popular in the exuberant '90s, aim to turn companies (and sometimes even whole industries) on their head and "transform" them. In effect, they change a company's basis of competition through a dramatic redeployment of assets.

The roster of companies that have favored transformational deals includes Vivendi Universal, AOL Time Warner (which changed its name back to Time Warner in October 2003), Enron, Williams, and others. Perhaps that list alone is enough to turn our readers off the concept of the transformational deal. (We admit it: We keep wanting to put that word *transformational* in quotes.) But let's dig a little deeper.

Sometimes what looks like a successful transformational deal is really a case of mistaken identity. In search of effective transformations, people sometimes cite the examples of DuPont—which after World War I used M&A to transform itself from a maker of explosives into a broad-based leader in the chemicals industry—and General Motors, which, through the consolidation of several car companies, transformed the auto industry. But when you actually dissect the moves of such industry winners, you find that they worked their way down the same learning curve as the best-practice companies in our global study. GM never attempted the transformational deal; instead, it rolled up smaller car companies until it had the scale to take on a Ford—and win. DuPont was similarly patient; it broadened its product scope into a range of chemistry-based industries, acquisition by acquisition.

In a more recent example, Rexam PLC has transformed itself from a broad-based conglomerate into a global leader in packaging by actively managing its portfolio and growing its core business. Beginning in the late '90s, Rexam shed diverse businesses in cyclical industries and grew scale in cans. First it acquired Europe's largest beverage-can manufacturer, Sweden's PLM, in 1999. Then it bought U.S.-based packager American National Can in 2000, making itself the largest beverage-can maker in the world. In other words, Rexam acquired with a clear investment thesis in mind: to grow scale in can making or broaden geographic scope. The collective impact of these many small steps was transformation.[14]

But what of the literal transformational deal? You saw the preceding list of companies. Our advice is unequivocal: Stay out of this high-stakes game. Recent efforts to transform companies via the megadeal have failed or faltered. The glamour is blinding, which only makes the route more treacherous and the destination less clear. If you go this route, you are very likely to destroy value for your shareholders.

By definition, the transformational deal can't have a clear investment thesis, and evidence from the movement of stock prices immediately following deal announcements suggests that the market prefers deals that have a clear investment thesis. In "Deals That Create Value," for example, McKinsey scrutinized stock-price movements before and after 231 corporate transactions over a five-year period.[15] The study concluded that the market prefers "expansionist" deals, in which a company "seeks to boost its market share by consolidating, by moving into new geographic regions, or by adding new distribution channels for existing products and services."

On average, McKinsey reported, deals of the "expansionist" variety earned a stock market premium in the days following their announcement. By contrast, "transformative" deals—whereby companies threw themselves bodily into a new line of business—destroyed an average of 5.3 percent of market value immediately after the deal's announcement. Translating these findings into our own terminology:

- Expansionist deals are more likely to have a clear investment thesis, while "transformative" deals often have no credible rationale.
- The market is likely to reward the former and punish the latter.

The dilution/accretion debate. One more side discussion that comes to bear on the investment thesis: Deal making is often driven by what we'll call the *dilution/accretion debate*. We will argue that this debate must be taken into account as you develop your investment thesis, but your thesis making should not be driven by this debate.

Simply put, a deal is dilutive if it causes the acquiring company to have lower earnings per share (EPS) than it had before the transaction. As they teach in Finance 101, this happens when the asset return on the purchased business is less than the cost of the debt or equity (e.g., through the issuance of new shares) needed to pay for the deal. Dilution can also occur when an asset is sold, because the earnings power of the business being sold is greater than the return on the alternative use of the proceeds (e.g., paying down debt, redeeming shares, or buying something else). An accretive deal, of course, has the opposite outcomes.

But that's only the first of two shoes that may drop. The second shoe is, How will Wall Street respond? Will investors punish the company (or reward it) for its dilutive ways?

Aware of this two-shoes-dropping phenomenon, many CEOs and CFOs use the litmus test of earnings accretion/dilution as the first hurdle that should be put in front of every proposed deal. One of these skilled acquirers is Citigroup's CFO Todd Thomson, who told us:

> It's an incredibly powerful discipline to put in place a rule of thumb that deals have to be accretive within some [specific] period of time. At Citigroup, my rule of thumb is it has to be accretive within the first twelve months, in terms of EPS, and it has to reach our capital rate of return, which is over 20 percent return within three to four years. And it has to make sense both financially and strategically, which means it has to have at least as fast a growth rate as we expect from our businesses in general, which is 10 to 15 percent a year.

> Now, not all of our deals meet that hurdle. But if I set that up to begin with, then if [a deal is] not going to meet that hurdle, people know they better make a heck of a compelling argument about why it doesn't have to be accretive in year 1, or why it may take year 4 or 5 or 6 to be able to hit that return level.[16]

Unfortunately, dilution is a problem that has to be wrestled with on a regular basis. As Mike Bertasso, the head of H. J. Heinz's Asia-Pacific businesses, told us, "If a business is accretive, it is probably low-growth and cheap for a reason. If it is dilutive, it's probably high-growth and attractive, and we can't afford it."[17] Even if you can't afford them, steering clear of dilutive deals seems sensible enough, on the face of it. Why would a company's leaders ever knowingly take steps that would decrease their EPS?

The answer, of course, is to invest for the future. As part of the research leading up to this book, Bain looked at a hundred deals that involved EPS accretion and dilution. All the deals were large enough and public enough to have had an effect on the buyer's stock price. The result was surprising: First-year accretion and dilution did not matter to shareholders. In other words, there was no statistical correlation between future stock performance and whether the company did an accretive or dilutive deal. If anything, the dilutive deals slightly outperformed. Why? Because dilutive deals are almost always involved in buying higher-growth assets, and therefore by their nature pass Thomson's test of a "heck of a compelling argument."

As a rule, investors like to see their companies investing in growth. We believe that investors in the stock market do, in fact, look past reported EPS numbers in an effort to understand how the investment thesis will improve the business they already own. If the investment thesis holds up to this kind of scrutiny, then some short-term dilution is probably acceptable.

Develop Good Relationships with Targets

We've stressed the importance of doing your homework. Let's assume that you have your basis (or bases) of competition firmly in mind, you have your list of appropriate targets in hand, and you are prepared to develop a strong investment thesis in response to opportunities that arise. Yet another kind of homework needs to be ongoing—building relationships with your targets.

As noted, outstanding acquirers create and work a pipeline of priority targets, each one with a customized investment thesis. At the same time, they actively look for opportunities to "win over" attractive prospects. In other words, outstanding acquirers systematically build a relationship with each target, and are therefore positioned to get to the table as soon as (or even better, before) the target goes on sale. By this stage, canny acquirers are likely to have months, or even years, invested in the prospective deal. As a result, they are often willing to pay a premium, or act quickly, because they know precisely what they can expect to achieve through an acquisition.

Private companies tend to sell themselves to people they know and like. At uniform-supplier Cintas, therefore, an employee is assigned to keep in touch with each target, often over a period of years. The deal team ensures that Cintas employees are staying in touch with the targets and are in a position to help Cintas decide when to pull the trigger on talks. Indeed, the deal team sometimes even "puts a bullet in the gun" by giving senior executives a compelling reason to write or contact the target company, based on changes in the marketplace or at the target firm. This consistent, sophisticated monitoring increases Cintas's chances of pouncing on opportunity—and winning the competition—if a company decides to sell itself.

Focus on the Right Size and the Right Frequency

Because this is a chapter about the "how" of mergers, we need to restate an important lesson from the previous chapter. Our global study revealed that the most successful acquirers do a lot of deals, that their average deal size is small, and that they do deals more or less continuously. So this is an important piece of the "how": Think small and act often.

What's the evidence for these assertions? Based on our research, we can sort frequent buyers into four groups and quantify their relative success:

1. Constant buyers, who buy consistently through economic cycles
2. Recession buyers, who increase their buying during recessionary times
3. Growth buyers, who buy principally in periods of economic expansion
4. Doldrums buyers, who buy in the just-bumping-along periods between recession and growth

Of these four groups, the constant buyers are by far the most successful, outperforming the growth buyers by a factor of 2.3 and the doldrums buyers by a factor of 1.8. (See the appendix, figure A-2.)

We can also assert that the companies that enjoyed the highest returns were the ones that systematically bought companies that were only a small fraction of their own size. U.S. firms that focused on small deals—in other words, buying companies that averaged less than 15 percent of their own size—outperformed firms acquiring larger companies (a third or more of their own size) by a factor of almost six. Conversely, the worst performers tended to make big bets. We observed a similar, although less pronounced, pattern in Europe, where firms that focused on small deals outperformed firms acquiring larger companies by a factor of 1.8.

Putting together the earlier sections of this chapter with these research findings, the prescription is clear. Do your homework. Develop a strong investment thesis, based on a clear strategy and an understanding of your basis of competition—and then be prepared to act on that homework. Go after targets that you already know intimately, and with whom you've developed strong relationships. Go to the table frequently, but take small bites.

These steps are prerequisites for answering the next critical question: Which deals should you consummate, and which deals should you walk away from? In the next chapter, we will ask and answer that question and show how the investment thesis can be an invaluable guide through the thickets of due diligence.

3

Which Deals Should You Close?

This chapter focuses on the second of our four key decisions: Which deals should you close, and—by extension—how does due diligence help you to make those choices?

Let's imagine that you've done all the steps we recommended in chapter 2. You've identified your core, and you've figured out promising ways to build upon it. You've articulated your investment thesis, which is well grounded in your business's strategy. You've cultivated your deal pipeline, and—by paying attention to attractive targets—you've brought some interesting deals into view.

Now, before you move forward, you should conduct your due diligence. To execute your second critical decision—which deal to close—you need to ask and answer three questions:

1. Does the investment thesis hold? We're assuming that you've developed a strong investment thesis. But will this proposed investment deliver on that thesis? Does a close inspection of the actual goods—customer lists, cost and revenue data, the company's management and physical plant—give you confidence that your thesis works?

2. What is the deal's stand-alone value, based on a rigorous analysis of cash flow under a range of scenarios?

3. What is the true value of synergies, beginning with near-in cost synergies, moving out to revenue options, and subtracting negative synergies?

The most disciplined deal makers zero in on the big questions—the ones that, once answered, will demonstrate whether or not there is a match between the target company and their investment thesis. They build a proprietary, bottom-up view of a target company; they quantify the company's stand-alone value, based on a rigorous understanding of cash flows; and they assess the scale and timing of synergies realistically. They also build cooperative relationships with their target companies, in part to ensure that the diligence phase is thorough and productive.

Finally, throughout the due-diligence process, they test what they are learning against their predetermined "walk-away" criteria. If and when one of those criteria is met, they do what the name implies: They walk away.

Before tackling our three key questions, as well as the issues of cooperation and walking away from deals, let's look at an example of due diligence in the context of a leading private equity firm. As noted previously, we believe that skilled private equity companies—firms that invest heavily in due diligence because their main raison d'être is buying and selling other companies—are among the best in the world at taking the risks out of a proposed investment. So let's look at the discipline that they apply to their trade.

TAKING THE RISKS OUT

Benoît Bassi is a careful man in a risky business. As a managing director at Bridgepoint Capital, a top private equity firm, he spends his time searching for deals in Europe's emerging private equity marketplace.

Bassi, who is based in Paris, may devote many months to finding a deal he can take to his partners. In a typical year, he starts with one hundred fifty investment ideas, which he eventually whittles down to just a few. "[O]nce we get to [year] end," as Bassi explains, "we may end up with three files, which is a very good year. Two is a good year, while one is an okay year."[1]

When Bassi finally finds a deal that he feels good about, he invests a lot personally to see the deal through to its appropriate conclusion—which, as we will see, doesn't always mean a purchase. In December 2000, Bassi was feeling very good about a company he had spent months courting for his €1.6 billion fund, Bridgepoint Europe 1. The target company was a fruit-processing business considered "non-core" by its owner, French wine-and-spirits giant Pernod Ricard. To invoke our own terminology, Bassi had developed a strong investment thesis: Capitalize on the worldwide growth in demand for yogurt by investing in a well-positioned, well-run manufacturing asset. He was looking for an important supplier to that industry that could be used as a platform to supply other market segments.

For the purposes of this book we'll call the Pernod subsidiary FruitCo. It was the world's leading producer of the fruit mixtures that are used to flavor yogurt, and these flavors, in turn, make it possible for yogurt makers to earn a premium price in the market. Western consumers were spending 5 to 10 percent more on yogurt each year, and the market was growing faster still in the developing world, particularly Latin America and Asia. Not only did FruitCo have the number-one market share globally; it could also boast of strong profitability, a tradition of strong R&D and innovation, and manufacturing excellence.

Bassi could see great opportunity to expand the business into adjacent categories, such as ice creams and baked goods, as well as into new channels, such as food service. Strong profits, high growth, a great reputation within the industry, room for expansion, and an owner divesting mainly to focus its portfolio: In FruitCo, Bassi thought he had found a winner.

After subjecting his investment thesis to a grueling five-hour session with his partners, Bassi got the okay to investigate the acquisition. To the outside observer, it seemed like easy sledding from that point on: Look at the books, negotiate a price, close the deal, and celebrate a hard-won victory. Four weeks later, however, Bassi found significant daylight between what his investment thesis required FruitCo to be and reality. "When we got in there to do our diligence," he explains, "what we thought we knew turned out to be wrong." Bassi himself killed the deal.

Unfortunately, this kind of disciplined diligence is an exception. In our recent survey of two hundred fifty global executives, in general breakdowns in due diligence and disconnects between findings and executive decisions scored high on the list of reasons for disappointing deal outcomes. Specifically, with the benefit of hindsight, two-thirds of executives realized that they had overestimated the synergies available from the deal. Half discovered the target had been dressed up for sale. Half believed that their due-diligence process had failed to highlight critical issues in the deal. (Obviously, many of our respondents admitted to more than one problem!) Overall, only 30 percent of executives expressed satisfaction with the level of discipline in their due-diligence process. (See figure 3-1.)

So what steps can business leaders take to discipline their decision—whether that decision is to move forward or to walk away?

To find the answer, we looked at best-in-class corporate buyers in our Global Learning Curve Study and interviewed winners. Likewise,

FIGURE 3-1

Why Deals Break Down

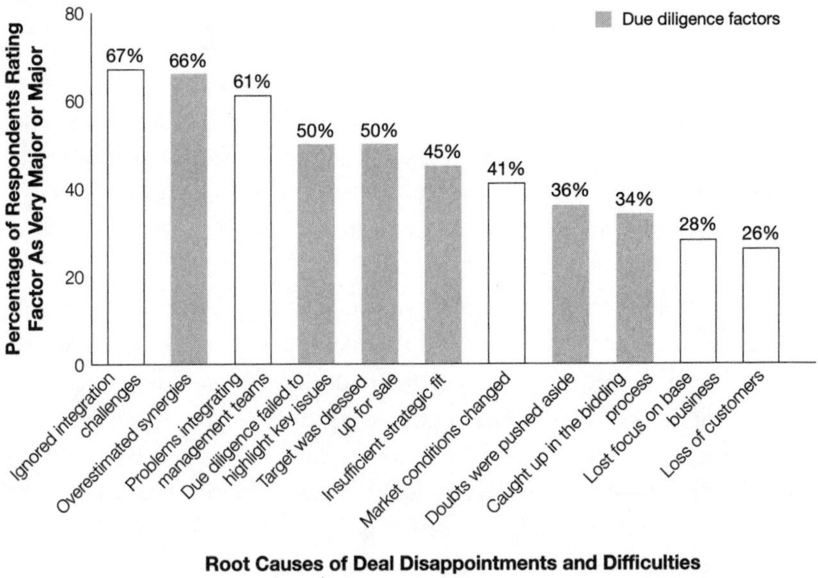

Source: Bain & Company Survey, fall 2002 ($n = 250$).

we looked again at the techniques employed by private equity firms. Our overarching finding, from both sets of practitioners? They ask and answer the big questions in due diligence. Yes, they "sweat the small stuff," but only in the context of our three key questions—the first of which is, does the investment thesis hold?

DOES THE INVESTMENT THESIS HOLD?

The best private equity buyers start with one question: Why would we want to own this asset? The answer to that question, as noted in the last chapter, serves as the centerpiece of your investment thesis.

Now is the time to test the reasoning behind your answer by asking a few big questions about why or how this business can earn you superior returns in the future. Getting the big questions right, and then answering them rigorously and dispassionately, is the first and most critical step in cracking the due-diligence code.

Sometimes people mistake rigor for negativity. Far from it! In fact, rigor can lead a company to make a strong acquisition that it otherwise would have passed up, and that others may already have passed on.

That's what happened, for example, when the private equity firm Centre Partners looked into buying a fishing company called American Seafoods in the late 1990s. At the time, the company, which caught and processed Alaskan pollock and other species in the U.S. waters in the Bering Sea using seven fishing trawlers, was owned by a Norwegian parent company. When the U.S. Congress enacted a law that made it illegal for a foreign concern to own companies fishing in American waters, the Norwegian parent was forced to sell. The question was, should Centre Partners buy?

Although American Seafoods had experienced a jump in profits in 1999—its earnings before interest, taxes, depreciation, and amortization (EBITDA) hit $60 million that year, up from an annual average of approximately $26 million in the three preceding years—the fishing business did not, at first blush, seem particularly attractive. Historically subject to wide swings in supplies and prices, and also under increasingly tight regulation, it seemed doomed to returns that were both volatile and potentially weak. But when Centre Partners sent in a highly skilled due-diligence team—combining experts in consumer products, fishing operations, and marine biology—it found that American Seafoods' profit boom wasn't merely a blip. In fact, it appeared sustainable.

Centre Partners asked and answered a key question: Just how competitive was the biomass of the Alaskan pollock fishery? To get its answer, the firm conducted a global analysis of the health of major fisheries. It discovered that the total biomass of the U.S. Alaskan pollock fishery was expected to grow in coming years, while the biomass of competing fisheries—Russian Alaskan pollock and Atlantic cod, most notably—would probably continue to decline rapidly. As supplies of pollock and cod fell, U.S. Alaskan pollock's market share would likely increase.

That was good news, from a revenue and pricing standpoint. But the news got even better when the due-diligence team looked more closely at trends in fish prices. Although pollock prices had recently increased as overall supplies fell, they remained well below the levels of competing whitefish such as cod, tilapia, and hoki. As a result, there seemed little chance that pollock would be subject to significant price competition for the foreseeable future. A huge Japanese market for pollock roe, meanwhile, remained strong, and supplies were falling. This had already led to a sharp and sustainable increase in roe prices—a trend that seemed likely to benefit American Seafoods well into the future.

Based on the results of the due-diligence analysis, Centre Partners made a successful bid for American Seafoods. The acquisition turned out to be quite a catch. Within three years, EBITDA grew to $109 million, and the private equity firm had recapitalized the company and sold a portion of its stake. In the process, Centre Partners realized nearly four times its initial investment and retained control of the business as it sought to further grow revenue and increase profits. By January 2004, it was exploring an initial public offering.

Surprisingly, most executives involved in deals do not take the kind of care that Centre Partners did in asking and answering the big questions. We mentioned in chapter 2 that of those executives interviewed in the Bain M&A survey, an astonishing 43 percent began the deal process without defining a clear investment thesis. Worse, of those who did define an investment thesis, half acknowledged that the thesis had failed within three years of signing the deal.

Due diligence is important. It offers your best opportunity to confirm, improve, or abandon an investment thesis. The process should tell you as much about the quality of your thesis as it does about the quality of the target company and its industry. And, as we'll see, it may tell you how to make a good acquisition better.

Experienced and successful deal makers build their own independent, bottom-up view of a target company's value. Bain Capital (not legally related to Bain & Company) may be the most successful private equity firm in business today. It was founded in 1984 and today manages $16 billion of assets, which it has put to use buying and turning around household-name companies like Burger King, Domino's Pizza, Houghton Mifflin, Duane Reade, FTD.com, and Sealy.

John Connaughton, a managing director with Bain Capital, stresses that his firm's edge begins with independence—with the perspective of an outsider looking at an industry with a fresh eye. "We have oftentimes been in situations where management teams tell us that an industry is growing at 4 percent, when it looks to us like it is actually declining," Connaughton observes.[2] He believes that too many practitioners doing diligence accept industry reports and other third-party information as fact. Bain Capital, Connaughton told us, does not. "The target's growth forecasts are often based on research reference after research reference," he says disdainfully, "with no one really trying to determine what the true drivers of growth in the industry are. We throw out the secondary research associated with the outlook for the business, and build our point of view from the bottom up."

When Bain Capital conducts primary research on an industry, therefore, it is not simply looking to verify growth rates and margins. According to Connaughton, the firm is looking "for value gaps associated with people not performing to their competitive position. Once we find those opportunities, we look for means not just to boost performance to [the sector] trend line, but to outperform."

In other words, Bain Capital is looking to make money by running the business differently. This ability to find the value gap (between a company's high potential and its relatively low performance) is one key to Bain Capital's success. "We are true believers that competitive position and differentiation ought to drive superior profitability," says Connaughton. "We don't like to buy businesses that are number-six players, and we don't necessarily find that we win auctions for number-one players that are already realizing their full potential. But we find that we often win when we define a situation where there is a competitively well-positioned company that is being run poorly." So an outside-in perspective not only gives an acquirer a proprietary understanding of the attractiveness of a given industry; it may also reveal specific ways to improve the performance of a company.

The Four C's

Given the need to do independent research to confirm or refute the investment thesis, you may well be asking, "Is there a system that ensures that I ask the big questions?" We use the framework of the Four C's to make sure that the search for what you don't know and should know is conducted in a systematic manner. To see how the Four C's work, let's return to Benoît Bassi's fruit-and-yogurt investment. Why did he walk away from the deal? Had Bridgepoint discovered something sour in the dairy sector?

Not exactly. The target was indeed well positioned in an expanding market, and in a region—Latin America—where appetite for its products was growing. But a key tenet of the original investment thesis—that FruitCo could win on cost leadership and the ability to grow faster than competitors—did not stand up to the scrutiny of four weeks of rigorous due diligence. Bridgepoint reached its decision by doing what all disciplined acquirers do: It tested the investment thesis from the bottom up.

Although bottom-up tests of a strong thesis vary on a case-by-case basis, the lines of inquiry that Bassi followed are typical of what any top-tier investor tends to ask. We refer to these as the Four C's:

1. Customers
2. Competitors
3. Costs
4. Capabilities

We use the Four C's to "pressure-test" an investment thesis when we are helping clients review potential deals. Here's how we apply this discipline: First, we look at the target's customers, both to assure ourselves that the business is stable and to identify ways of maximizing profits. We draw up a map of the market, sketching out its size, its growth potential, and how it breaks down by geography, product, and segment. Which segments are most promising? Which ones are most vulnerable? We work very hard to understand the buying process, paying particular attention to the role of price, the perceived value of premium offerings, and loyalty effects. What is the profit impact of increasing retention? Is it likely that, postacquisition, the target can increase its prices?

In general, we find the issue of pricing flexibility to be a reliable indicator of the health of a business. In the postmerger environment, you want flexibility, and the ability to command higher prices provides just that. Bain Capital's Connaughton, though, cautions that buyers frequently have too rosy a view of their postdeal pricing power, especially if there are cost savings on the near horizon. "People believe that margins will continue to expand," he explains, "not realizing they will have to give back a reasonable proportion of [cost savings] to the customer [in price reductions]."

We also quantify the profitability of customers. Who, exactly, are the most profitable customers? What is the cost of attracting profitable customers? How should we do it? We further segment customers to discover what different products and services the merged company might offer them. Has the target acquisition fully penetrated some customer segments but neglected others? Could the target adjust its offerings to grow sales? Is a valuable customer segment defecting to a competitor? If so, why?

Finally, a careful examination of the customers also involves an in-depth understanding of distribution channels. What range of channels is possible for each product or service? Do some offer superior economics? How do the target's channels match up with our own?

In analyzing a target's customer base, it's important not just to take the company's word for it. Call up the most important customers, or—even better—visit them. The information you uncover this way can be eye-opening.

Customers matter so much that some experienced buyers will not buy a company unless the target company has a strong customer list. Robert Kohlhepp is the vice chairman and former CEO of Cintas Corporation, which has used hundreds of small, "tuck-in" acquisitions to help build its leading position in the uniform business. In an interview, he stressed customers as the key factor in deciding on the merits of an acquisition:

> The number-one thing in most cases is the quality of the customer list. Our mind-set is that we can build new plants, hire new management, or promote management from our own company. But to buy a company that has a bad customer list—you might as well not buy it at all.[3]

Second, after analyzing a target's customers, we investigate opportunities to achieve differentiation and preempt competitor moves. We start by assessing the relative performance of the target and its competitors. What are the competitors' relative market share, revenue, and profit by geography, product, and segment? Does each competitor make the profits that are implied by its relative market share? Is the target underperforming operationally? Are its competitors? Is the business correctly defined?

We then look at the pool of available profits and decide whether the target is getting a fair (or better) share of the industry's profits.[4] Where in the value chain is the profit concentrated? We perform a classic SWOT analysis, examining each competitor's strengths, weaknesses, opportunities, and threats. We also role-play how competitors will react to the acquisition, and how that might impact the business.

Third, we analyze the target's strategic cost position, relative to its competitors, and identify opportunities for cost reduction. Do competitors have a cost advantage, and if so, why? Is the target performing better or worse than we would expect, in terms of cost, given its relative market position? What is the best cost position we could reasonably achieve? We also determine how low we can take costs by instituting best practices. This requires benchmarking: looking at how other business units or companies perform similar activities.

For companies in multiple businesses, we might look at potential for cost sharing, although this often turns out to be one of the harder things to assess in a diligence process. Among other things, we assess whether the benefits of sharing costs with other business units might outweigh the lack of focus that often results from this kind of initiative. We also look at allocated costs to determine which products and customers actually make money and which don't. (Target companies can be surprisingly forgiving on this particular score; acquiring companies should not be.)

When we look at the fourth, and often overlooked, "C"—capabilities—we document the special skills or technologies that the business possesses that (1) intersect with the business unit's core competencies, and (2) create specific, recognizable value for customers. Which investments in technology or people will advance either or both of these ends?

This knowledge, in turn, provides the basis for understanding which products a business unit should manufacture itself and which should be bought from another company. Assessing capabilities also involves looking at what organizational structures will enable the business to implement its strategy most effectively—an important input to planning merger integration. We also examine how all other aspects of the organization (such as compensation, incentives, promotion, information flow, authority, and autonomy) align with the strategy.

The key here lies in remembering that you are not just buying a P&L and a balance sheet. You are buying a human endeavor with all the strengths and fallibilities that go with it. You must be in a position to appraise the intangibles of an organization, such as managers' expertise and innate ability to get the job done, or better yet, to respond to coaching from you to improve their performance.

Successful firms approach the Four C's assessment with just as much rigor as they would a legal or environmental assessment. Due diligence is, in effect, an audit, one that ranges far beyond the limits of a traditional financial audit. (See table 3-1.) Bridgepoint's Bassi says that during due diligence, his firm conducts a thoroughgoing audit of the target company's human capital. "Even a management audit is done systematically," he elaborates. "A management audit means people are audited—the way they work together, and how they fit with our strategy."

TABLE 3-1

Tools for Testing the Four C's

Tool	Questions Addressed
Market mapping	How big is my market? Who are my competitors?
Industry pricing	Do I have pricing power?
Industry profit pool analysis	Who makes money in the industry?
Relative cost position	Am I low cost?
Customer/product profitability	What products and what customers drive my profitability?
Company SWOT (strengths, weaknesses, opportunities, and threats)	Where should I invest?
Customer/employee loyalty	Am I buying a good book of business?
Synergy analysis	What is my margin of safety?
People assessment	Can I rely on the team?
Systems assessment	Will I have the information to manage the business?

Source: Bain & Company.

So why did Bassi bail on FruitCo? First, he tested his thesis that FruitCo would make money by growing scale and competing on cost. What he learned was that although the company boasted considerable global scale—number one in the world!—regional scale turned out to be the more relevant driver of cost position. Moreover, when Bassi studied FruitCo's potential competitors—including companies that played in similar product markets, such as jams and preserves—he found that they were better positioned than FruitCo to share costs and build regional scale. As an aside, we should note that developing a good understanding of how scale—local, regional, or global—affects a business is a common stumbling block in diligence exercises.

Meanwhile, Bridgepoint did a thorough check on the company's customer lists. It was unhappy to learn that FruitCo was exposed to two dominant customers who were determined to control the preparation process in all the countries in which they operated. These customers (which included huge global yogurt producer Danone) wanted more control over their suppliers and their costs, in part because they were convinced that they had been gouged by fruit-preparation companies in the past. With such important customers so deeply suspicious of the very business FruitCo was in, Bridgepoint could not help but be concerned about the sector's credibility.

This led, naturally, to a test of price and revenue forecasts for FruitCo's product. In its conversations with customers, the firm learned that while the market for yogurt in Latin America was indeed growing, profitability was plummeting because the product was becoming more of a commodity. Bridgepoint concluded that this decline in profitability was irreversible, because both the company's customers and their customers proved unlikely to tolerate increased prices. Again, this downward trend boded ill for FruitCo.

What about capabilities? Well, with so many cracks appearing in FruitCo's cost, competitor, and customer scenarios, it began to be obvious that even the strongest internal capabilities at FruitCo couldn't save the original investment thesis from crumbling. The jury—Bridgepoint's diligence team—came in conclusively, and it came in against FruitCo.

The best diligence teams know that numbers on a page go only so far in telling the story. To test whether your investment thesis holds, you have to spend less time in data rooms looking at computer printouts, and more time in the field interviewing customers, suppliers, employees, creditors, and competitors. Joe Trustey, the managing partner at Summit Partners, a top-tier private equity and venture capital firm, tells us that he and his colleagues are "fanatical about reference checks. It would not be unusual for us to call a hundred customers in the course of an investment, hoping to speak to fifty of them, and planning on spending an hour with each of those fifty."[5] And Trustey takes pains to track down the customers who aren't showing up on the official radar. He explains:

> The reference checks are only as good as the source. So we have to figure out how to go beyond the list that was provided to us by the target's management team. Because we cold-call [to generate investment ideas], we get to know a lot of people that end up being customers or competitors of our targets. We tap into that network. Most of the time they tell us things we already know, but every now and then we get a [new] kernel of truth.

When Ronald Reagan negotiated nuclear-arms deals with the Soviets during the Cold War, his mantra was "Trust but verify." The private equity equivalent is—in Trustey's words—"Doubt everything."

At the same time, says Trustey, he and his partners try hard to keep their attention focused on the important variables in a given deal. He estimates that they spend 90 percent of their time on what he calls "strategic due diligence." By contrast, corporate buyers may field large teams tasked with assessing everything from the 401(k) plan to real estate and as a result spend less time focused on the business itself. As Trustey comments:

> We outsource everything except the focus on the business. We think it's more efficient to have a team of five focused on the big questions, than a team of forty covering all the waterfront.

But Bassi at Bridgepoint cautions against invoking the word *strategic* to cloud the key issues in a due-diligence process. Corporations undertaking due diligence, he says, very frequently illustrate the maxim that a little bit of knowledge can be a dangerous thing. "When you work for a corporation and you buy something you think is in your core business, or fits with your core business, you assume you know what you are buying," he observes. "By contrast, we [private equity investors] have to rediscover everything. There can be a certain arrogance in corporations, which causes them to make silly mistakes."[6]

In short, private equity firms like Bridgepoint, Bain Capital, and Summit Partners offer a crucial lesson to strategic buyers: Know what you don't know. Then use due diligence to test your investment thesis, and learn what you don't know.

So what happened with FruitCo? After rigorous due diligence, it became very clear to Bridgepoint that the gaps between the FruitCo commercial environment and the plan presented by management to further develop the company could not justify the price requested by the selling party. Bridgepoint decided not to pursue the deal, and it was eventually picked up by another investor. The ultimate verdict, of course, will not be known for years—but it seems likely that Bridgepoint's decision saved its investors from a deal that faced a strong headwind, and in which the odds of success appeared low.

Due diligence isn't the kind of activity that sets pulses racing. It is often perceived as the preserve of the back-room bean counters—not worthy of the attention of the titans and rainmakers who write corporate history, out there on the front lines of business. But as the Bridgepoint example shows, when a firm is contemplating an acquisition, there is simply no better place for that firm's top minds to be focused. In this phase of deal making, due diligence is the best way to be spending managers' time and investors' money. The best acquirers now realize that investing heavily in due diligence—especially strategic due diligence—vastly increases their chances of avoiding expensive mistakes and of creating real value for shareholders.

Rushes to Judgment

Before moving on to our next key question, let's look at an instance in which due diligence was short-circuited.

In chapter 1, we examined the troubled merger between Newell and Rubbermaid. Rubbermaid—a multibillion-dollar, global, multi–product line business—approached Newell with an exclusive deal that had to be completed within just three weeks, after which (the Rubbermaid board said) it would launch a public auction process.[7] When you consider that it took Bridgepoint four weeks to assess the Four C's at FruitCo, a relatively small, single-product company, the Rubbermaid time line practically guaranteed an impulse purchase. It was in the same spirit as one of those time-limited holiday sales: Buy now, or you're going to wish you had.

On reviewing this deal, our conclusion is that Newell management raced through the due-diligence process so quickly that it was unable to test the Four C's adequately. One key mistake, for example, came in the realm of valuing customers and their associated revenues. Only after the deal closed did Newell begin to discover the excessive price discounting and promotional activity that had been going on at Rubbermaid prior to the acquisition. Because retailers had become accustomed to Rubbermaid's "real" price—as opposed to its list price—instituting long-overdue controls on pricing had a negative impact on sales.

In addition, competitors' footholds in Rubbermaid's markets turned out to be far more secure and numerous than Newell had assumed. Rubbermaid's recent history of poor customer service was to blame: Over the years, smaller competitors had taken better care of key retail customers, had established a creditable track record, and were not going to give up their hard-won shelf space without a fight.

And there were cost issues growing out of strategic differences. Newell failed to recognize that while its own strategy was to compete on the basis of low-cost production, Rubbermaid competed on the basis of brand strength. True, both companies sold "everyday-use" products to roughly the same customers. But their cost points and competitive advantages were poles apart and could not be brought together easily.

Finally, Newell's leaders were disappointed with Rubbermaid's capabilities—ranging from distribution problems all the way up to the quality of management. Newell's managers had paid top dollar for what they thought they were buying—a premier company that would bring consumer brand-building skills to Newell—and were bitterly disappointed in the rather run-down company that their prize acquisition turned out to be.

These are the perils of cursory due diligence—and sadly, stories like this, full of oversights and ensuing frustrations, are all too common. The Newell–Rubbermaid saga illustrates what happens when inadequate effort is expended to test a deal's investment thesis. Newell should have insisted on more time to develop a complete picture. If Rubbermaid persisted in its threat to go the public-auction route, well, fine: Someone else should have paid too much for a company that didn't want to be scrutinized. Newell should have walked away.

WHAT IS THE STAND-ALONE VALUE?

On to our second key question: What is the stand-alone value?

Even the most elegant investment thesis ultimately must translate into concrete benefits—in terms of revenues and earnings—or it will be worthless. Those benefits, in turn, must be modeled into realistic cash flow estimates of the business. This is the cornerstone of establishing the target's stand-alone value.

Of course you will want to thoroughly integrate your new acquisition into your existing business, and of course you want to understand the bottom-line benefits of that integration, if and when it is finally successful. But meanwhile, your due-diligence process must first establish a baseline—that is, your target's value under "business as usual" conditions. Here's the watchword to keep in mind: Most of the price you are paying reflects the business as it is, not as it may be after you own it. All too often, acquirers take just the opposite stance. They decide, consciously or unconsciously, that the fundamentals of the target are unattractive relative to the likely sale price, so they go looking for synergies in order to justify the deal.

We asked Summit's Joe Trustey to cite the major reasons why he has walked away from deals. He gave us four:

1. Financial projections that are not credible
2. Historical financials that aren't conservative (for example, accounting practices regarding revenue recognition, inventory policies, and bad-debt treatment that put the best possible light on the business)
3. Uncertain cash flow
4. Bad reference checks on management

Note that the first three reasons relate directly to the deal's standalone value. And of all of the reasons for walking away from a deal, weak cash flow is easiest to overlook. Says Trustey: "We have learned through hard experience that cash flow is everything. If you do not believe the cash-flow model, don't do the deal." All good private equity buyers stress the importance of understanding a company's historical and prospective cash flow.

Admittedly, it can be tough to get a clear understanding of the true value of the company you hope to acquire. As we have seen, it's not always in the seller's interest to give you the full picture. Look at it from the other side of the table: When you are attempting to sell your house, don't you do your best to cover up all those cosmetic blemishes? Multimillion-dollar corporate deals are no different. In fact, there are a number of ways for sellers to artificially boost revenues or reduce costs to extract the maximum price for their asset. We call this "perfuming the pig," and we've listed some of these techniques in the accompanying box.

The only way to ensure that you are not fooled into buying something that has been sweetened for sale is to rigorously evaluate the historical and prospective cash flow of the company you are buying, stripping away all such accounting tricks. The result of all this work should be a comprehensive cash-flow model for the business.

Over the years, we have created some truly gigantic Excel models to support our diligence efforts, and the models that have worked the best for us tend to have a number of characteristics in common. First,

PERFUMING THE PIG

Dating back to the days of the barter economy, when farmers would do their best to exaggerate the health and understate the age of the animals they were selling, people have dressed up assets to make them more attractive.

But just like the buyer in the medieval marketplace, your job as an acquirer is to see through all the tactics that companies employ to buff themselves up for sale. As you get more experienced in deal making, you'll probably want to add to the following list:

- ***Stuffing distribution channels to inflate sales projections.*** For instance, a company may treat as market sales many of the products it sells to distributors—which many not represent recurring sales.
- ***Using overoptimistic projections to inflate the expected returns from investments in new technologies and other capital expenditures.*** A company might, for example, assume that a major uptick in its cross selling will enable it to recoup its large investment in customer relationship management software.
- ***Disguising the head count of cost centers by decentralizing functions so you never see the full picture.*** For instance, some companies scatter the marketing function

they are built on a credible set of market-demand, market-share, and margin inputs that both the buyer and seller agree on. Second, they allow for the flexibility to anticipate changing market and competitive conditions. For example, we use these models to assess how changes in the price environment and sales volumes will affect the business and to factor cost inputs. Finally, we make the models compatible with the company's accounting systems so that the models can be used to track actual performance more or less in real time.

As promised at the beginning of this book, we are not going to get overly technical in our discussions. We are interested here in discussing the methodology of what goes into your cash flows, rather

among field offices and maintain just a coordinating crew at headquarters, which hides the true overhead.

- *Treating recurring items as extraordinary costs to get them off the P&L.* A company might, for example, use the restructuring of a sales network as a way to declare bad receivables as a onetime expense.
- *Exaggerating a Web site's potential as an effective, cheap sales channel.*
- *Underfunding capital expenditures or sales, general, and administrative costs in the periods leading up to a sale to make cash flow look healthier.* For example, in many manufacturing industries, postponing machine renewal by a year or two will not be immediately visible in the books but will overstate free cash flow by misleading the investor about how much regular capital a plant needs.
- *Encouraging the sales force to increase sales while hiding costs.* A company looking for a buyer might, for example, offer advantageous terms and conditions on postsale service to boost current sales. The product revenues will show up immediately in the P&L, but the lower profit margin on service revenues will not be apparent until much later.

than how you build the model. The old saw—"garbage in, garbage out"—was never more applicable than in merger calculations. You don't want to see garbage in your spreadsheets. If you want to know how to build a good spreadsheet, consult one of the several good texts available that run through the mechanics of how to do cash flow analysis. We recommend, for example, *Valuation* by Tom Copeland, Tim Koller, and Jack Murrin.

Does this process seem long-winded? Unfortunately, it needs to be. There is no shortcut to finding out a company's true value: exactly how and where it makes money, and how much. And as with the customer base described earlier, often the only way to see what's really happening with cash in and cash out—to look beyond the reported numbers—is to send a due-diligence team out into the field.

That's what Cinven, another leading European private equity firm, did before acquiring Odeon Cinemas, a U.K. theater chain, in 2000. Cinven has built its reputation on the detailed analysis it applies to every deal. When it decided to bid for Odeon Cinemas, it planned to combine Odeon's operations with ABC Cinemas, which Cinven already owned. But Cinven had three strong reasons for thinking long and hard about buying Odeon. First, Odeon was three times the size of ABC, which in itself would make integration very challenging. Second, combining the two businesses would work only if Odeon was a strong, attractive, stand-alone business. (This was the key assumption behind Cinven's plan to create value, but at the start of the due-diligence phase, it was not clear whether this was indeed the case.) And third, Cinven needed to establish whether Odeon was worth the £325 million price tag that industry analysts were expecting.[8]

Richard Segal, CEO of Odeon at the time of the deal, said, "The plan going forward is not based on cost-cutting but on significant investment. It will be about growing admissions, increasing spend per customer, and at the same time optimizing the synergies that bringing two companies together will inevitably create."[9]

Rather than just looking at revenues and costs at an aggregate level, Cinven sent a team of analysts into the field to "hang out at the movies" in a feet-on-the-street effort to figure out how to generate cash flow at each theater. Painstakingly, they went through every cinema site in order to understand the distinctive profit-and-loss dynamics of each location. This enabled them to paint a location-by-location picture of market conditions and competitor activity, including the number of admissions, revenues, operating costs, and the kinds of capital expenditure that would be required over the next five years.

During the exclusive phase of the deal, Cinven drew in Odeon's management as part of an iterative process designed to challenge the business model—and, by extension, to test assumptions about the potential value of the target. They did this by holding four one-day meetings in which all parties went through each of the sites and agreed on the most important levers of growth—for example, providing substantial capital investment to grow admission and increase spend per customer, or extracting synergies by leveraging the increased purchasing power and streamlining the structure.[10]

This detailed process gave both sides a clear, bottom-up understanding of the true financial potential of the business as well as a road map specifying how profits might be boosted postacquisition. It also enabled Cinven to negotiate a price that reflected the deal's true value: £280 million, or some £45 million less than the analysts had initially estimated. Cinven was then able to use the deal-derived road map to manage and track the business postacquisition. What did Cinven find? By 2003, the business was performing slightly ahead of the original plan.[11]

Selecting the right metrics can be helpful in accurately valuing the base business. Private equity companies are masters at this. They use performance measures to help them zero in on what really drives the target's ability to make money.

As suggested earlier, they resist the temptation to measure everything, and instead home in on the two or three financial indicators that most clearly reveal a company's value. As a rule, they tend to watch cash more closely than earnings, knowing that cash remains a more reliable barometer of financial performance. (As recent history has painfully illustrated, corporate earnings can be manipulated.) And they prefer to calculate return on invested capital (ROIC), which states the actual returns on the money put into a business, rather than fuzzier measures such as "return on accounting capital employed" or "return on sales." We hasten to point out, however, that managers in private equity firms avoid imposing one set of measures across their entire portfolios. They prefer to tailor measures to each business they hold.

To see how effective this can be in practice, let's look at Texas Pacific Group's 1996 purchase of Beringer Wine Estates from its parent Nestlé. Winemaking is an asset-intensive business, and therefore one that private equity buyers like Texas Pacific Group (TPG) would normally shun. The TPG managers leading the deal quickly recognized they would need to rethink the measures used to gauge Beringer's past performance as well as its true potential. In assessing Beringer's performance, Nestlé had focused on return on assets (ROA) and economic value-added (EVA)—the measures that it applied to all of its businesses. But while those measures made sense for most of Nestlé's units, TPG felt that they weren't the right ones for Beringer. (The reasons are technical: Those measures pull asset depreciation and amortization out of earnings, even though they're not really cash expenses. And while it's essential to age wine in cellars to achieve a quality level sufficient to command a premium price, ROA calculations penalize companies that hold on to inventory.[12])

Focusing on more appropriate yardsticks—operating cash flow, cash margins, and growth—enabled TPG to value Beringer on the basis of those factors that actually exerted the most influence on cash flow. With this accurate—and positive—picture of Beringer's stand-alone value in hand, TPG closed the deal. And the deal turned out to be a good one: Beringer subsequently thrived under TPG ownership, achieving a ninefold return on initial investment within five years.

After—and only after—you feel satisfied that you know the stand-alone value of a target company, you can begin to focus on the kinds of synergies (both positive and negative) you can expect from the deal.

WHAT IS THE TRUE VALUE OF SYNERGIES?

Fair warning: We are now entering one of the most dangerous territories in the deal-making world—synergy.

Many deals have failed largely because of an overoptimistic evaluation of a deal's revenue-boosting promise. In fact, the very notion of "synergy" has been all but discredited because of the number of times it has been used to justify acquisitions that subsequently went sour.

How widespread is the problem? According to Bain's M&A survey, two-thirds of acquiring executives said they had overestimated the synergies available from combining companies, and that this prospective exaggeration had been an important factor in a deal outcome that was ultimately disappointing.

Based on what you've read so far, you can understand why business leaders so often find it difficult to make realistic judgments about the synergies that an acquisition will deliver. In the cranked-up environment of a takeover—think Rubbermaid—cost-saving synergies are often overestimated in terms of value and underestimated in terms of how difficult they will be to achieve. Revenue-generating synergies, in most cases, are even harder to capture.

This long record of shortfalls and disappointments has led some companies to take the extreme approach of not including any synergies in the valuation of a company. For example, Fiserv—an information-management-technology company that serves financial companies—evaluates opportunities almost solely on a stand-alone basis; it claims that it pays for synergies only about 5 percent of the time.[13]

We view Fiserv's approach as too extreme. Ignoring positive synergies will lead companies to pass on deals that they should make. And conversely, ignoring negative synergies (and yes, there are such things!) lures companies into bad deals.

Positive Synergies

Let's look first at the happier side of the equation. "Positive synergies" is what people usually mean when they refer to synergy—the case of one plus one adding up to three, or better.

We like to depict positive synergies as a set of concentric rings. (See figure 3-2.) The synergies in the center ring typically come from the postmerger combination's duplicative, non-customer-facing functions, such as legal, treasury, human resources, and the like. You're sure to get most of these, and there is little risk in getting them.

One ring out are the shared operating costs, such as distribution, sales, and regional expenses. Most companies get the majority of

FIGURE 3-2

Synergy Valuation

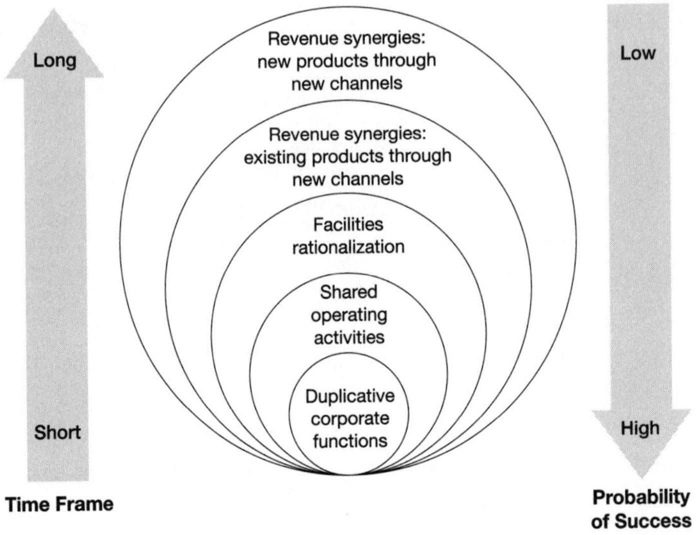

these, although the risk of affecting customer relationships often requires the company to move more slowly (and therefore realize savings later). Farther out lie savings from facilities rationalization, which typically involve significant people and regulatory issues. In the outer rings lie revenue synergies, starting with increased sales of existing products through new channels, and moving to the most distant (read "least sure") circle of all: revenues from new products through new channels.

Capturing the value that is nested in each circle may generate huge rewards. But the painful truth is that the farther from the core these cost or revenue synergies lie, the more difficult they will be and the longer they will take to capture. Part of your assessment, therefore, should focus on (1) the speed with which you think the synergies can be realized and (2) the level of investment that it will take to realize them. By the way, the news resulting from such a careful scrutiny is not always bad. In some cases, companies can make a more attractive bid to the target's shareholders not because they can identify greater value-creating opportunities than the other bidders, but because they know they can realize that value more quickly or less expensively.

In short, for each ring, we recommend assigning a probability of success, the necessary investment, and a timetable. From this, you calculate expected values that you can model into your cash-flow forecasts.

If you are going to assess the value of synergies—and as already explained, we believe that you should—then getting this calculation right is critically important, since it has major implications for the price you are prepared to pay for the new business. At a maximum, your walk-away price should be the sum of the stand-alone value of the business plus the expected value of the synergies. Ideally, it should be somewhere in the middle.

Consider the way Kellogg evaluated synergies in setting a price for Keebler. (See chapter 1 for the previous discussion of this case.) When Kellogg CEO Carlos Gutierrez was putting together this deal, his investment thesis argued that getting Kellogg snacks delivered through Keebler's DSD system provided the most compelling reason for doing the deal. But another pillar of the deal, according to Gutierrez, was cost savings. By measuring those potential savings carefully, he was able to better judge the value of the deal. He told us, "We came up with a realistic cost-savings target [and] did our own projections of what we felt [Keebler's] value was if we owned them, and what their intrinsic value was. On the basis of that we developed our walk-away price."[14]

Note that in valuing the acquisition of Keebler, Gutierrez focused on cost synergies. He left potential revenue synergies to be calculated and pursued after the deal was (or wasn't) completed. To us, that's the way to treat elusive, outer-ring synergies. Work hard to get them, if and when you get the chance, but don't count or build them into your walk-away price.

Negative Synergies

The temptation in deal making is to see and count the things you like, and to not see and not count the things you don't like. But you can't have it both ways. If you're going to identify and quantify the positive synergies, you have to do the same for the negative ones.

A negative synergy is just what it sounds like: the case where one plus one equals less than two. Almost all deals involve at least some negative synergies, which you can probably find if you go looking for them.

One common mistake is to create a valuation model that sums up the revenues of the two companies, plus the synergies, without subtracting an estimate for revenue erosion (a negative synergy). How many shared accounts will you lose when you combine customers simply because some of those customers won't want such a large piece of their business with one provider? (One plus one just got to be less than two.) How likely is customer service or order fulfillment to slip as you merge back offices—and how much will that slippage impact sales? And what about the trusted and talented employees who inevitably leave during the postmerger integration process? Do they have accounts associated with them, and will you lose those accounts? And what of the almost inevitable loss of momentum in the base business, as managers focus on integration and cost cutting? There's probably a dollar amount that should be associated with that by-product of a merger.

The impact of ownership change, too, should be factored into your valuation model, particularly when you are acquiring a business from a larger parent company. Has the acquired business enjoyed a favorable cost position due to its privileged relationship with other companies within the parent organization? Has it been getting its raw materials, for instance, at more attractive rates than you'll be able to achieve in the open market? What about shared services, such as IT? These can sometimes turn into large, unanticipated costs, postacquisition.

We've already alluded to the risk of losing management talent and key employees. Not only will this erode revenues, but it will also force you to spend money to replace these people. You may face cultural clashes as you rebuild the organization. Meanwhile, your competitors aren't just sitting out there; they're moving to take advantage of any weaknesses you may reveal in the wake of the merger.

Even the best acquirers face negative synergies—sometimes even as a result of being virtuous. An executive who left Kellogg after its merger with Keebler told us that Kellogg ran into negative synergies when it decided to put new-product launches on hold in order to focus on integration in the aftermath of the merger. In other words, by keeping its well-intentioned promises to itself about achieving cost synergies, Kellogg wound up paying a price on the revenue side.

Cases in Point: Synergies Real and Unreal

Let's flesh out our discussion of synergies with two stories from real life. One is inspirational; the other cautionary.

Royal Bank of Scotland's acquisition of National Westminster Bank (NatWest) is a textbook example of how a realistic assessment of near-in cost synergies can be a powerful tool in creating significant shareholder value. During late 1999 and early 2000, NatWest was the target of two unsolicited hostile takeover bids by dueling Scots: one from the Bank of Scotland (BoS) and the other from the Royal Bank of Scotland (RBS). At the time, NatWest was the fourth-largest bank in the United Kingdom, though its stock price had been sliding due to a reputation for poor management.[15]

RBS was half the size of NatWest in terms of assets and net income, but was viewed as one of the most technologically advanced banks in the industry. The firm had grown organically and also through a series of smaller acquisitions—in other words, following the formula we recommend.

The strategic motivation behind this new deal was to grow in size and gain critical mass in the rapidly consolidating U.K. market. RBS managers also believed that applying their bank's own best practices to a much larger customer base would enable it to benefit from economies of scale and enhance profitability.

Before they embarked on the bidding process, RBS leaders studied the potential cost and revenue synergies in great detail. Cost savings included the elimination of duplicated support activities, while revenue benefits comprised the combination of brands, customers, products, and skills. As a result of this up-front investment of time and money, RBS was able to compute the value and timing of these savings and bid a realistic price for NatWest. Having a crystal-clear picture of NatWest's stand-alone value as well as a realistic understanding of the synergies likely to result from the deal gave RBS the edge in what turned out to be one of the most hard-fought takeover battles in the United Kingdom. On March 6, 2000, RBS acquired NatWest for £21 billion.

Since then, RBS's meticulous due diligence has continued to pay off. Because RBS had a thorough understanding of its target company and the market, it was able to draw up a clear business plan to capture savings postacquisition. In fact, the combined entity was soon achieving annual benefits of £300 million more than plan.[16] Not only have savings and synergies been larger than anticipated, they also have come faster.

Most banking mergers are, at their heart, cost plays. This is interesting because the basis of competition in financial services—that is, the ability to earn superior sustainable financial returns—is all about customer loyalty. It was Royal Bank of Scotland's ability to use technology to better satisfy customers, and thereby win a larger share of wallet, that made this deal so successful. Taking costs out in and of itself is generally not a compelling enough reason to justify a merger premium.

By contrast, the recent wave of media combinations has consisted mostly of revenue plays, predicated on nebulous revenue synergies that in most cases have not panned out. Vivendi—which we cited in chapter 2 for its faulty investment thesis in buying media properties—is only the most egregious example of faulty due diligence and exaggerated estimates of synergies.

Vivendi was founded in 1853 as a French water company, Compagnie Générale des Eaux (CGE). Though it was one of France's largest utilities, its line of business remained pretty much unchanged for more than a hundred years—that is, until the first half of the 1980s, when CGE started to expand and diversify into international water operations, waste management, energy and transport services, and telecommunications and media. By 1998 the company had changed its name to Vivendi, and in June 2000, it became Vivendi Universal after the US$34 billion merger with Canal Plus and Seagram, the Canadian owner of Universal Studios and Universal Music.

As noted in chapter 2, the driving force behind the transformation of Vivendi into a global media empire was the company's then-chairman, Jean-Marie Messier. His plan was to marry the best content in the world with distribution across all communications platforms, from television to mobile telephones. By joining the production capabilities of Universal Studios with the distribution of cable-television companies Canal Plus and USA Networks, Messier hoped to create a vertical entertainment giant. The giant would produce and distribute television shows and movies. It would cross-promote that content. It would tame the Internet and put it to work for Vivendi. Synergies (and new and increased revenues) would abound.

Two years after its largest acquisition, however, the synergies had yet to materialize. The integration of content and distribution Messier dreamed of just didn't happen, and the idea that Internet service would drive synergies from the rest of the group turned out to be no more than a dream, as the vision of content being piped from the Internet portal Vizzavi—Vivendi's joint venture with Vodafone—came to naught.

As the trouble closed in around him, Messier increasingly had to defend his strategy in front of irate investors. And increasingly, he began to acknowledge that at least some of his acquisitions—such as the purchases of Maroc Telecom or MP3.com, Inc., which together cost Vivendi some $3 billion—weren't central to the company's strategy.[17]

Meanwhile, curiously, Vivendi's stake in the original water utility seemed to have been forgotten. (Does your investment thesis, or your estimation of synergies, simply ignore whole pieces of your business? If so, that's probably a bad sign, since an investment thesis by definition should make your existing business stronger.) Indeed, Messier wrote in his memoir, *Mon vrai journal,* that his failure to sell off the utility businesses was one of his six fatal errors of leadership.[18] Only some years after the company embarked on its media and telecommunications acquisitions spree did Vivendi—under the new leadership of Jean-René Fourtou—begin to sell some of its utility interests. (Jean-Marie Messier left the company in July 2002.)

Vivendi Universal finished 2001 with a €13.6 billion loss, the largest corporate loss in France's history. Operating profits were positive, but Vivendi had to take a goodwill write-off of €15.2 billion, reflecting the reduced value of many of its acquisitions. Investors were furious. In April 2002, a Bloomberg news report captured the strength of feeling against Messier's strategy by quoting a hapless Vivendi investor: "Messier hasn't created anything since taking over. . . . He's acted more as an investment banker than a manager."[19] In fact, Messier used to be a banker (at what is now Lazard LLC), and it's fair to infer that his years of training on the other side of table influenced his deal-making decisions.[20]

Of course, not all Vivendi's losses can be attributed to overly ambitious synergy expectations. Deal fever, lack of a good investment thesis, and intermittent lack of due diligence also contributed mightily. But without a doubt, the company bet too heavily on alleged synergies between traditional media and novel technologies like the Internet, and paid heavily for that bet.

Deal makers have an obligation: to create value. When they scrutinize a potential deal and can't make it make sense, they have a second obligation: to walk away.

BE READY TO COOPERATE

While we're on the subject of obligations, here's a third one: to cooperate with the leaders of your target company to the fullest extent possible.

We say this not in the spirit of the Golden Rule, but rather, from a practicality standpoint. It should be clear, based on the preceding discussion of due diligence, that the acquiring company's success depends in large part on an intimate knowledge of the target company. In most cases, you simply can't get close enough to do due diligence on a company without its cooperation. An adversarial posture almost always backfires.

Conducting due diligence effectively means making the seller part of the solution, not the problem. It requires persuading the seller to help you and not your competitors. Working positively with the target's management team is likely to make due diligence far less onerous and far more effective. Persuading the target's shareholders and managers that you are the most suitable acquirer may help you win an acquisition battle, and therefore may prevent you from overbidding and overpaying for the target.

As Joe Trustey, one of the savviest acquirers in our study, says: "We walk away from a target whose management is uncooperative in due diligence. For us, that's a deal-breaker."

BE PREPARED TO WALK

Our closing thought for this exploration of due diligence is a distillation of much of what we've said earlier: Be prepared to walk.

The buyers we have come to respect say that even when they have poured hours of their own time and effort into a deal, and have (in their own way) answered the three questions we find critical to due diligence, they are prepared to walk away from the deal at any point if they begin to have strong doubts about the deal's value.

Randall Mays, the CFO of Clear Channel whom we met in chapter 2, is one of our disciplined corporate buyers. He has set up a clearly defined process to guarantee objectivity around the walk-away decision (which we'll explore in detail in chapter 6). He lets his deal team call the plays from the field but keeps on top of the situation from the sidelines. If a target fails an objective test of due diligence, headquarters dispassionately uses its veto power.

Trustey of Summit considers such level-headedness the core strength of private-equity firms:

> We are less emotionally tied to the deal than many corporate buyers we've competed against. If we miss this deal, we know that we'll get the next one. It's more difficult for corporate buyers to adopt that mentality.[21]

More difficult, perhaps, but certainly not impossible. Much of the discipline you find in private equity firms gets down to a matter of process and of discipline in applying that process consistently. The best acquirers teach us that we need mechanisms to ensure that all the tough questions get asked, and that we make the necessary judgments in an unsentimental manner.

As Bassi, Mays, and Trustey all note, the most successful corporate acquirers and private equity companies adopt formal checks and balances to make sure their assessment of a target is on the money. An investment committee, which has no involvement in the day-to-day examination of the proposed acquisition, may be charged with making the final decision. Some acquirers have discovered that a good way of keeping a dispassionate eye on things is to put together a decision-making body of trusted individuals who are less attached to the deal than the deal's proponents in senior management may be. Going a step further, some companies assign a "red team" to every serious deal prospect. The job of the red team? To play devil's advocate, and try to kill the deal at every turn.

For example, Bridgepoint assembles a team of six managers who represent four constituencies. One of these is a prosecutor who plays the role of devil's advocate. The second one is a less-experienced manager whose involvement is a key part of training. The third group comprises two veterans—senior managing directors who no longer have any hierarchical function at the company, and who therefore cannot be undermined by corporate politics. The final members of the panel are managing directors who still have an operational role. "That makes quite a balanced whole," says Bridgepoint's Bassi. "Is it perfect? I don't know. But it works."[22]

The bottom line is that meaningful, rigorous due diligence saves you money. Cinven saved up to £45 million on the Odeon deal, compared to market estimates; Bridgepoint appears to have saved itself from a costly investment in FruitCo. Superficial due diligence, by contrast, is expensive. Vivendi learned the hard way that you can't overinvest in due diligence (and Vivendi went on to learn a brutal lesson in the cost of misapprehending synergies). Due diligence is your most important risk-management tool.

If you've done your due diligence right—if you've thoroughly tested your investment thesis, determined the target's stand-alone value, and ensured that the (positive) synergies are real—you're ready to pull the trigger and close the deal. See How the Private Equity Firms Do It for a summary of best practices.

And then, of course, you have to master the details of how best to integrate the target company into your own. As you'll see in chapter 4, we believe that good integration is all about determining which parts of the business need to blend right away and which can be left alone for the time being. If you're as focused on getting this right as you were about answering the big questions in due diligence, you'll have an excellent chance of fulfilling the deal's promise.

HOW THE PRIVATE EQUITY FIRMS DO IT

1. Test the investment thesis from the outside in. Take stock in the field, where customers, suppliers, and competitors labor.
2. Believe only assumptions that you can translate into concrete results that can increase shareholder value.
3. Repeat the mantra that "cash is king." If you cannot model a benefit in terms of cash flow, you should not count it.

Meanwhile, closing a good deal can be a gratifying experience indeed. Let's look again at the experience of Bridgepoint's Benoît Bassi. One year after turning down FruitCo, his due-diligence team checked out yet another potential investment: pest-control company Eurogestion. Again, Bassi initially liked what he saw. He explained his deal rationale to us: "Altogether, our investment thesis [suggested] that we could increase margins from 9 percent to 12 percent with external growth in Europe and Australia, and in the same way make acquisitions in important countries." This time, though—in contrast to the FruitCo deal—he continued to like what he saw.

Bridgepoint decided to close this deal and acquired the company in November 1999 for €75 million. Just as Bassi had hoped, Eurogestion served as a platform for a successful pan-European and Australian pest-control business. In the summer of 2002, Bridgepoint sold Eurogestion to ISS, a Danish facilities-services group, for €155 million, more than twice its purchase price. "It was great," said Bassi, savoring the sweetest result of due diligence. "What counts in this industry isn't just earning money. What counts is to return it to investors."

4

Where Do You Really Need to Integrate?

Integration means bringing two companies together in productive ways. Using the language of the last chapter, it is the process of delivering on a particular deal's investment thesis. And while every integration—like every merger—is different, a number of guiding principles apply across almost all integration efforts, and they revolve around a central question: Where do you really need to integrate operations as opposed to letting each entity simply carry on separately? The answer lies in a set of decision principles, which we will group into four main categories:

1. ***Plan for ownership***. Ideally, acquirers should plan for ownership and launch their integration planning months before the deal is publicly announced. (Indeed, we will argue that certain aspects of integration should begin in due diligence.) Many of the toughest integration decisions will be about people: choosing the best talent from each company, selecting the executive team, and thinking about who will stay and who must go. Management should link this process tightly to the deal's investment thesis and to the synergies and cultural issues identified during due diligence.

2. ***Integrate quickly where it matters.*** Integrating in every direction at once isn't practical or effective. Yes, speed is paramount, but you have to focus on the right issues. Being highly selective about where you integrate is the best way to reduce friction and extract value. Ultimately, the extent of integration should reflect the investment thesis. In some areas, it may be counterproductive to integrate—now, or even in the long term.

3. ***Put culture high on your leadership agenda.*** Leaders of merged companies need to retool their corporate culture in a way that is consistent with the investment thesis. Scale deals demand more cultural integration; scope deals require less. Whatever path you choose, you need to use hard tactics—organizational structure, compensation incentives, and a shared decision-making system—to address cultural integration.

4. ***Maintain firepower in the base businesses.*** Even when you have planned for ownership, properly focused integration efforts, and paid full attention to cultural issues, mergers can exert a gravitational pull on employees. Many of your brightest and most ambitious young managers will perceive the integration planning and leadership team as strategic—the place to be—and will want to involve themselves. But the best acquirers reinforce the first three principles of successful integration by keeping line management focused on minding the store.

We will consider each of these imperatives in turn. First, though, let's set the stage by considering an interesting example of integration, one that included both predeal and postdeal elements.

JONAH SWALLOWS THE WHALE

Greg Lawton, the chief executive of Johnson Wax Professional (JWP), takes his fiduciary responsibilities to his shareholders very seriously. That's a good thing, because at JWP the shareholders tend to have one another's phone numbers—and to use them. Founded in 1886, the company is owned by the family of the late Sam Johnson, the fourth-generation chairman emeritus. So when Lawton and Sam Johnson's son Curt wanted to acquire Anglo-Dutch conglomerate Unilever's commercial-cleaning-products business, they had to go to the heirs of the Johnson fortune and ask permission to borrow $1.6 billion.

The Johnson heirs asked a lot of hard questions about how their company—an informal, family-owned business based in Racine, Wisconsin—was going to manage Unilever's DiverseyLever unit, a Netherlands-based, command and control–oriented business that was more than a third larger than JWP.

"I thought they were crazy trying to pull this off," Sam Johnson told us, "but they stuck with it, told everyone they could do it, and they did it."[1]

If there was ever a high-stakes corporate-integration exercise, this was it: highly leveraged personal fortunes at risk, Americans buying Europeans, and the little company buying the big guy. And while both companies had institutional cleaning businesses and operated in complementary regions around the globe, their corporate cultures could not have been farther apart. JWP, with sales in 2001 of $1.1 billion in floor-care and housekeeping products and services, was entrepreneurial, intuitive, and informal. DiverseyLever, at $1.5 billion in 2001 revenue, was highly structured and bureaucratic in its approach to business and its decision-making process. JWP and DiverseyLever were about as different as two companies in the same market can get. So some observers no doubt held their breath when, in May 2002, JWP completed the acquisition of DiverseyLever.

And how have these unlikely bedfellows fared? So far, they've thrived. Why? For one thing, having had lots of practice in integrating a number of small acquisitions, Greg Lawton understood the importance of deciding where he really needed to integrate people and functions. Months in advance of the deal's announcement, he launched extensive integration discussions and made the tough choices about who from each organization would join the top management team.

Second, those previous deals had taught Lawton to start the integration with Diversey by targeting a few key operations and forcing consolidation only in areas where integration truly created value.

Lawton understood that cultural alignment had to be a top priority. He decided early on where a common culture really mattered—among the merged company's new leadership, for instance. So, before the deal was even announced, he developed decision-making procedures that encouraged executives from both companies to work together.

Throughout, Lawton kept a sharp eye on both companies' base businesses, not only keeping customers informed of merger plans, but also making sure that employees not involved in the integration would stay focused on their jobs. Through these key steps, JWP overcame the difficulty of blending two very different companies without significantly distracting the operating teams that were out there earning money. The integration went off with few problems, and the retention rate of both major accounts and top managers was almost 100 percent.

Failing to focus on the integration issues that matter can jeopardize even the most promising deal, a lesson General Mills learned to its dismay when it stubbed its toe on the acquisition of Pillsbury in 2001. The deal thesis appeared sound: General Mills had marketing savvy and new-product-development expertise; Pillsbury was a player in high-growth consumer-product categories. At the time, analysts forecasted that revenue synergies would boost sales between 4 and 5 percent and push up the stock price between 11 and 15 percent. But these ambitious goals were slow to materialize. General Mills had difficulty integrating its direct sales force with Pillsbury's brokered sales force. Instead of focusing on this challenge—which all knew to be the key driver of value in the deal—management became distracted by the overall deal.

Integration is tough, but you can increase your chances of success by understanding what drives a successful integration. Eighty percent of respondents in Bain's survey of two hundred fifty global executives involved in M&A identified avoiding the General Mills–Pillsbury trap as vital to integration success, asserting that integration efforts must be "highly focused on where the value is in the merger." (See figure 4-1.) The other top reasons for success cited by executives were

- "cultural integration addressed early on and actively" and
- "best people selected to lead combined entity, irrespective of which company they come from."

FIGURE 4-1

Why Merger Integrations Succeed

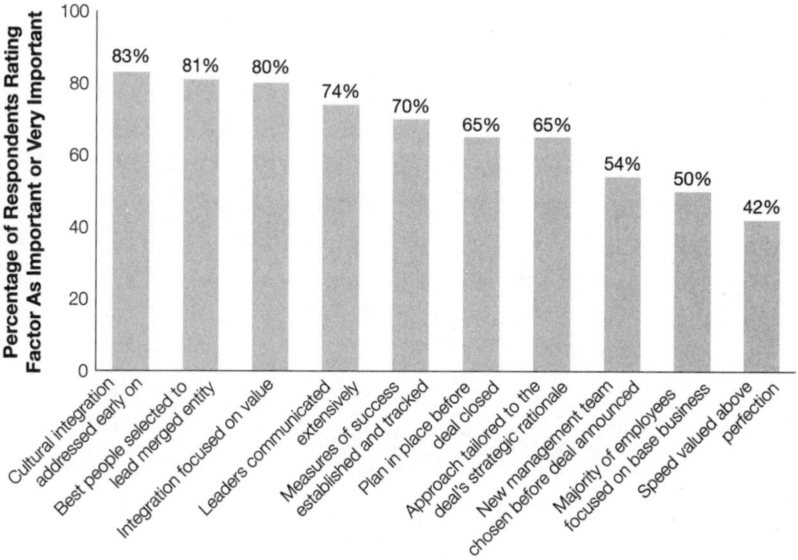

Source: Bain & Company Survey, fall 2002 ($n = 250$).

Now let's begin our in-depth review of the four key principles of successful integrations, beginning with issues that can—and should—be considered even before the ink is dry on the deal.

PLAN FOR OWNERSHIP

In our view, the first day of due diligence is the first day of integration planning. Integration feasibility and cost arguably are the biggest determinants of an acquisition's ultimate success or failure. It is impossible to perform a thorough due diligence and develop a fair price without taking them into account.

That said, too often companies do not think seriously about integration until after a deal is announced, or even closed. Almost half the executives interviewed in the Bain M&A survey believed they did not create a clear road map that outlined the necessary next steps during due diligence. A third of them felt they should have spent more of their time (a third more time, according to the survey) during due diligence on planning their postmerger activities.

Delaying integration planning until after a deal is announced is a serious mistake. If you don't know the mechanics of how a deal is going to work, how can you comfortably make the decision to invest? The best acquirers know that by translating the investment thesis—opportunities to improve the base business and the synergies—into a series of simple instructions, they force themselves to bridge the gap between the theory of how a company will come together and the practice of making it happen. They can assess whether they have accurately measured the merits of a deal and understood the risks involved in achieving its value. In fact, it is not uncommon to find acquirers adjusting their cash flow model after they've had a chance to do their real homework.

What's more, by mapping out all the steps that will be required for integration, you put yourself in a good position to make realistic estimates of how much integration will cost. Many enthusiastic buyers underestimate the likely costs of integration, and therefore neglect to figure those costs in their overall valuation of a deal.

A careful assessment of integration costs can even save you from making a bad deal. In a dramatic case, Toronto-based O&Y Properties Corp. and Vancouver-based Bentall Capital Limited Partnership called off their merger in 2003 after totaling up the true cost of synergies. What went on here? O&Y is one of Canada's largest real estate companies. The Reichmann family, which controls O&Y Properties and its sister company, O&Y Real Estate Investment Trust, has been involved in industrial and commercial real estate development for the past forty years, most notably the 2.7-million-square-foot First Canadian Place in Toronto in the 1970s, New York's 8-million-square-foot World Financial Center in the 1980s, and the highly leveraged, initially troubled, construction of London's Canary Wharf in the late 1980s and early 1990s.

In O&Y's proposed deal with Bentall, the synergies had looked irresistible: O&Y managed properties in eastern Canada, and Bentall had properties across the West. In addition to complementing each other geographically, the two companies thought they could rationalize expenses over a larger portfolio and also have representatives and people in every major North American city. Yet after due diligence, both sides realized that the synergies they'd reap in combining their real estate services businesses were too low to offset the considerable costs of integration. Bentall president Gary Whitelaw was quoted as saying his company had grown "increasingly concerned that the scale of the integration could divert resources away from our primary objective. . . . The merger risks would have been significant, demanding increased management attention and resulting in larger integration costs than at first may have been thought."[2] The deal broke up, and the business press applauded O&Y and Bentall for protecting the interests of their respective investors.

Planning for ownership and integration not only informs your decision to do the deal and at what price, but also helps you to achieve results quickly. There is little time to plan integration once a deal is completed. One useful—but daunting—rule of thumb is that companies have a grace period of about a hundred days after a deal closes to take hold of the business and begin delivering on the promise of the deal. After that, analysts and shareholders alike began to voice their skepticism (if they weren't skeptical already!).

Recall the example from chapter 1 of Kellogg's acquisition of Keebler. CEO Carlos Gutierrez knew that getting Kellogg's snacks into Keebler's direct-to-store delivery (DSD) system was his top priority, and he wasted no time making sure that would happen. He therefore used due diligence to jump-start the integration process. As Gutierrez told us:

> After we signed the deal in October of 2000, literally the next day we had nine teams of people together, ready, planning out things like the transfer to DSD. . . . We closed the deal in March of 2001, and we hit the ground running, because we had teams of Kellogg and Keebler people ready to go.[3]

In fact, just three days after completing the acquisition, Kellogg was taking actions to increase sales and efficiencies. "By moving aggressively, we will help maximize the great potential of this acquisition," said David Mackay, executive vice president of Kellogg Company and president of Kellogg USA at the time. "Our ability to act immediately is based on an exhaustive study of all our marketing and operating systems by teams of Kellogg and Keebler people."[4]

Note the inclusion of the target company's managers in the preclose integration planning. This is essential to devising the best possible integration plan and also to bringing the target's management team on board. Bridgepoint's Benoît Bassi underscores the importance of including the target's management when mapping out integration strategy during due diligence. "Before we buy, we discuss an action plan with the [target's] management. We try to get buy-in for the 'attack plan' before the deal closes. We used to determine the strategy, then put the documents in the cupboard. Now we are transparent."[5] This kind of transparency reduces initial confusion and friction and ensures that each member of both the acquirer and the target's management team knows his or her destination on day one.

Initiating integration during due diligence offers a good opportunity to anticipate some of the thornier issues that a merger might create and develop strategies to tackle them. High on this list are cultural issues (which we'll come to later in this chapter). Integrating disparate cultures can create a set of problems that are much less tangible than merging distribution channels or rationalizing software, but are no less important to address. Though it may be tempting to view cultural differences as a bundle of "soft issues" with correspondingly soft solutions, this is a mistake. Our research shows that it takes hard tactics to wrestle down soft issues. If the cultural integration issues seem intractable in advance, this may be an adequate basis for screening out an acquisition altogether.[6]

Particularly important to look at early on is how well the two management teams are likely to integrate with each other. Internet hardware and software giant Cisco Systems, which integrated no fewer than sixty-three acquisitions between 1997 and 2002, applies an interesting "integration screen" during due diligence. Cisco has designated what it calls a "Culture Cop" to vet targets. Among other things, a Cisco senior vice president—the Culture Cop—draws up a list of apparent stress points in the target's recent history—events such as expiring patents, pending litigation, failed product launches, personnel problems, and so on. Then the Culture Cop plays out these scenarios, going over the responses the target's management team made to these stress points and deciding whether Cisco would have responded in a similar way. This is an effective way to assess how well the new team will blend with Cisco managers.[7]

The sooner managers identify cultural snags, the more informed they can be about whether to proceed with the acquisition and at what price. They'll also be better equipped to address any cultural issues that come up in the wake of the acquisition. Even deals that involve apparently clashing cultures can create value in some cases, if the difficulties are identified early and resolved with diplomacy, wisdom, and urgency.

Beyond culture, CEOs face more tough decisions before the deal is announced, and certainly before it closes. These include everything from the highly emotional—for example, naming the new company and determining the location of headquarters—to the operationally important, including creating an organizational structure and assigning roles and responsibilities to senior managers. This last task—picking leaders—is at the beginning of the critical path to deal success. A first (and usually unpleasant) task is to distinguish between managers who will support the merger and those who will interfere.

Sometimes acquiring companies engage in wholesale layoffs that are motivated, at least in part, by cultural concerns. ("All these people are working against us!") But all too often, this is a mistake. If the real problem is localized in a few levels of management or a particular geography, these are the offenders to go after. When you're trying to promote integration, whom you let go usually matters more than how many you let go.

Let's move on to the flip side of this coin—the positive side—which involves assigning the right people to the right jobs. Obviously, this calls for a fundamental understanding of who's good at what, but it also calls for some sensitivity in "power sharing" between the acquiring and the acquired. Let's look again at JohnsonDiversey, which got this aspect of integration right.

JWP's Greg Lawton communicated who the members of a new management team were the day the deal was announced to the public and employees. To determine who would manage the new company, Lawton had spent more than one hundred hours with Diversey executives, getting to know them well in advance. "Surprise number one," says Lawton, "was the personal time investment that I had to make to pull off the selection and shaping of the team."[8] He assured the staffs of both companies that there would be balanced representation, and he based his selections on culture and values as well as management talent. Also, in the months before announcement, Lawton set up the integration team and resolved what the company name would be.

Then, between the announcement and close of the deal, Lawton and his counterpart at DiverseyLever, Cetin Yuceulug, made integration their priority and jointly took systematic steps to address it. Lawton launched the integration program office comprising executives from both companies who focused full time on the merger. At the same time, he identified other executives who would continue to operate each company's existing business—as we will see, a critical step in any well-conceived integration strategy.

By the time the deal closed, the integration team had developed an explicit, objective process for how the new company would be created, and made inroads into realigning both companies' operations. They also had chosen middle managers from both companies for key jobs, articulated clear lines of authority, and established formal procedures that allowed managers from Johnson and Diversey to work together effectively.

The JohnsonDiversey deal is a great example of planning for ownership around people. Now let's look at an example of planning for ownership around process. In chapter 2, we described the combination of Jefferson Smurfit and Stone Container—two giants in the box-making industry—as an example of a merger of equals that reflected a clear sense of how to leverage their basis of competition. This clear thinking continued through their integration phase, which was both highly disciplined and comprehensive. Smurfit and Stone each had extensive corrugated and mill operations, and their merger was predicated on obtaining scale economies. Consequently, the leaders of the two companies knew there would be G&A rationalization as well as significant opportunities for standardizing best practices across mills, optimizing production capacity, and combining purchasing. To achieve all this, they developed a merger-integration process aimed at quickly cutting overlap operations and making the best use of each company's operations. Importantly, divisions that did not overlap—Stone's bag business and Smurfit's folding carton division—were left untouched during the initial merger phases.

Before the close, the firms identified a range of such opportunities. They assigned joint teams of Smurfit and Stone people for every sector of the business, and they began working to map the physical plants that overlapped and could be combined. By the time the deal closed, executives knew exactly where to look to consolidate manufacturing capacity. (Of course, personnel issues moved in parallel to these process issues.) This allowed them (as part of a detailed financial plan) to announce the closure of 17 percent of their U.S. containerboard mill capacity as well as 33 percent of market pulp capacity within seven days of formally merging in November 1998.[9]

During this process, senior management actually identified ways to cut more costs in areas like purchasing than they had originally calculated in due diligence. They also identified superior practices that could be shared to enhance the merged firm's operations. Smurfit's container plants, for example, were more cost efficient than Stone's, while Stone's paper mills were better run than Smurfit's. By rationalizing high-cost capacity and refocusing production to meet the needs of higher-margin customers, Smurfit-Stone increased its average price per square foot of containerboard within ninety days of the merger, thereby quickly boosting profitability as it implemented other changes over the course of a year.

Getting the Word Out

Planning early for ownership is a precondition to a successful integration. But the next step is also critically important: *explaining what these plans mean and how they will help the combined company compete more successfully*. Obviously, there are both internal and external audiences for these messages. This argues for engaging a variety of media and spokespeople—although without losing the *focus* of the communication and corner office *control* of the communication. This kind of focus and control, says organizational psychologist Daniel

Holland, is critical: "The biggest mistakes that CEOs make are either to communicate nothing, because there are so many moving targets, or to delegate communication two or three layers down, which ends up causing more confusion."[10]

At JohnsonDiversey, even as their financial teams were hammering out the details of their complex deal, chief executives Greg Lawton and Cetin Yuceulug were jointly developing a vision-and-values statement to convey the goals of the merger to employees. They also commissioned a video designed to profile the new entity's guiding principles and direction. On the day that Lawton announced the deal to Wall Street, he rolled out the video to the staff worldwide.

Shortly thereafter, Lawton took his management team off-site to review both the intent of the deal and the historical values of both organizations as well as to foster a sense of common purpose. This culminated in the collective drafting of a two-minute speech about the firm's values and strategy that any executive could give to employees—the "elevator version," in other words.

In Lawton's case, careful planning led to productive communication. Conversely, a ready-fire-aim management approach is almost always full of communication peril. Shortly after Northwest Airlines merged with Republic Airlines in 1986, for example, CEO Steven Rothmeier sent a memo to Republic's staff saying: "The workday begins at 8 A.M. . . . there are no exceptions. . . . The workday ends when you have completed your work. . . . Officers should be in the office at least Saturday mornings for two Saturdays a month minimum."[11] Not surprisingly, staff morale plummeted. Shortly thereafter, passenger complaints climbed to more than double the industry average, and shortly after that, bookings slumped. Perhaps it's a stretch to connect all these dots—but it's not a stretch to assert that Northwest would have benefited from a more sophisticated and less autocratic approach to its postmerger communications.

Yes, some companies are compelled to present their vision under difficult circumstances, and this necessarily complicates the communications challenge. Consider, for example Hewlett-Packard's proposed merger with Compaq Computer Corporation in 2001. Under intense pressure to convince investors that the companies would be better off together, HP and Compaq conducted extensive predeal analyses of exactly how the integration would proceed. Investors received thousands of pages of materials, and many attended Q&A sessions with HP chief executive Carly Fiorina and her counterpart at Compaq, Michael Capellas.

Interestingly enough, the very heated and very public debate of the deal's merits—both in the courts and on the news—forced HP and Compaq to make difficult decisions about the integration phase (and especially about who would lead what) long before the deal actually closed. It also forced HP to execute an intense, internal communications program to win the hearts and minds of its employees.

In this case—and, we would argue, in most cases—planning for ownership, and making and communicating tough decisions early, paid off. Despite uneven market reaction to the merger, HP delivered on its short-term integration promise. In 2002, the first year of the merger, HP managed to cut its costs by more than $3 billion, beating its target of $2.5 billion in cost savings by 2004.

In sum, planning for ownership and integration begins during due diligence. Yes, there's a chance that time invested up front in adequately exploring integration requirements will be "wasted" if the deal falls through. But there's also the chance that your integration planning will keep you out of a bad deal—and the certainty that the deals you do close will work far better.

WHERE DOES INTEGRATION REALLY MATTER?

To know where to integrate, you have to revisit the underlying investment thesis for the deal. Investment theses cluster around at least one of three aims: active investing, growing scope, or growing economies of scale. A deal either enhances the core in some way or it represents a completely new platform for active investment, separate from the core business. If it enhances the core, it is intended to either grow the scale of a company's operations (by adding similar products and/or customers), or plug a gap and expand a company's scope of operations (by adding one or several new products, customer segments, channels, or markets).

These three types of investment thesis form a spectrum, with active investing on one end and growing scale on the other. (See figure 4-2.) As one moves along the spectrum, the extent of an acquirer's

FIGURE 4-2

Integration Extent Versus Deal Rationale

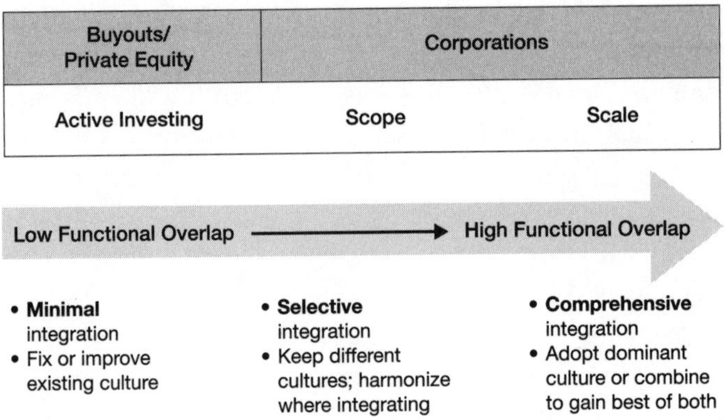

integration effort needs to increase. If an acquired company is meant to be the first plank of what will be a new platform, it will probably require the bare minimum of integration—say, inserting some management talent from the acquirer and extending financial-reporting requirements. The first deal in a new sector by a private equity fund, for example, may fall in this category.

Moving along the spectrum, deals that enhance the scope of a core business will need to be integrated only in discrete areas. An acquisition that expands a company's product scope, for example, may require extensive integration in distribution and customer service, but not necessarily in manufacturing and R&D. What's more, in a scope-enhancing deal, the best approach may be to keep cultures separate, or to impose a new corporate culture only on those operations that directly overlap.

At the other end of the spectrum, deals intended to grow scale require extensive integration, not only of overhead functions but also in operations. Success here requires full integration of all activities to capture the value that inspired the deal, value such as reloading plants, lowering administrative costs per employee, or consolidating vendors to lower purchasing costs.

Once you know where to integrate, accelerate. Speed and focus go hand in hand to get results. Although only 42 percent of respondents to Bain's survey rated "speed valued above perfection" as a critical approach to integration success, some of the best acquirers rank speed number one. As Citigroup's Todd Thomson puts it: "I think the biggest mistake everybody makes in deals is not integrating rapidly enough. The reality is the faster you integrate, the better. Everybody in the acquired company is sitting around waiting for you to do something, and when you don't, good people get demotivated."[12]

In that spirit, Citigroup integrated the 350-plus branches of acquired Golden State Bancorp into its California retail operations in just one quarter. Explains Thomson:

> We integrated people, we integrated the systems, we changed the branding, we changed the incentive systems. We did all of that in three and a half months. There are retail banks today that made acquisitions four or five years ago that still have not integrated their systems and, in some cases, their branding, and they are all dying because of it. It doesn't get any easier in the future. . . . The sooner you integrate, the sooner you make the decisions, the better.

Selective Integration

Let's look at a few examples of "selective integration."

Illinois Tool Works Inc., a frequent acquirer, is one company that has mastered the art of selective integration. ITW's main aim is to squeeze value out of complementary assets, rather than generating synergies by blending operations. Based on this strategic objective, W. James Farrell, who became CEO of ITW in 1995, spent over $6 billion to buy more than two hundred mostly small, mostly private companies over six years. Today, the Glenview, Illinois–based company manufactures everything from plastic soda bottle carriers to paint sprayers, operates in forty-four countries, and employs 48,700 people.

ITW keeps its acquisitions almost entirely independent. It focuses on a simple model for boosting the stand-alone efficiency of its acquisitions; it calls the core of this approach its "80-20 process." The idea is that companies obtain 80 percent of their revenue from the top 20 percent of the products they sell to a small number of key customers. Accordingly, ITW consists of some six hundred small, highly specialized businesses whose local managers have broad authority to manage their units with little assistance from headquarters—provided, of course, that they live by the 80-20 rule, focusing primarily on top customers and products.

Like most good scope acquirers, ITW integrates control functions rather than operations. Headquarters handles taxes, auditing, investor relations, R&D support, and some centralized HR functions. Otherwise, the businesses are self-supporting, with headquarters helping to point them in the right direction. Farrell's charge to his units is to squeeze the lemon: simplify production, continuously improve processes, and make sure you are increasing earnings. The parent allows companies to set their own financial targets, although it expects them to increase profit margins annually. Farrell reinforces this goal through a compensation system that awards bonuses based largely on increased margins.

Is selective integration working? Indisputably. From the time Farrell took the helm in 1995, the deals he has struck have helped ITW to more than double revenues to $9.5 billion in 2002. In that same period, the company's stock price has more than doubled.

Another example of selective integration is the relationship between Morgan Stanley and Dean Witter. Morgan Stanley paid $10 billion to merge with Dean Witter in 1997, forming MSDW. Pundits widely predicted friction between the two Wall Street giants. Morgan Stanley's hierarchical management style stood in contrast to Dean Witter's irreverent, fast-paced culture, and there were also giant gaps in pay scales. "The Four Seasons meets Burger King," one journalist wrote of the deal.[13]

But Morgan Stanley and Dean Witter correctly figured that there would be little friction if the two cultures avoided rubbing up against each other. They based their approach to integration on their shared investment thesis—to broaden product scope and gain revenue from cross-selling in just a few key business units. The combined firm therefore defined its integration challenge as creating a peaceful coexistence of cultures that maximized each unit's performance. MSDW consolidated the executive suite and folded Dean Witter's minor underwriting and equity research operations into Morgan Stanley's blue-chip investment bank. Out of a total of forty-eight thousand jobs, only three hundred were cut.[14]

A key driver behind the projected revenue growth that drove the deal in the first place was the prospect of adding Morgan Stanley products to Dean Witter's retail portfolio. The merged companies—under their new combined name—pursued new opportunities in this realm, including online brokerage, asset management, and the credit card business. The investment bank, by contrast, continued to refer to itself as Morgan Stanley, since Dean Witter brought nothing new to this business. It continued to operate pretty much as it always had. According to an investment banker at a rival firm, Morgan Stanley's investment bankers "barely acknowledge that [the merger] has happened."[15] And because of the compelling logic of selective integration, they didn't need to.

In 2001, despite suffering an industry downturn, the combined firm MSDW reported higher profit margins and return on equity than its four main competitors. By December 2003, almost seven years after the deal was announced, and despite some hard intervening years, MSDW's stock had more than doubled—significantly outperforming its primary rival, Merrill Lynch, whose stock was up only 19 percent.

Fully Merging Market Share

The strategy of integrating rapidly, but only where it matters, makes sense in all deals. Yet as deal theses become more complex, integration matters in more places. Attempting to grow market share using a merged company's business requires a more extensive effort than simply adding a new product line.

The experience of Philips Medical Systems, the medical-device unit of Koninklijke Philips Electronics N.V. of the Netherlands, shows how—in a deal aimed in large part at growing scale—selective integration can give acquirers an edge. Philips Medical makes imaging products, such as X-ray equipment and MRIs, and competes fiercely with rivals Siemens Medical and GE Medical Systems. Between 1998 and 2001, Philips Medical acquired four companies in rapid succession. Its rationale? With medical costs rising and hospitals forming large buying groups to cut costs, Philips needed greater market share in core products and a broader product line to stay competitive. The acquisitions moved Philips from a distant third-place position to parity with Siemens, the number-two player, and filled gaps in its product line.[16]

Yet capturing the true benefits of this roll-up required a major integration effort. In October 2001, with the last of the deals completed, Philips deployed seventeen "synergy search-and-rescue" teams over an intense six-month period. The mandate of the integration teams—which spanned numerous operations—was to identify the greatest potential for both cost savings and revenue increases.

First, the teams developed and clustered an initial list of about five hundred synergy initiatives. They then pursued the highest-payback tasks, such as integrating individual product lines. And at the same time, they delayed the longer-payback ones, such as redesigning the imaging-technologies supply chain. To better assess where the company stood and where opportunities lay, Philips benchmarked the best practices of its own internal operations as well as those of its competitors. They set standards based on how rivals marketed individual products and how their cost structure and profit margins compared. Philips quickly incorporated targets for each synergy initiative into the annual budgets.

Throughout the process, William Curran, former CEO of Philips Electronics North America, which oversaw Philips Medical Systems, kept his colleagues focused on the bigger prizes that lay before them. "I admit that we paid less attention to the teams where the cost synergies were small," says Curran. "We were off doing the job where the money was." Philips Medical Systems' secret to avoid the incessant cries for help on the little stuff? Empowerment. "Once the person who was going to lead the function was appointed, the phones stopped ringing," explains Curran.[17]

After five and a half months, teams had identified *three times* the synergies originally quantified. The largest synergies and savings came from IT integration; the next largest from combining the sales and service staffs that sold CT scanners, X-ray equipment, and MRIs. Says Curran of this and similar interventions: "Those were the ones where you really wanted to hit the accelerator."

Another source of savings came from aggressively reducing costs within the individual business lines—including, for example, consolidating operations of the multiple ultrasound product lines into one business. And on the other side of the coin, Philips delayed long-payback efforts, such as integrating the sales force for products that required different selling skills, including nuclear medicine and patient-monitoring technology. Explicitly, the company decided to wait until management had the capacity to take on such large, longer-payback challenges. By focusing on integrating where that effort would have an immediate impact on costs and the bottom line, Philips was in a position to begin methodically planning to tackle the more difficult cross-product-line opportunities that would take years to capture.

The upshot? Philips Medical surpassed its announced goal of achieving €230 million in synergies by 2004. In fact, in February 2004, it announced it had achieved €342 million in synergies in the two previous years.[18]

WHERE DOES COMMON CULTURE COUNT?

Companies like Philips Medical, Morgan Stanley Dean Witter, and Illinois Tool Works excel at extracting value from their deals. But their ability to do this almost always derives from their skill at mobilizing and motivating key employees. This brings us to the third of our four key principles of integration: putting cultural issues high on the leadership agenda.

Former General Electric chairman Jack Welch frequently tells the story of one of GE's worst deals: the 1986 acquisition of Kidder, Peabody. Buttoned-down GE failed miserably in its attempts to mold freewheeling broker Kidder into a typical GE unit. Instead of giving Kidder's talent the space to succeed, GE nitpicked about expenses and imposed GE-style strategic planning on Kidderites, for whom such practices were alien. GE further antagonized Kidderites by replacing their much-loved leader, Ralph DeNunzio, with Silas S. Cathcart, a former tool-and-die company CEO and a newcomer to Wall Street. The result: Kidder's top managers departed in droves, leaving a trail of scandal. GE's $600 million investment produced only $250 million in earnings before GE finally got its money out by selling Kidder to PaineWebber in 1994 for $670 million and a 25 percent stake in the merged company.

The Kidder debacle inspired Welch to think harder about issues of postmerger integration, particularly in the cultural realm. With Welch's blessing, GE Capital—GE's finance unit—developed an approach to mergers called the Pathfinder model, which has generated a remarkable track record when it comes to integrating acquisitions. Pathfinder reflects GE's (newfound) belief that in integrating acquisitions, as much attention must be paid to scaling culture as to business; therefore, the system involves a cultural-integration machine designed as carefully as any GE assembly line.[19] By all accounts, the process is thoroughgoing: Companies that go through the Pathfinder process come out indelibly stamped with the GE logo. As Welch told a forum of senior executives at *Fortune* magazine's 2002 leadership conference in Chicago, "At GE, we said one thing when we got a company: 'You're acquired. Welcome. Here's the finance system; here are the rules. We hope you'll like it and you'll stay.'"[20]

We note that this is straight-ahead cultural assimilation, which works in GE's scale mergers, but assuredly is not the optimal approach to every merger. (One size does not fit all.) In fact, Bain & Company research suggests that cultural-integration strategies should spring from the cultural starting point of the merged entity—that is, from the investment thesis that inspired the deal in the first place. Different investment theses call for different approaches to cultural integration.

To better understand the impact of cultural issues on merger success, Bain & Company studied 125 deals greater than $1 billion consummated between 1996 and 2000. Our analysis confirmed a phenomenon that we've seen increasingly in thirty years of M&A consulting: Cultural-integration issues can make or break deals.

The Bain study categorized deals by investment thesis, and found that all deals, scope or scale, in which management proactively addressed cultural-integration issues showed better results than deals in which management was inattentive to those issues. A proactive approach netted a 5.1 percent higher stock price twelve months after deal announcement compared with sector indices, while there was a 2.4 percent underperformance in deals where senior leaders failed to identify and negotiate cultural hurdles.

Addressing culture proactively in scale cases, where complete integration usually spells success, had the highest payoff. When we broke out scale deals, we found that those that ignored cultural issues identified in the transaction performed 8 percent below sector indices, which is more than three times the average underperformance for all deals that ignored culture.

No matter what the investment thesis for the merger, getting cultural integration right requires bursts of leadership energy from the outset. In fact, it will never again be quite so important. William Curran of Philips reflected on the risks of delaying cultural integration: "When you make the acquisition, people understand: 'I work for a different company now; a lot of stuff is going to be different.' . . . And when [change] doesn't happen, the old culture just gets reinforced and really gets set, and it gets really hard to change it."[21]

So speed is essential to successful integration, particularly when dealing with parties that have cultural differences. Philips paid a price for waiting to integrate its four acquisitions simultaneously, three years after the first acquisition was announced. "The concrete had set much harder at the earliest acquisition," says Curran. "It made the changes needed for some of the integration projects more difficult." Less so for the last of the four deals, which closed within weeks of the company kicking off its integration effort in October 2001: Reports Curran, "Sales and service were reorganized immediately."

Hitting culture early and from the top is key. How, exactly, is this done? We have seen a spectrum of approaches that work, ranging from hands-off to complete assimilation. In almost all cases, however, executives should plan on using some combination of hard tactics, such as performance indicators and compensation, to underscore the importance of cultural integration. (See box, Cultural Integration's Hard Tactics.)

CULTURAL INTEGRATION'S HARD TACTICS

Effectiveness in the "soft" realm of culture almost always requires the use of hard-nosed tools—and sometimes even blunt instruments. These may include, for example:

- ***Decision making:*** Successful acquirers unambiguously designate who will make which decisions, and how. Early on, they set highly visible examples of how they intend to change decision making.
- ***People selection:*** The newly merged organization requires the appointment of managers who fully buy into the new vision and culture. The best acquirers don't hesitate to make the tough "people decisions" quickly—even with incomplete information—and then cascade this priority downward through the organization.
- ***Key performance indicators:*** To ensure follow-through at all levels, leaders must rapidly adjust metrics to the company's new vision and strategy. Even soft issues can be tracked successfully, allowing management to monitor progress.
- ***Compensation system/incentives:*** An acquiring company can change a culture rapidly if it creates an incentive system that (1) reflects the new vision and (2) rewards employees for meeting the company's new performance goals.
- ***Promotion/career development/performance-evaluation processes:*** After the company has put the new management team in place and changed compensation and incentives, the HR department should redesign its own systems so that they support and reflect the company's new culture.
- ***Internal and external communication:*** Successful acquirers continuously and consistently reinforce key messages on vision, strategy, and culture.

Building Bridges

As noted earlier, when a deal reflects a strategy of active investing, the amount of cultural integration needed tends to be minimal. But in mergers designed to broaden product or geographic scope, the choices get trickier and more numerous. Sometimes the right answer is selective integration; sometimes it's blending cultures to create a new, overarching ethos.

The best deal makers tend to base this decision on the needs of their customers. In the case of JohnsonDiversey, where the deal was in large part inspired by cross-sell potential, the combined companies needed to blend cultures to share and serve each other's customers. CEO Greg Lawton therefore took pains to create a "bridging culture" in a way that worked for both companies.

Shortly after the deal was announced, Lawton held a meeting of his integration team, which included executives from both companies. The cultural gulf between the two camps was immediately apparent. One of the biggest surprises, recalls Lawton, was how differently the two groups tended to execute. Johnson's corporate culture was entrepreneurial and unstructured; its representatives tended to arrive at the meetings with a relatively open, problem-solving mindset. DiverseyLever executives, by contrast, showed up with briefs and formal written proposals, and quickly dominated the discussions. Lawton says his company's approach "seemed to be much quieter and more reflective, in the face of a decision-making bulldozer that was coming at them from the DiverseyLever side."[22]

These differences weren't good or bad, Lawton reports—"just different." At his urging, his team adopted a three-step process to bridge the cultural gap, most critically with regard to the approaches to decision making at the two companies. The first step was to help members recognize their differences and to talk about them without labeling them. Next, the team developed a way to make decisions that both teams could accept, which amounted to a compromise between Johnson's informal style and DiverseyLever's preference for structure. The final step was to cascade this new approach down both companies, with the top team "walking the talk" and encouraging others to follow.

Five months into the effort, Lawton could point publicly to early signs of success, including the retention of major accounts and top managers and the ability to keep aggressive synergy plans on track despite a challenging business environment.

JohnsonDiversey's nuanced approach to cultural integration worked well for its scope-enhancing deal, but subtlety and gradualism are rarely the right solution for scale deals. Scale mergers require maximum integration, and often call for tough decisions very early in the game. The key word here is early: If acquirers don't quickly develop a solid platform for integration success, they can rapidly lose momentum (and market value) as competitors steal customers, employee morale plummets, and key executives flee.

One company that is well aware of the need to move quickly toward cultural integration is British Petroleum. John Browne, BP's chief executive, had feared that industry consolidation would leave his company behind. Between mid-1998 and the spring of 2000, therefore, BP closed a series of transactions (totaling $120 billion) that brought BP, Amoco, Arco, and Castrol into a single company with a market capitalization of about $200 billion. The acquisitions were the first in what became a series of transactions in the industry, as competitors Exxon, Chevron, and Total followed suit with their own scale-oriented acquisitions.

After observing the costly mistakes made by other companies that had taken a hands-off approach to integrating their scale-motivated investments, Browne decided that "you have to have clarity with an acquisition. You can't let these things just work themselves out."

"Of course, the benefit from transactions comes partly through cutting costs," he adds. But to capture all the benefits, he asserts, "you have to create a single organization—with common processes and standards, common values and a way of working, which everyone can recognize."[23]

Browne moved swiftly to achieve this goal. Within one hundred days of closing the Amoco deal, he had filled all the top management jobs and completed most of the staff reductions—including ten thousand layoffs—and startled some Amoco executives by imposing BP's structure and management style on the new company. Meanwhile, he also set a course for efficiency improvements by establishing some very tough targets. "We set strong goals, and [expected] our people [to] innovate to get the right answer," Browne said.

BP's assimilation of Amoco was so thoroughgoing that it inspired an insider's joke: How do you pronounce BP–Amoco? Answer: BP. The Amoco is silent. Some senior executives at Amoco quit in frustration. Even so, BP achieved its projected $2 billion in cost savings within the first year—that is, twelve months ahead of schedule. Its stock emerged as a top performer, rising nearly 11 percent during the first hundred days, and outperforming the oil-and-gas stock index by 17 percent one year after the deal was announced.[24]

In this integration process, John Browne didn't win many friends. Without a doubt, though, he mastered the enormous complexity of scale integration. A key reason? He made the tough decisions on cultural integration early.

MAINTAIN FIREPOWER IN THE BASE BUSINESSES

Let's summarize where we've come so far. The first three principles that guide successful integrations tend to focus on the process of integration itself:

- plan for ownership,
- integrate quickly where it matters, and
- put culture high on your leadership agenda.

Our fourth principle refocuses attention on the wellspring—on the wealth-generating businesses that made all this deal making possible in the first place. Our survey respondents (as well as our own experience) underscore the importance of maintaining firepower in the base businesses.

In many cases, the roots of failure or success are put down during the period immediately surrounding a deal's announcement. Think about it: From the moment the two companies first begin their merger dance, they expose themselves to rejection not only by the other party, but also by their own customers and employees. At the same time, executives involved in both sides of the negotiations become preoccupied with the financial terms of the deal, and especially with how the merger will affect their own jobs. Anxiety runs high. Workloads become oppressive as merger-related tasks are piled on top of normal duties. People who don't know or trust each other must start making critical decisions together. In this turbulent context, people often respond by ducking tough decisions on budgets, strategic plans, organizational charts, and people.

At the same time, like gravity, integrations exert an inexorable pull on employees. For better or worse, people are drawn to the action—and almost inevitably, they take their eye off the business-as-usual ball. Meanwhile, most combinations result in some degree of inefficiencies, bleeding from small wounds (e.g., lost accounts here and there), and a certain amount of cannibalization. For all of these reasons and more, revenue dips are almost inevitable in the integration phase.

A McKinsey study argues that revenue deserves more attention in mergers. The study of 160 acquisitions made by 157 companies in 1995 and 1996 found that only 12 percent of acquiring companies achieved organic growth rates ahead of their nonmerged peers, and 42 percent of companies actually lost ground in postmerger years. Too many companies lose their revenue momentum as they concentrate on cost synergies or fail to focus on postmerger growth in a systematic manner.[25]

Successful acquirers understand this phenomenon. Many build short-term revenue dips as negative synergies into their deal model and valuation, as discussed in chapter 3. Many also launch initiatives to provide special care and feeding to critical employees and accounts, since integration is frequently the period when competitors will work furiously to steal customers and talent.

The good news for acquirers is that this fourth overarching principle is the easiest to apply. Keeping the organization focused on the base business requires nothing more than applying the competitive tools you use every day: setting priorities, checking in regularly, and asking tough questions.

As a rule, great acquirers respond to the minding-the-store challenge with three basic tactics:

- Walk the talk.
- Use the 90-10 rule.
- Let the line "steer."

Walk the Talk

The senior management teams at consistently successful acquirers set an example in terms of how much attention they pay to customers between announcement and closing. If the top brass focuses on the base business, reports will follow their lead. Such was the case when department store giant Sears, Roebuck acquired catalog retailer Lands' End in the spring of 2002. When the Sears deal was announced, the Lands' End executive team spent extra time listening to the customer. They read the e-mails coming in from customers, and they got regular reports on what questions were being asked of their call-center employees.

They also made sure that the integration effort did not distract the company from the core job at hand: getting ready for the all-important Christmas season. Only weeks into the integration planning, David Dyer, then CEO of Lands' End, made a point of putting a number of integration efforts on hold in order to prevent distractions from hurting the base business.

At Singapore-based Keppel Offshore & Marine (KOM), the top brass likewise walked the talk. KOM is a global leader in the construction and conversion of offshore rigs and specialized vessels. It was formed in 2002 through the integration of Keppel FELS, which builds and repairs offshore rigs, and Keppel Hitachi Zosen, which repairs ships and converts container ships into floating storage vessels for offshore oil. These two companies, both majority owned by the Keppel Group, competed against each other premerger. The merger offered powerful synergies through consolidating procurement and subcontracting, coordinating sales and marketing, and eliminating redundant overhead.

To motivate all workers to embrace the integration effort's bottom line, KOM's CEO, Choo Chiau Beng, set up integration incentives. In the combined company's first year, he handed out 10 percent of all integration-related savings—which totaled close to 20 million Singaporean dollars—not only to members of the integration team, but also to others who had contributed heavily by keeping the base business humming. People got between one and three months of extra compensation in addition to their regular bonus. Choo knew rewards spoke louder than words when it came to proving that working toward a successful integration was in everyone's best interest.[26]

Use the 90-10 Rule

The key point here is to use only a small, highly respected, and dedicated team to drive the integration—10 percent or less of employees in any function—so that at least 90 percent of employees can focus solely on running the business, especially in customer-facing functions. To limit distraction, some firms remove the members of the integration team entirely from their existing jobs.

Smurfit-Stone didn't go to that extreme. Nevertheless, the company carefully analyzed new and continuing employee roles in advance. Based on that review, it established who would do what, and how, and where, with an eye toward leaving critical people in the field so that they could service and retain key customers throughout the merger process.

About fifty people—fewer than 10 percent of the 624 employees at Smurfit-Stone's corporate headquarters—worked part time on integrating general and accounting oversight functions. At the vertically integrated paper mills, which were focused solely on production, the ratio and part-time nature of involvement was similar. The top four managers from Smurfit and from Stone—all either heads of the business units or regional managers—and a handful of logistics and finance types worked together to integrate operations. Day to day, they continued to supervise operations that manufactured and moved corrugated sheets to Smurfit-Stone container plants; in addition, they dedicated between 20 percent and 50 percent of their time to the integration effort. Meanwhile, the mill managers themselves spent less than 10 percent on integration.

Smurfit-Stone took a different tack at the container plants, which sold converted sheets directly to customers, than it took at its paper mills. There, senior managers stayed focused on the base business, while a very small but dedicated team of six spent 100 percent of its time merging the plants. The plant integration team also included one of the regional managers, who was pulled out of his job to reorganize the regions, and who later became head of the business unit. The rest of the senior managers, notably, spent very little time on integration, apart from staying informed and submitting relevant data to the integration team. Instead, they kept their sights trained on making sales and serving customers.

Let the Line "Steer"

This last principle may sound counterproductive, but it's actually a wise investment of resources in store-minding. Smart acquirers often designate their line executives as members of a steering committee for the duration of the integration. Why? The direct benefit is a line team that has a clear and early line of sight into any major changes that are in the offing, and is confident that its voice will be heard at the appropriate moment (i.e., early). But the indirect benefit is keeping the hands of those line executives on their respective tillers. At Sears, for example, the merger leaders took great pains to ensure that the key executives of Lands' End had early and frequent reviews of any proposed changes that the integration teams were recommending. The Lands' End line executives knew from the beginning that Sears would not implement any changes without their approval, which freed them to stay focused.

Keppel's Choo set the stage for an effective integration by naming the organization's new leaders early. As he explained in an interview:

> Establishing a clear organization very early, both in terms of the structure—how the business was going to be put together—but also very much in terms of the key twenty-five

> people, was critical to our success. In fact, the CEO, COO, and CFO were clear on the day the merger was announced. A month later, the twenty-five top people were clear, and that was still three months before the close.[27]

Having established his top leaders, Choo then set up a steering committee of line executives. This ensured commitment to the integration from the business lines, without distracting the line executives from running the business. Because the line was part of the decision-making process, these executives were comfortable with the integration's directions and targets. Choo explains:

> The steering committee consists of people who have day-to-day decision-making power. Because [it] consists so largely of all the line executives, they do the questioning on how [the integration] will impact them and the organization, and they [select] whom to put on task forces. It's so important to have them [agree from the start on important issues]. You need the key decision makers on board to do a successful integration.

What were the results of Choo's decision to pay extra attention to the base business during the difficult period of transition? On a micro level, the newly combined company won an order during the integration process itself—one that the firm's leaders felt they clearly would not have won premerger. This gave a big boost to the integration effort and redoubled employee focus. Moving up a few powers of magnification: Despite the kinds of incremental costs that are associated with any merger, Keppel achieved record results in 2002, with combined revenues up 35 percent and profits up 169 percent over 2001. Keppel exceeded its synergy targets by 100 percent within six months of the deal close.

In the end, Keppel, JohnsonDiversey, BP, Philips Medical, and Morgan Stanley Dean Witter know from experience what many deal makers have suspected all along: that successful merger integration can make or break a deal's trajectory.

But they also know something that only a much smaller group of companies understand. Just by throwing a few switches at the right moment, in the right direction, they can vastly improve their odds of integration success. Companies give themselves an advantage when they start integration planning well before a deal's announcement, when they integrate quickly in directions where it matters most to sales and profits, and when they proactively address cultural integration. And they can press their advantage by keeping a firm hand on the base business. If they throw these switches at the right moments, acquirers can bring their deal objectives within sight sooner, and with greater levels of satisfaction all around.

How will you know you've arrived? Beyond financials, Greg Lawton at JohnsonDiversey tracks cohesion. "If you closed your eyes and listened," he says, recalling a celebratory team dinner after the merger integration, "you would have thought you were back in the single company."[28]

5

What Should You Do When the Deal Goes Off Track?

Let's face it: No deal ever works out exactly as expected, so you have to be prepared to make the decision to intervene early and decisively when the unexpected occurs. If you got the "how" of picking your targets right and nailed which deal to close and where to integrate, you're on the right track. But you still need a contingency plan. You need to make your fourth critical decision: What should you do when the deal veers off track after closing?

Why should you worry? It is true that for the lucky few, a merger will turn out even better than anyone ever anticipated. Hidden jewels surface after the deal closes, boosting the transaction's value far above management's forecasts. There is no postmerger revenue dip; in fact, revenues and earnings increase dramatically. The stock price of the combined entity soars. Life is good.

For a larger and far less fortunate minority, however, postdeal explorations uncover the proverbial "perfumed pig": a business that was dressed up for sale. The acquirer has paid too much, and—in extreme cases—there is no way to cover, or recover from, the mistake.

The vast majority of acquirers, and acquisitions, fall somewhere in the middle. In these cases, once the books are fully open, the new team is in place and at work, and the full implications of the business acquisition are revealed, a succession of tough little problems begins to crop up. At one end of the spectrum, these problems are like weeds in your front yard: They won't kill you, but if you don't deal with them, you're likely to have more of them soon. At the other end of the spectrum, they're like grubs: Left unchecked, they'll kill your lawn.

To switch metaphors: When you enter into a marriage, you can expect that there will be a certain amount of friction, on topics ranging from the sober to the silly: money, kids, in-laws, toothpaste tops, and toilet seats. According to John Gottman, coauthor of *The Seven Principles for Making Marriage Work,* one of the top predictors of marital success is a couple's ability to repair problems that arise between them.[1] Without frequent air-clearing conversations that sort out minor differences, resentments fester and can destroy the original reason two people chose to live together.

It's like that in corporate marriages, too. The more effective acquirers expect things to go wrong—although even they can't say just where the train will go off the rails—and they ready themselves to correct course. They set up mechanisms for diagnosing and repairing problems.

Less effective acquirers are always surprised when things go wrong—and are therefore unprepared to deal with problems. This ad hoc approach to problem solving can have the most serious of consequences: Our survey suggests that many of the top reasons for the failure of marriages between companies relate to poor handling of postdeal problems. To put into perspective the challenge of dealing with a merger that has come off the rails, let's return to Newell Rubbermaid. This was the "merger from hell" that we first encountered back in chapter 1. In the years following the merger, things continued to go wrong, and a series of CEOs and managers tried desperately to turn the business around.

What kind of things went wrong? Key managers left, cost synergies never materialized, new-product introductions were late, competitors continued to take share. Large purchasers such as Wal-Mart resisted price increases, and the company lost credibility on Wall Street.

In January of 2001, Newell Rubbermaid hired Joseph Galli to take the helm. He was determined to succeed where others had faltered. His task? Achieve the potential that Daniel Ferguson had seen in the merger of Newell and Rubbermaid some two years before. Galli would be the third executive to try. Two of Newell's top executives, John McDonough and William Sovey, had worked hard over the prior year and a half to fix Rubbermaid's problems and get the company growing again, on both the top line and the bottom. Now it was Galli's turn.

At forty-three, Galli brought a fresh perspective to Newell Rubbermaid. He had enjoyed a rapid rise through the managerial ranks at Black & Decker, after which he had served as COO of Amazon.com. But he had never run anything close to what he was handed at Newell. Galli would have to activate the turnaround strategy and galvanize change at a $7 billion company with a serious merger-integration hangover.

As Galli said to us, "I think it was very simple to conclude the direction of the company had to change. It had to go from a growth-by-acquisition play that focused on commodity-oriented products. It had to morph into a product-development, brand marketing company." Galli found that Newell executives understood the changes required to fix the business—the question was, how to enact them? As Galli remembers, "The strategy fit. Everybody who looked at the issue thought this is exactly what we should do. But—and it's a big but—building that capability is not simple. It's anything but simple."[2] We will return to what Galli did in a few pages, but let's take a step back and look more broadly at this whole issue of dealing with the unexpected.

This chapter looks at three categories of deal-related problems, in ascending order of difficulty:

1. ***Problems that can be fixed through focused interventions.*** When you're operating in this realm, you're fixing problems around the margins—issues that are serious enough to demand attention, but not in the deal-breaking realm. Your investment thesis is largely substantiated in the wake of the deal, but some weeds appear in the lawn.

2. ***Problems that can be fixed only through transformations.*** These kinds of challenges may reflect faulty due diligence, or they may grow out of changing market conditions. Your investment thesis still holds, in whole or in large part, but the grubs have become all too visible and demand time-consuming treatment. In rare cases—including the Newell Rubbermaid situation—your company needs to transform itself, and its investment thesis, to be able to move forward in the deal.

3. ***Problems that can't be fixed.*** Sometimes, the only way out is to get out. Your investment thesis was wrong from the outset, or, external circumstances changed so radically that even the deepest intervention isn't going to help. The goal in such cases is to move expeditiously, humanely, and decisively—that is, leaving no loose ends. It takes discipline to get out of a relationship as well as to get into one.

We will devote considerable space to the first two kinds of problems—the two categories of fixable problems—and somewhat less space to the unfixable ones. This reflects our generally positive outlook as well as our conviction that rightly focused due diligence can keep you out of failed corporate marriages.

FIXING PROBLEMS THROUGH FOCUSED INTERVENTIONS

Let's look at the first of our three categories of postdeal problems: those that lend themselves to solution through focused interventions. In our consulting practice, we are frequently called in after a deal has been closed to sort out the unexpected. We have found that the "manageable problems" that arise postdeal usually crop up in three areas:

1. ***Organizational issues.*** You will end up with some of the wrong people in the wrong jobs. Expect it. At the same time, no matter how open your communications, the conspiracy theorists will be hard at work in your company, detailing how your nefarious plans will unfold to their listeners' disadvantage. Unfortunately, as with most paranoid visions, these

explanations will contain enough truth to confuse even normally right-thinking people.

2. ***Operational dysfunction.*** You should also expect lots of challenges on the operational level after a merger. Vendor problems, production problems, inventory problems, sales force problems, distribution problems, and human resource problems: You will soon have your own list.

3. ***Customer-service blunders.*** At some point after a merger, no matter how hard you try, you will let a customer down. This is apparently inevitable when two sets of customers—often with overlaps—are brought together in one system. You will miss a shipment, or send out a dramatically incorrect bill, or get confused about sales coverage. Believe us: You can't know in advance which of these gremlins will get you, but one or more of them will. Most likely, more than one.

Underlying all these issues will be concerns about information-systems compatibility and integration. Expect your CIO to be logging lots of overtime. Expect even routine, automated functions to go haywire as two management information systems become one. Once you look beyond these general rules of thumb, of course, the challenge is twofold: to detect problems and then to solve them. We have found that after a deal is completed, companies can greatly increase their chances of detecting trouble by

- eliciting feedback,
- establishing early-warning systems, and
- monitoring operations closely.

Then they can solve problems by

- reassuring customers,
- changing people,
- changing the business, and
- making change stick.

Let's look at each of these activities in turn.

Eliciting Feedback

In the last chapter, we argued that the leaders of an acquiring company need to obsess about communication. Obviously, we think that's a good thing. But we need to introduce a refinement here. Many executives conceive of "communication" as a one-way street: "I think large thoughts; the rest of you attend to those thoughts." In deal-fixing mode, however, it is absolutely critical to solicit and act upon feedback from your employees, customers, and suppliers.

This priority reflects the merger's life cycle. Think about it: Deals start small. A relatively small band of highly motivated executives and advisors make contact, negotiate the terms, conduct diligence, plan for integration, and close the deal. Yes, this deal team inevitably grows as the process unfolds, but—as we have argued in the last chapter—it still has to remain relatively small for the good of the company. (Somebody needs to be minding the store and making the money.) So throughout the early stages of the deal, most of the people involved share a similar mission, have a high personal investment in the outcome, and are generally bound by draconian confidentiality agreements.

Once the deal is announced, all of this changes. All of a sudden, a huge number of constituencies have varying degrees of interest in the deal. Many of these parties will question how this development is in their best interest. The press and the analysts will probe for weaknesses and will certainly publicize any that they may find. And of course, the market will weigh in with its own verdict (which, as explained earlier, will often be negative for the buyer).

After the deal is announced, therefore, the CEO has an obligation to go out and explain the transaction: to employees, customers, vendors, investors, media representatives, and the public at large. But this is only half of the communications challenge when it comes to deal fixing. The other half involves—to put it bluntly—shutting up and listening.

Let's look at an example of a somewhat complicated merger to highlight both components of the communications challenge. When Rick Wolford, the CEO of Del Monte Foods—a marketer of canned fruits and vegetables—agreed to merge his company with a set of businesses being spun off by H. J. Heinz, he faced all the usual issues of explaining a complex transaction to Del Monte Foods' employees, investors, and other stakeholders.[3] But he also faced an usual complication: The transaction structure meant Heinz shareholders would, in effect, own Del Monte Foods when the deal closed. It was unclear to Wolford (or anyone else involved in the transaction) whether Heinz shareholders would take kindly to waking up one day to find a big chunk of some other company in their portfolios.

As Wolford later told us, "We spent a lot of time thinking through how each constituency was going to react to this deal. I knew this would make Del Monte a better company, but I had to persuade my shareholders—and my soon-to-be shareholders—that this made sense."[4]

Wolford spent the better part of six months working through the communication plans for the deal. He personally oversaw the development of all the communication plans to his top executives, to his board, and to the investor community. And because this was a merger of equals, he spent a great deal of time visiting at Heinz and meeting with the executives who were coming with the deal in an effort to clearly define their roles.

Wolford made a point of eliciting different—even contradictory—ideas about the best way to structure and run the organization after the closing of the deal. As he explains:

> I knew there was no inherently right way or wrong way to run a business. Both companies had business systems that worked for them. What we had to do was to find one way to get things done for both businesses. The challenge was that if Del Monte said "tomato," Heinz said "tomahto." Whether it be organizational philosophy, distribution mechanics, sales strategy, or operating practices, if we did it one way, it seemed that Heinz did it the other.
>
> So we needed to listen, think through both sides, and then make a decision. Maybe it was the fact that we were so opposite in so many ways that made us stop and listen before we acted.

Wolford knew that he could not use raw power to get people to buy into a shared vision of the future. So he set up forums and teams to get feedback to him—quickly, and unfiltered. "I like to hear what people have to say," he says. "If you have a good argument and the data to back it up, I'll go with you." In other words, Wolford solicited feedback on his deal, heard the feedback, and then acted on it (in visible ways) when he came across a good idea.

We emphasize those three verbs because it's not enough to stop somewhere in the middle. In our experience, more companies are better at asking for feedback than they are at hearing what comes back in response. And—going to the next step—more companies are better at hearing these responses than they are at acting on them. In other words, the funnel narrows at each step.

Why? One answer is that more people know how to talk than to listen. Listening is an acquired skill. If you search the phrase *active listening* on Google, you will come up with more than 140,000 matches. In our practice, we haven't come across all that many accomplished listeners, even outside the deal context. And in the postdeal environment, listening (and hearing) are especially difficult. Unfortunately, that's when these skills are most needed.

Wolford reaped invaluable returns from investing up front in his organization. After the deal closed he had to face a host of challenges, including sales force coverage, customer issues, IT concerns, and distribution challenges. But none of these issues rose up to threaten the overall merger integration plan. By opening the lines of communication, he empowered line managers to identify problems quickly and fix them. Crisis averted!

Establishing Early-Warning Systems

The expression "canary in a coal mine" derives from the antique mining practice of keeping a live bird in a cage somewhere deep underground. If that sensitive canary expired and fell off his or her perch, it was a good indicator that the mine was filling up with poisonous or explosive gases—and therefore a hell of a good time to beat a hasty retreat.

Similarly, certain telltale signs can warn you of trouble ahead with your deal—but only if you arrange ahead of time to put the canary up on its perch, learn to read its behavior, and carefully monitor that behavior.

When you're doing a deal, it's important to have a very good understanding of the leading indicators of future performance for your business and to shorten your normal review cycle on these indicators so they'll flash a warning before your business can be substantially harmed. Ideally, you will have canaries to sense dangers in the three common problem areas listed—organization, operations, and customers—as well as a canary for IT, which touches all parts of your business. In each of these realms, you need to figure out which indicator is most important and what the most appropriate early-warning systems might be.

These choices derive from your understanding of what drives your company's success. If you are in a service business, where customer loyalty is extremely important, then customer feedback is likely to serve as your canary. If you're in a business where retaining and energizing highly skilled employees is of overriding importance, then the defection of key employees is the measure you have to watch most closely. And for all businesses, certain kinds of operational and IT indicators (most likely, the ones you have relied upon heavily in the past) will help you detect any emerging problems with the overall running of your business. Again, if you resort to "old-friend" indicators, consider whether you need to consult them more frequently or revise them in ways that give you a better way to probe your changed circumstances. (See table 5-1.)

TABLE 5-1

Checklist of Early Warnings

Where Things Go Wrong	Warning	Preemption
1. Customers	Call center spikes; e-mail increases	Communicate early with customers
2. Organization	Increased turnover of key employees	Launch broad-based employee listening sessions
3. Information Systems	Key data goes missing—for example, can't easily ID largest customers	Check in with information users inside/outside company
4. Operations	Financials deteriorate	Solicit customer feedback on shipment and reliability

Let's revisit the Sears acquisition of mail-order clothing retailer Lands' End and see how customer feedback signaled trouble in that case. You will recall (or perhaps you know from personal experience) that Lands' End's customers are fiercely loyal. Sears bought Lands' End mainly because it craved the catalog retailer's brand identity as well as affluent, loyal, and way-too-busy-to-fight-the-mall-traffic kinds of consumers.

Sears also understood that the greatest risk in the acquisition was that it might scare off those same coveted consumers. After all, these savvy consumers were likely to perceive a big difference between megaretailer Sears and the down-home folks from Dodgeville, Wisconsin. Customers had a strong, emotional bond with the Lands' End brand, which evoked a cheerful, tasteful, outdoorsy, natural-fibers simplicity; they were likely to be less excited about traditionally dowdy, polyester-inclined Sears.

To detect early any change in customer loyalty, therefore, the company stepped up its monitoring of customer calls and e-mail feedback at the Lands' End contact centers. Lands' End understood early on that many of its loyal customers were uncomfortable with the connection with Sears. The call center received more than twenty calls a day from customers saying they did not want to receive any marketing communications from Sears. Sears and Lands' End therefore kept their customer interfaces separate, with each retaining its own distinctive service style. Also, Lands' End sent a note to its customers explaining the takeover, and reassuring them that they would continue to receive the same high-quality products and service to which they were accustomed.

We made reference in this chapter to the kinds of companies that depend on highly skilled employees to stay ahead of their competitors. In such cases, retaining stars is key to future success. When these companies make a deal, therefore, they have to be sure to monitor their organization, since for them, keeping key people happy and productive is every bit as important as (and in some cases, even more important than) keeping customers satisfied.

Technology companies, whose bread and butter is intellectual property, always need to focus on retaining key employees when they make deals. In chapter 4, we introduced the example of Cisco Systems. As John Chambers, the CEO of Cisco, asserted:

> When we acquire a company, we aren't simply acquiring its current products, we're acquiring the next generation of products through its people. If you pay between $500,000 and $3 million per employee, and all you are doing is buying the current research and the current market share, you're making a terrible investment. In the average acquisition, 40 to 80 percent of the top management and key engineers are gone in two years. By those metrics, most acquisitions fail.[5]

So Cisco—which acquired more than forty companies between 1993 and 2001—judges the success of its mergers by its ability to retain key employees. Every month, the CEO gets a report on employee turnover figures, and if turnover spikes or begins to touch key functions, the senior team acts immediately to probe the trend and to address whatever kind of dissatisfaction lies behind it.

Monitoring Operations Closely

Problems with customers and employees tend to crop up soon after a deal is done. Operational issues, by contrast, can be much slower to develop. Sometimes they show up first as a shortcoming on the information technology side of the house, which may take a while to reach a flashpoint. But suddenly, you can't get answers to critical questions, such as, Who is our biggest customer? Which of our product lines are most profitable? One technology company we know of drew blanks on such queries for six months after rolling up several smaller firms in its sector. When the company finally straightened out IT snarls, it discovered that its biggest customer was its chief competitor, which was happily buying parts from the new units.

So, it's important for all companies to keep a close eye on their operations well after the merging companies integrate. That is especially true of deals where companies are doing a fair amount of integration and are expecting significant gains from a combined sales effort. Let's look again at Citigroup—which we see as a highly skilled acquirer—and explore how that company assessed and dealt with operational problems.

When Citigroup's joint chiefs conceived of the merger of Citicorp and Travelers Group, they told investors the deal was predicated on cross-selling opportunities: Citicorp banking customers would buy Travelers insurance and brokerage services from Travelers's Salomon Smith Barney. Sandy Weill, then chairman and CEO of Travelers Group, and John Reed, then chairman and CEO of Citicorp, planned to create a one-stop shop for financial services, and they forecast profits to grow by a staggering $1 billion. Unfortunately, as discussed in chapter 3, cross-selling usually proves tough to pull off. A year after the Citigroup deal closed, the investment thesis had yet to prove itself. Revenue growth fell far short of projections.

Todd Thomson, Citigroup's CFO, told us that when it comes to early-warning signals on the operational side, Citigroup tends to focus on financial performance—and in an interesting way. Citigroup defines short-term financial goals for acquired companies and builds them into the budget. This means, Thomson explains, that those numbers become highly visible:

> We track the performance. For any major acquisitions, I actually report the performance versus budget to the board for at least twelve months. I look at it monthly, and we talk about it within the management group monthly. From that perspective, everyone knows their numbers are going to be in front of the management committee and the board. They are scared to death because of that.[6]

Thomson also told us that Citigroup does a postclosing audit in order to check the quality of due diligence, and that the firm's M&A group does a deal review on the one-year anniversary of the deal. By doing both short-term and long-term monitoring, Citigroup learns not only about the state of an acquired company, but also about the accuracy of its own projections.

Once it detects a problem, Citigroup takes swift action. For example, rather than ignoring its cross-sell shortfall, Citigroup's leaders faced the disappointment head-on, and tested all the sources of value assumed in its investment thesis. Their conclusion: They weren't wrong in anticipating cross-sell synergies, but they were far too optimistic about the timetable for realizing them. In June 1999, John Reed spoke candidly to the press, telling *BusinessWeek,* "I would lie to you if I said we have booked tremendous incremental customer revenue by exploiting the various channels. . . . It's premature. I would guess that would take two to three years."[7]

Having recalibrated its expectations, Citigroup went on to fix its problems. The company pacified shareholders by delivering ahead of forecast on another aspect of the deal's promise—cost reductions—and pointing to progress on the corporate side. Then, still convinced that its investment thesis remained sound, Citigroup redoubled management efforts to solve the cross-selling problem.

What sets successful acquirers like Citigroup apart is their ability to take swift and decisive action to fix postdeal problems. Whether the issues concern customers, a hamstrung organization, or faltering operations, the pattern is the same: Disciplined acquirers don't dwell on the past. They admit mistakes and move on, communicating openly about their actions. They also realize that a problem in one area may find its solution in another. For instance, an organizational shortcoming may be at the root of poor operational performance—and therefore, the answer may lie in a change of personnel (see the section Changing People). When you appreciate such linkages, you are more likely to make good decisions under pressure. Let's turn to how companies deal with the pressure to get things right.

It is critically important when things go wrong to reach out to your customers to fix things as quickly as possible. You need to be aggressive in dealing with their issues. We've already touched on this in the context of Sears and Lands' End, but let's look at another telling example. Kellogg's acquisition of Keebler, introduced in chapter 1, shows that it pays not only to fix problems quickly, but also to communicate immediately with affected customers.

You will recall that this acquisition was almost a reverse merger, in that the overarching thesis for the deal was that Kellogg would profit by putting its snacks through Keebler's direct-store-delivery system. But Kellogg didn't just want Keebler's distribution system—it also wanted its SAP technology platform. That was all well and good, except for the fact that Kellogg moved too fast in its initial distribution-center conversions. When it converted the first distribution center, Kellogg's "order fill" (that is, the percentage of orders that were successfully filled) dropped from the high 90 percents to the low 70 percents. "We had a crisis," admits CEO Carlos Gutierrez.[8] It didn't last long. Gutierrez quickly saw that the conversion team needed to take much more care in bringing each distribution center live, so Kellogg developed a system whereby the team worked on a distribution center until it was ready to go live. Then—and only then—would it move on to the next one.

During this difficult period, what did Kellogg offer its affected customers? "A lot of phone calls, and a lot of face-to-face discussions," Gutierrez says. "Fortunately, we fixed the problem in a matter of a couple of weeks." By acting quickly and addressing customers directly, Kellogg got its SAP integration back on track.

Changing People

Rapid response often involves personnel changes. That's because no matter what kind of deal you have done, good management will make all the difference. In our survey, 97 percent of executives who had been through a bad merger agreed that strong management is one of the keys to successful integration.

If you find that weak management is undermining your merger, you need to put aside the gentler approaches that may work under normal business conditions. Executives who usually prefer to give people time to find their feet may have to be less tolerant. Those who don't like to judge new people in their first few weeks may have to make swifter decisions about new arrivals from an acquired company. These tough decisions are made doubly difficult when those people who aren't making the grade are old friends or longtime associates.

When it came to cross-selling, as described previously, Citigroup clearly had a problem. After the announcement of the merger in April 1998, the combined share price had dipped more than half by the start of October.

As it turned out, however, Citigroup was able to regroup from its troubles with Travelers because it was able to trace its operational failure all the way back to its source. In this case, problems integrating the overlapping parts of Citicorp's corporate arm and Travelers' investment bank—Salomon Smith Barney—showed up as a delay in establishing a joint approach to serving key clients. Finally, Weill and Reed traced this delay back to the senior management team in charge of putting the two sides together. Personality clashes and historical allegiances were preventing the team from addressing tough integration issues.

Having established the root cause of the problem, Weill and Reed took action. They said goodbye to a popular top executive, James Dimon, which was a difficult and courageous decision. Weill and Reed weathered the ensuing publicity storm, admitting this was a painful move while at the same time asserting forcefully that the restructuring was necessary. By March 1999, the market had rewarded their candor and tenacity, when the stock price climbed back to what it had been at the time of the merger's announcement.

Changing the Business

When Weill became the single chief executive of Citigroup after Reed retired, he continued to respond quickly when problems arose, even when it meant admitting an error and retracing his steps. Consider, for example, his handling of a disappointing performance from Travelers's property and casualty business, noted earlier in this chapter.

After Citigroup's false start in cross-selling consumer products, renewed efforts began to pay off in 2000. But by 2002, Travelers Property Casualty still wasn't jelling. In fact, it was losing money on Citibank customers. Weill candidly told *Money* magazine in June 2002, "The people who ended up taking our insurance policies were those with the greatest risks."[9]

Adding to this disappointment was the fact that, by Citigroup standards, the property and casualty business was generating a relatively low return on equity. Faced with this double whammy, Weill acted quickly and forcefully. He spun out Travelers Property Casualty in 2002 in an IPO of 23 percent of the company, which raised about $4 billion. Citigroup kept a 9.9 percent stake in the business, with the rest being distributed to existing Citigroup shareholders. Weill got an indirect advantage from his expeditious action as well. After the terrorist attacks of September 11, 2001, property and casualty share prices had risen in anticipation of ensuing rate hikes; these prices partly account for the princely $4 billion take.

Sometimes a changed business results in a changed industry. Take the case of Jefferson Smurfit's purchase of Stone Container, discussed in chapters 2 and 4. Michael Smurfit was a veteran acquirer who had systematically bought capacity when the containerboard market was close to rock bottom. Smurfit described Jefferson Smurfit Group's secret formula as "acquire, rationalize, repeat."[10] The company's acquisitions of Container Corporation of America in 1986 and Cellulose du Pin in 1994 both complemented the acquirer's capacity at a bargain price.

However, at the time that Jefferson Smurfit made moves to acquire Stone Container, it hit economic and industry turbulence. The bottom fell out of the Asian market, and the containerboard market began to drop toward life-threatening lows. Smurfit had to decide quickly whether to stick with the deal or pull the plug. Fortunately, Michael Smurfit had thought through various contingencies. For example, he could put a stand-alone Stone Container on the market and thereby cut his losses. But most likely, in that scenario, someone would pick up the assets and keep operating—at a competitive advantage, since the new entry would have little or no debt. This would help push the whole industry (including his own company) into a prolonged downturn.

But Smurfit spotted some room to maneuver. If he could reduce costs in the combined Smurfit-Stone by $350 million, the combined company could survive the storm even with rock-bottom containerboard prices. At the same time, by dramatically reducing Smurfit-Stone's capacity, he could take some teeth out of industry overcapacity and thereby minimize the bite of a market slump.

Smurfit quickly drew up a plan to cut $350 million of costs from the combined companies, and then went ahead and closed the deal on Stone Container. He immediately announced his cost-cutting plan, along with mill and plant closures that would reduce total U.S. containerboard capacity by 5 percent. These bold moves pulled Smurfit-Stone back from the brink of failure and helped ensure the deal's success.

Smurfit-Stone's capacity reduction and cost cutting saved the day. In other industries—for example, those in which branding, product innovation, and service levels play a bigger role—focusing solely on cost cutting in a downturn won't do the job. Because you still have to grow your core business, you need different kinds of contingencies—around increasing customer and supplier loyalty, forming alliances, or reaching beyond your company borders to access new ideas.

Making Change Stick

Making tough decisions is one challenge; making them stick is another. Change is effected through people. This sometimes means changing people, as described earlier; but at other times it means holding on to people—or at least, creating a kind of continuity that can survive the departure of key individuals. Philips Medical Systems, introduced in chapter 4, had good people in place early in the process of acquiring four businesses. Then, in the midst of the integration effort, a string of planned retirements meant that the parent company had to replace several top executives, including the CEO, during the integration. This leadership turnover, former CEO of Philips Electronics North America William Curran told us, hampered the pace of integration:

> We not only lost people from the business we acquired, but also from the acquiring business. You have to be very careful with changes like these. As you work through planned leadership changes, some other people leave as well. Time marches on. Because integration is a multiyear effort, some of the people you thought were going to be on your team, simply won't be.[11]

It's inevitable: Sometimes leaders critical to the integration leave. Wise acquirers therefore line up lieutenants as potential successors for key integration roles. Similarly, they take care to document not just the gist of their decisions, but also the rationale behind those decisions. Sometimes a clear recitation of a debate and its outcome is the most powerful tool for continuity, especially in the wake of a departed leader and the absence of a clear successor.

FIXING PROBLEMS THROUGH TRANSFORMATIONS

The second of our two overall categories of problem-fixes comprises what we call "transformations." Transformations don't involve a process of nipping and tucking around the edges; instead, they entail fundamental organizational overhaul. They can be the result of poor due diligence, or they can arise as a result of a dramatically changing competitive context. Markets change; competitors make moves of their own. These changes may force the acquiring company to go through a rapid evolution.

The best acquirers plan contingencies based on worst-case scenarios. When problems arise—which they almost always do—they look for the incremental fix. When that doesn't work, they test the investment thesis and the underlying basis of competition again: Did we get it wrong, due to either poor due diligence or some sort of earthshaking shift in the marketplace?

If the answer is yes—we got it wrong—then there are only two choices: transformation or divorce. Transformation, as we see it, involves four overarching tasks:

1. Cutting your losses by fixing your core business
2. Turbocharging your management team
3. Working the balance sheet
4. Redefining the strategy and then implementing the new strategy

Experienced turnaround artists will recognize that these are, in fact, the building blocks of turnarounds that take place well away from the merger marketplace. But because they are so often associated with troubled mergers, we will run through them here, drawing on yet another complicated Del Monte story for our illustrations.

This story involves not Del Monte Foods—introduced earlier as an example of a merger-related communications challenge—but two other Del Montes: fruit producer Del Monte South Africa and Del Monte International. (We should explain, as an aside, that the proliferation of companies called Del Monte—there are actually five—is a by-product of one of the least disciplined deals of all time. In the late 1980s, a leveraged buyout of RJR-Nabisco, chronicled in *Barbarians at the Gate,* broke up and sold off Del Monte—once part of Nabisco—to pay down debt.[12]) Vivian Imerman, major shareholder of Del Monte South Africa, bought Del Monte International (DMI) to safeguard his own Del Monte's produce-distribution channels. In the process, he and his colleagues set up the kinds of early-warning systems advocated earlier.

Shortly after the acquisition, three of the early-warning signals that Imerman's due diligence had identified began to blink simultaneously. Imerman remembers, "The scale of the problem wasn't apparent even after six months' due diligence. Shortly after we bought DMI, the environment changed in the retail trade, with supermarkets' power changing."[13]

Consolidation among European retailers began to squeeze manufacturer margins. Imerman says, "We did identify this as a possibility during due diligence, but it was difficult to assess how quickly things would change. And the knock-on effect in the supply chain was horrendous." At the same time, currency shifts in Asia and Europe adversely affected the Asian side of DMI. "We were squeezed on the cost and selling side," says Imerman. Finally, one more shock—a glut of pineapples on the market—delivered a blow to produce prices.

Unfortunately for DMI, the warning lights flashed only shortly before the company was in full crisis and the share price began a treacherous slide. Imerman quickly realized it was too late for troubleshooting; DMI was already off the rails.

Executives who discover that one of their acquisitions is in danger of collapse—whether as a result of postdeal shocks, as was the case for DMI, or owing to a failure of due diligence—must decide whether to retreat from their position and sell the ailing company or move into turnaround mode. In DMI's case, a sale was not a sensible option. As Imerman puts it, "Strategically, there was no doubt about the fit of the businesses of Del Monte International and Del Monte SA."

What's more, DMI's collapse would have had serious consequences for the parent company, which still had to worry about its distribution channels. So Vivian Imerman moved into turnaround mode, commissioning a full strategic review of the business, "from the seedling to the finished product on the shelf," as he puts it.

As noted, corporate turnarounds—whether or not they're related to a recent merger or acquisition—require a discipline of their own. The first of our four prescriptions is to reduce your losses by fixing your core business. Imerman's review concluded that DMI should capitalize on its core strength, the Del Monte brand, cutting out minor brands and reducing costs across the board. The review also pointed to some deep operational cuts, an overhaul of DMI's distribution strategy, and other drastic changes in the way the company competed.

Our second prescription is to turbocharge your management team. In other words, replace dead wood with stars, and provide incentives aligned with business success. Imerman saw that DMI did not have the management team it needed to see his plan through. "Existing management had been in the business a long time," he explains. "They weren't capable of change. They were not prepared to embrace a new strategy, even though some said they were." Rather than wait to see whether the old guard could change, Imerman changed his entire management team except for one person, bringing in self-starters who could adapt to new ways of doing business. Looking back, he concludes, "The team change was absolutely essential. We had to change the whole mind-set."

Our third prescription is to work the balance sheet, selling off noncore businesses and assets to raise cash to invest in your core business. Under Imerman's direction, but with input from others, DMI worked its balance sheet hard. As he recalls:

> We had a lot of noncore businesses—tea, some private-label juice businesses, biscuits, confectionery—and they were good profit contributors. I was quite amazed when we came to the conclusion that we should sell those businesses and use the proceeds to pay for the restructuring.

Imerman raised some $70 million through the sale of peripheral businesses. "The cost of the whole exercise was paid for out of noncore assets," he reports. "We used no shareholder money."

Fourth, we recommend redefining the strategy and then implementing that strategy. With his new team on board, Imerman implemented a three-year plan to restore the business to an even footing. Eighteen months later, he sold DMI for €680 million, more than four times its market value in the depths of the crisis.

For an in-depth look at an example of redefining and implementing a strategy to fix a troubled merger—as part of a larger transformation process—let's return to the unhappy merger of Newell and Rubbermaid.

Fixing Newell Rubbermaid: A Transformation Chronicled

You will recall that postmerger, when Newell finally lifted Rubbermaid's veil, the deal makers discovered a perfumed pig. Rubbermaid had been very successfully dressed for sale. Newell Rubbermaid's longtime CEO and original champion of the Rubbermaid deal, Daniel Ferguson, later admitted that Newell paid too much for Rubbermaid.

Even more troubling, though, was the fact that the two businesses—the acquirer and the acquired—turned out to be fundamentally incompatible. Rubbermaid was a consumer-oriented innovator, accustomed to offering the premium product in each of its categories. By contrast, Newell was a low-cost, high-volume supplier of more-ordinary household products. The two companies' products might end up next to each other on a laundry-room shelf, but the economics of getting them there were very different. This fairly basic fact unfortunately came as a surprise to Newell.

When there's a fundamental mismatch between two merged companies, the choices are (1) to get a divorce or (2) to stay married by rethinking the strategy for the whole enterprise.

Newell chose to stay married to Rubbermaid. To be sure, this resulted in part from the fact that Newell had determined that Rubbermaid would command only a very low price on the market. But more important to Newell's decision was Galli's confidence in his ability to turn Rubbermaid around, even if that meant rethinking parts of the larger Newell strategy. Let's return to how Joseph Galli, the new CEO, set out to transform Newell Rubbermaid.

Galli began by announcing his intention to continue the Newellization process that John McDonough had begun. His priorities included improving customer service, reducing corporate overhead, tightening financial controls, and implementing some deep cost cutting. In May 2001, Newell Rubbermaid announced a major restructuring program that would cut three thousand jobs worldwide (6 percent of the combined company's total) and close several manufacturing sites.

But when the overall investment thesis is in question, cutting costs may not get you nearly far enough. Even as you're taking steps to stop the bleeding, you probably need to be revisiting your basis of competition to figure out what has gone wrong. In Galli's case, that meant facing up to the fact that the company could not be two things at once. Either it would focus on low-cost production, which was Newell's original strength, or it would embrace Rubbermaid's focus as a marketing-oriented product innovator.

Galli also found that, although many of his Newell colleagues intellectually understood the changes required to fix the business, people didn't know how to act on that understanding. There were at least two huge obstacles. First, Newell managers didn't have the right background to manage Rubbermaid. As Galli explains, "The managers who were put in place from Newell to go over and manage Rubbermaid were really financial managers, folks with an accounting background and an operations background. There were really no marketing or product-development people who were in Newell and shipped over to Rubbermaid."[14]

Second, Rubbermaid talent had been heading for the exits even before the deal with Newell surfaced. Under former CEO Stanley Gault, Rubbermaid had built a stellar reputation for innovation. But the company had begun to drift, to the point where its core competence for innovation wasn't nearly as strong as it used to be. Then when the deal closed, many of the talented people who had stuck with Rubbermaid took a look at Newell's track record and determined (with ample justification) that innovation wasn't going to be as highly valued as keeping costs low. "You had a case here where the innovation capability really was not in place because of that exodus," Galli explains, "and whatever vestiges were still in place were gone relatively [quickly] after the acquisition, after the accounting-oriented folks took over."

Newell saw that in order to rescue its marriage with Rubbermaid, it was going to have to innovate significantly in its base business. In other words, the acquiring company consciously decided to alter its investment thesis to fit a new reality. (We are reminded of that cautionary voice-over on those old TV science shows: "Hey, kids—don't try this at home!") And in order to do that, it was going to have to take a step that many companies trying to retrofit a troubled merger find themselves taking: hiring new kinds of people for the job. Not surprisingly, those people tend to come from businesses that are already succeeding in the areas where the troubled company is coming up short.

For Galli, that meant hiring people from companies that were proven winners in mass-market innovation. Because of the wide gulf between Newell management's expertise and the skills the combined company would need, Galli had to make wholesale management changes. These changes continue today, says Galli:

> We've hired, at this stage, over one hundred and twenty people at the VP and president level and up who have come in from outside of the company. Most of those folks came out of my Rolodex. [Many] came from Black & Decker, but some came from Amazon, and some we brought in from other companies like Johnson & Johnson, Dell, Procter & Gamble, Stanley Works, Danaher. So we brought a mixture of people into the company that had skills in the areas that we needed.

In all, Galli made 141 management changes at the vice-president level and above. "The fact is," recalls Galli, "we had to move aside 120 out of the top 150 people in the company. There was a lot of bitterness over this change in direction."

In this same time period, Galli introduced an incentive scheme designed to align executive interests with a set of specific promises the company had made to the investment community. These included, for example, sales growth of 5 percent per year (excluding acquisitions) and 15 percent return on investment. Galli also laid plans to broaden Newell Rubbermaid's employee stock-ownership scheme.

As new people arrived at Newell, Galli gave them not only strong incentives, but also a clear understanding of exactly how Newell planned to get back on track. As part of this effort, he created an intensive program that put—and still puts—groups of twenty-five to thirty leaders through a six-day "boot camp" in leadership development. Built around a highly practical curriculum, it is in many cases taught by Galli himself. "It teaches people our product-development process, branded marketing, account management, globalization, inventory turns, how you manage working capital and fixed capital," he explains. "All the fundamentals."

So, Galli's first priority was hiring and training the right kinds of people. At the same time, though, he had to create a system to set corporate goals and measure performance. He did this by rolling out what he calls an "operating cycle," which is essentially a twelve-month calendar that forces Newell to set strategy, review the organization, review operations, set budgets, and evaluate performance. As he elaborates:

> This operating cycle has been powerful, because it used to be that there was all sorts of ambiguity around how we run the company. "When do we see the CEO?" "When do we review our business?" Talent became tied up with one-off meetings. Everything was ad hoc. Now there is always room. We can call a meeting now, and within an hour we can get all the key people from around the world. But the reason for that is because the talent is so clear [about the company's agenda] between operating-cycle sessions.

Transformations, by definition, are disruptive. Once the self-transforming team has its members in place and its goals clear, it needs to look again at the issue of culture. Most likely, there are one or more camps who are feeling bruised, battered, or unloved. How will the organization deal with this rent in the cultural fabric?

At Newell, Galli very explicitly set out to reset the company's culture, to capture benefits for the business as a whole. Remember, his chief goal was to create a company that was dedicated to product innovation on a mass-market scale. So what did he do? He worked the culture not only from the top, but also from the bottom.

"We had too many people in the company who were isolated from the market, from the customer," says Galli. He therefore decided to create a recruitment program called Phoenix—named for the mythical bird that periodically rises from its own ashes—which took all of Newell Rubbermaid's fresh hires from colleges and put them out in Wal-Marts and other retail stores, where they would rub shoulders with sales clerks and customers and get a street-level feel for their products. "They really learn the business from that," says Galli. He adds:

> We've already hired over fifteen hundred [into Phoenix] in the last eighteen months, and three hundred have already been promoted to their second or third job. Any college graduate we hire is a Phoenix. We bring them in, we train them vigorously, and we tell them that in addition to the results we expect, we are developing them into the future roots of the company. So then we wind up with one culture and not thirty-seven.

In order to save the marriage between Newell and Rubbermaid, in other words, Galli needed not only to activate but also to redefine the strategy of the whole company. This transformation involved making Newell act more like Rubbermaid had traditionally performed—that is, making the combined entity a consumer-oriented company. (In a sense, the corporation was "Rubberized" after it was "Newellized.") Galli grabbed onto the most valuable part of the Rubbermaid acquisition—the Rubbermaid brand itself—and held on tight.

As of this writing, Newell Rubbermaid's transformation is moving forward in fits and starts. By December 2003, Newell Rubbermaid shares were down since Galli's arrival two years earlier. But by mid-February 2004, they were up 19 percent over their price at the time Galli came on board. The company has made noteworthy strides in free cash flow. From 2001 to 2003, it generated more than $1 billion in free cash flow, a dramatic improvement over the $160 million it generated from 1998 to 2000.[15] Galli is doing many of the right things, but sometimes you have to look at the question, Should we undo the deal?

UNDOING THE DEALS YOU CAN'T FIX

In a spirit of optimism, we have devoted the majority of this chapter to the deals that you can fix, either through focused interventions or transformations. Sometimes, though, the range or intensity of post-deal problems indicates a fundamental flaw in the portfolio strategy itself. If tackling these large problems seems to hold no greater promise than damage control, the best response may be to retrace your steps out of the woods, and undo the deal.

For executives who build their reputations on the deals they do, backing out can be one of the toughest decisions of all. "It's very hard for a company to admit it's making a mistake," says Blair Effron, vice chairman of investment banking at UBS Warburg. "They get very emotionally tied to their assets." The strong temptation, therefore, is to try to make the deal work. "Most good managers have the confidence to think they can turn a business around," Effron continues. Unfortunately, such confidence often leads only to a delayed sale and lost value. "What you generally find is that the divestiture strategy is made eighteen months to two years too late."[16]

A case in point is BMW's £1.7 billion acquisition of the U.K.'s Rover Group in 1994. The deal shows just how badly things can go when a poor investment thesis is coupled with hasty due diligence. BMW's appetite for a radical fix came only after six years of draining coffers and resources to salvage an anemic acquisition.

The problems began with a faulty philosophy: In the early 1990s, conventional wisdom held that only car companies able to produce around two million cars a year would survive. According to this argument, any company producing fewer cars would fail to achieve the necessary economies of scale and so would lose its independence to a larger automaker. This struck a chord with Bernd Pischetsrieder, then chairman of BMW's management board, who aspired to grow BMW into the ranks of the auto industry superpowers and to expand its range of product offerings. But an aspiration is not the same thing as an investment thesis. And if BMW had a clear investment thesis, it did not share it with equity analysts or shareholders.

Given the premium positioning of the BMW brand, he was convinced that BMW had no choice but to expand, either by building its own new brand or by acquiring a ready-made mass producer. The first option was dismissed as being too expensive and time-consuming. Rover, said Pischetsrieder at the time, was "the only alternative left in terms of size, suggested or perceived price, and presence in the necessary market areas, geographically as well as in terms of market segmentation."[17]

The idea that Rover was the last automaker up for grabs fueled momentum among BMW leaders, and they embarked on a race to the finish line. After a breathtaking round of clandestine meetings between the two parties, Rover's managers physically handed over all the information BMW needed to value the company on January 16, 1994. Just ten days later—a time scale that makes the Newell–Rubbermaid deal seem positively leisurely—the automakers signed the deal at the offices of BMW's lawyers in London.

BMW's abbreviated due diligence had failed to discover that Rover was a dog of a deal. BMW's next mistake—and it was a prolonged one!—was to ignore the warning lights that were flashing for the better part of six years. Somewhat cowed by the howls of indignation that went up from the British public after the takeover—the British hate it when the Germans best them at either soccer or cars—BMW tiptoed around this sleepy hound instead of tackling the problems of Rover head-on. Meanwhile, Rover's managers remained in place, doing pretty much what they had always done, when in fact an active restructuring was called for. The results? The business limped along unprofitably, year after year.

After coping with myriad acquisition pains, including a failed integration process, demoralized workers, a drain of engineering resources from BMW to Rover, and unsuccessful turnaround efforts, BMW finally had enough. The Rover unit lost £800 million in 1999 alone. By then BMW had invested £2 billion in Rover and faced the prospect of having to invest an additional £3 billion over the next three years.

After six long years, Pischetsrieder's successor, Joachim Milberg, concluded that Rover and BMW were mutually incompatible. It was time for divorce. In making the decision, BMW was finally able to turn this sour deal into a moneymaker. How? BMW sold Rover to a group called the Phoenix Consortium for the royal sum of £10. Then,

Milberg sold Land Rover to Ford in May 2000 for £1.8 billion. Finally, BMW kept the production facilities in Oxford and the rights to the Mini model, which, with BMW's attention, has turned into a smash hit. In the end, BMW recovered from its investment in Rover, but this was a tortuous way to regain financial footing. It should have undone the deal sooner.

By contrast, Liechtenstein Global Trust (LGT) was far more proactive in cutting its losses in the wake of its overly ambitious takeover of Chancellor Capital Management.

LGT, a European-based private bank, had expanded beyond its core European business into retail, and then institutional, asset management around the globe. LGT's acquisition of faraway New York–based Chancellor Capital Management vaulted the combined company into the upper echelons of global asset-management firms. The deal looked good on the surface: Chancellor boasted a powerful institutional sales force, a highly disciplined and proven investment approach, and an excellent reputation among pension-fund consultants. But even as the deal closed, LGT's chairman, HSH Prince Philipp of Liechtenstein, had begun to see the problems inherent in such a large-scale acquisition, so far removed from LGT's historical core:

> I felt very uneasy. I wondered if we weren't taking on too much. Already my management team and I were having problems managing LGT: Management feuds were frequent among our businesses, and our financial performance was erratic. How could we expect to improve things by adding a huge, unfamiliar business to our portfolio?[18]

Soon after the deal, Prince Philipp's early-warning system told him his instincts were right. The portfolio mismatch soon led to management disagreements between Chancellor and LGT. Within two months, these disagreements had escalated into full-blown warfare. The two most senior executives at Chancellor essentially demanded the right to take over LGT's entire U.S. asset-management business, which the parent felt those individuals were ill-equipped to do. And, as Prince Philipp remembers, "If they didn't get what they wanted, they threatened to organize a walkout." At the same time, the senior

LGT executive who had led the charge to buy Chancellor left the company. This precipitated a downward spiral of more departures, additional morale problems, and stagnating performance.

No one recommends a quick resort to divorce. But when companies find themselves trapped in a failed marriage, they must consider the full range of strategic options, including exiting all or part of the business. In these cases, it often helps to bring in a fresh eye. The people whose careers—and pride—are hitched to the deal are unlikely to make objective decisions. Conversely, they are far more likely to allow sentimentality and turf considerations to creep in.

Atypically, at LGT the leader of the deal also led its undoing. Prince Philipp called for a no-holds-barred review of the tangled situation that the merged company found itself in. This review revealed that although the asset-management business had been growing, it was weak in most of its markets. LGT's costs in asset management were way out of line with those of competitors. Not only was LGT's asset-management business still in a relatively weak position after the acquisition, even stronger competitors were emerging as the market consolidated globally. LGT had little hope of gaining ground without adding more, and even larger, asset-management acquisitions to a business that was still in the early stages of a very difficult integration.

At LGT, letting go paid off. In January 1998, the bank was able to take advantage of an upswing in the asset-management market and make a high-value sale to one of the consolidating global leaders. LGT restructured its business portfolio and sold the combination of Chancellor and its own asset-management business for more than $1 billion, generating more than $800 million in profit for its shareholders.

Finding a high-value solution certainly helped reduce the pain and minimize any lingering sentimentality about the failed Chancellor deal. Prince Philipp, for one, was happy to swallow his pride: "Did we feel foolish, agreeing only a little more than a year after acquiring Chancellor to divest the entire business? No. I, for one, felt relieved. In my heart, I knew that this was the right decision, and I also knew that there is nothing so foolish as to throw good money after bad."[19]

A final caution: even if it appears that the right answer is to retreat from the partnership, don't let up on discipline when evaluating your options. By this stage, some managers may well be desperate to shed their unwanted "spouse," and may miss the creative options that could turn a troubled situation into a financial victory. Disciplined acquirers put the past behind them, accept sunk costs for what they are, and consider all the possibilities. Options may include unbundling the company and selling the parts separately, spinning off the acquisition in a management buyout or buy-in, or even looking for new alliances and partnerships that would render the acquisition more valuable.

GETTING BACK ON TRACK

Again, getting back on track is all about discipline and the willingness to look at reality in a clear-eyed way, see things as they are, and then act on that understanding.

Successful acquirers know what they should do when the deal starts to derail. They anticipate postdeal problems, set up sensors to detect them, and tackle them as soon as they emerge. They let go of the past, admit their errors, and take tough, decisive action to put their deals back on track. They pick the right people to lead their business, even if that means bypassing or replacing long-serving executives. They learn to distinguish between the deals that present the inevitable glitches and those that present more serious problems. In the former case, they launch focused interventions. In the latter case, either they move swiftly into turnaround mode or they make the tough decision to retrace their steps.

Sometimes, saving a troubled deal can vindicate the original decision to acquire. At Newell, Joe Galli—who put the company back on track—credits Dan Ferguson with having the original vision and understanding of portfolio needs to make the deal in the first place, difficult as it turned out to be. Says Galli:

> I think in the end, Dan should get a lot of credit for having had the courage to stand up and say, "Wait a minute, we have to completely change leadership and direction," even though there was limited support among folks who had known Dan for years. Many of the people Dan has worked with, col-

leagues who have worked with him for decades, were violently opposed. And Dan stood up and said, "We have to do this." That takes a lot of courage.[20]

But as Joe Galli's efforts to rescue the Newell–Rubbermaid deal amply illustrate, getting a troubled deal back on track requires more than courage. It requires the discipline to expect the unexpected and the determination to reset the course for merger success.

6

Organizing for Decision Discipline

So far, we have focused mainly on closing a deal and surviving the immediate aftermath of that deal. We have walked through the four critical decisions you have to get right in order to successfully complete a merger, fight the fires that are likely to ignite in the wake of that deal, and conduct a far-ranging postmerger integration: financial, operational, and cultural.

But just as one great game does not make an athlete's career, so one great deal rarely serves as a foundation for sustained shareholder value. To be great, you need to be able to repeat your deal-making success over and over again. You need repeatedly to ask and answer astutely: How should we pick our targets? Which deals should we close? Where do we really need to integrate? And what should we do when the deal goes off track?

High-performing acquirers are consistently successful, we believe, because they have organized their M&A functions to create discipline around these four critical decisions. To do so, they first have to answer three basic organizational questions:

1. ***Who makes deals happen?*** The winners build a standing, experienced deal team that works hand in hand with the line

to identify, screen, close, and integrate deals. This allows the company both to create opportunities proactively, consistent with the strategy, and to strike rapidly when the right deal becomes available. The deal team is responsible for institutionalizing the process, with clear guidelines for the purchase and integration of acquisitions. The line is responsible for developing its strategy and for scanning the horizon to look for new growth through acquisition opportunities. The deal team updates its codified guidelines at the end of each deal through a postmortem.

2. ***Who evaluates opportunities?*** The deal team applies a set of standards to each transaction, making sure that it meets minimum hurdles. In addition, the best-practice acquirers commit line expertise. They make sure that line management—the people who ultimately end up with the job of absorbing the new company—get involved early, in all parts of the process, from the decision to buy to the estimation of synergies to the integration itself. And they hold the line managers accountable for long-term results.

3. ***How do you prepare to walk away?*** The most successful acquirers always set a walk-away price, and dispassionately prepare themselves to do just that: walk away, even at the last minute, if the deal's investment thesis fails to pan out. They insist on high-level approval, and put in place a decision-making process that clearly delineates who in the company recommends deals, whose input should be solicited, and who decides yea or nay in the final instance. And they often use the compensation system to ward off ill-considered acquisitions.

In this final chapter, we will look at what it takes to institutionalize success. To help us understand how the best acquirers organize for decision discipline and thereby standardize their deal-making prowess, let's look first to the Swiss food giant Nestlé and its peripatetic CEO, Peter Brabeck.

NESTLÉ: A TEXTBOOK ACQUIRER

In 2000, Brabeck attempted an ascent of the Matterhorn: Switzerland's most famous peak. Only a short distance from the windblown summit, under whiteout conditions, Brabeck abandoned his climb.

Why? He didn't want to risk his life. A wise choice, of course—but one that he says was driven more by a sense of professional obligation than by concern for his own safety. "The risk was too high for the responsibility I have," he explained to *Time* magazine.[1]

Brabeck applies the same restraint to his company's deal making. In the same year that he declined to take a gamble near the flinty peak of the Matterhorn, he also kept his company at the merger equivalent of base camp while arch rival Unilever bought Bestfoods, and U.S.-based Kraft took over Nabisco.[2] These moves threatened Nestlé's prized position as the world's largest food company. Nevertheless, Brabeck declined to jump into the merger fray. "I would not make an acquisition," he explained, "just to remain the biggest food company in the world."[3]

So there are limits on the kinds of risks Brabeck is willing to take. And yet, a thoroughly cautious man doesn't even think about setting foot on the Matterhorn—and the fact is, Peter Brabeck has taken his share of risks as the CEO of Nestlé. He has built the Swiss giant into the preeminent food company in the world today in part by focusing his base business on its historical core, but also by systematically augmenting his businesses with a series of smaller, well-thought-out acquisitions.

Brabeck's success was by no means preordained. He took the helm at Nestlé in June 1997, and some executives wondered whether the intellectually inclined Brabeck would be tough enough, and practical enough, to get the company back on a growth track. Under the leadership of his predecessor, Helmut Maucher, Nestlé had become a very reliable but very dull company. Volume growth had fallen to 2.7 percent, well short of the firm's long-established (and often-achieved) target of 4 percent.[4] Net profit remained under 6 percent, and the stock price was increasing at an anemic 3 percent a year in a bull market.

Perhaps even more disconcerting, competitors were out-innovating the traditionally pioneering Nestlé. The company was relying on incremental innovations to its existing product lines—that is, making existing customers a little happier—rather than making new customers happy and old customers much happier.

As it turned out, Brabeck and his team were more than up to the task, and their ability to organize and institutionalize for deal success was a linchpin to this success. They began by outlining a two-pronged corporate strategy: Nestlé would allocate resources to its core brand positions, and at the same time invest R&D dollars in new "good-for-you" food technologies. Ironically, this was less a revolution and more a return to the classic formula that had made the 137-year-old company a world-beater in the first place.

The company's overarching plan for growth became the bedrock out of which each subsequent deal's investment thesis was carved. The approach, now institutionalized, works as follows: Nestlé conducts an annual review of each strategic business unit. The goal of this review is to set strategic direction, and—as M&A head James Singh told us—"identify where we need to improve on the specific strengths and competencies in each specific product category."[5] Based on this analysis, Nestlé's management team determines where it can bolster its business, both organically and with deals. In other words, says Singh, the company's M&A activity is an "outgrowth of the business strategy."[6]

Like most successful acquirers, Nestlé has a core deal team, headed by Singh, that is in charge of all acquisitions. Once Nestlé's management team sets targets and strategies for its strategic business segments, Singh's M&A team begins its work here. "We try to get involved in terms of how M&A activity can help each business unit achieve its strategic objectives," he explains. "Whatever we do here in M&A is an outgrowth of those discussions and the decisions that are made with respect to strategic direction for each of those businesses."

To ensure that it accomplishes its goals, Nestlé has structured the acquisition process with a standard template and clear acquisition criteria against which major investments must deliver. Those criteria are written down and communicated to all. Singh himself ensures that everybody understands the criteria before starting to screen and evaluate prospects. "We would walk away from a deal if we thought that the deal did not meet those criteria," he says.

At the same time, Singh continues, the company's standard template must serve as a stimulant, rather than an impediment, to deal making. In other words, it must lend itself to being adapted to the specifics of a particular transaction. As he explains:

> You could do exactly in Eastern Europe as you did in the U.S., and do it splendidly, yet miss something specific to the local environment in terms of local practices, customers, legislation, controls, et cetera. We try to use a standard template to make sure that we cover the key aspects, but we do not treat it as sacrosanct, honoring every aspect of it. We want the template to be stimulating the process.

In previous chapters, we've cautioned about the perils of "deal fever." One way that Nestlé kills deal fever is through the involvement of CEO Peter Brabeck. Nothing gets bought or sold unless he approves the move, and would-be acquirers within the company know full well that their ideas will ultimately be subject to Brabeck's critical eye. In fact, Singh believes that senior-management leadership and support are a key success factor in M&A. "The CEO and the key executives in the business units provide leadership for the entire acquisition and integration process. And they provide me with the support and clarity to get the job done," says Singh. "That creates an obligation for communication with the executives to be frequent and relevant, so that direction can be given before you get too far down the process."

When the time comes to evaluate a prospect, Nestlé pulls operations people into the acquisition process. It also brings finance people from the strategic business units and geographies into the process to assist in the financial evaluation; and on international transactions, Nestlé requires the local-market CEOs and CFOs to be involved in the process. (Most best-practice acquirers follow this pattern of gradually expanding involvement, and it is a requirement at Nestlé.) Singh describes how the process works:

> The people in the geographic zones and the strategic business units become part of an M&A team that we put together. We try to get the requisite competencies. More importantly, we make sure that the people who are going to be running the business are an important part of the team that acquires the business. On large transactions, Nestlé requires the strategic business-unit heads to participate in the whole due-diligence process, attending the management presentations, visiting the data room, and understanding the synergies.

Ultimately, the line managers, operators, and finance people are responsible for estimating the potential business synergies, with guidance from the M&A team. "We work hand in hand with the line managers," says Singh, "to make sure there is clarity with respect to the objectives—for example, which factories are going to be closed, what capital investments will be made, and so on."

The relevant executives are not only involved; they ultimately have to sign off on the acquisition proposal, including the valuation. Says Singh: "As a matter of fact, we would not necessarily recommend buying a business, no matter how attractive it might be, if the operational management was not prepared to support it."

As we've seen in previous chapters, closing the deal is only half the story; integration and postdeal problem solving are the other half. Nestlé evaluates the achievement of the acquisition objectives through its postaudit review process. The company used to do postmortems on an ad hoc basis, but experience has convinced it to implement a more formal postaudit review process as an operating norm. Nestlé now conducts reviews of all of its major investments, including acquisitions and divestitures, for two to three years after it makes them. These reviews compare the results achieved with the objectives around synergies, growth rates, management structure, and so forth that the company had set during due diligence.

As Singh explains, "That adds a different discipline to the process, because it requires active involvement and real commitment. As soon as the acquisition is done and announced, it becomes part of the long-term strategic plan." And if the deal goes off track, it is the responsibility of both the central management team and the local line operators to find ways to create the value that the company promised at the time of the acquisition.

The postdeal review process also allows Nestlé to continuously monitor a deal's progress against the targets agreed upon at closing. "The important thing is that we understand what we are doing and don't by chance find out that the deal has gone astray," says Singh. Nestlé bases its definition of success not only on how well it delivers on specific targets, but also on how much it learns from the acquisition. "You hope that the key learnings would be an indication of success," says Singh. "Capitalizing on the technologies, the brands, and the management skills that you have acquired in the process is a critical success factor in achieving high-quality, sustainable growth."

Between 1998 and 2001, through a succession of acquisitions and divestitures, Brabeck, Singh, and their colleagues effectively remade Nestlé. For the most part, they targeted companies that were relatively small, which as we've seen is a hallmark of the successful acquirers in our study. Each deal, moreover, bolstered Nestlé's position in clearly defined ways. As a result, the company built tremendous scale around its strong brands and its technologies, fully realizing the benefits of being the world's largest food company. And, like most successful acquirers, Nestlé's leaders institutionalized a program of deal making. Like the other best-practice acquirers in our study, they bought frequently and methodically, focusing on each deal's long-term strategic value, rather than the short-term market perturbations created by the deal.

And in short, it worked: Between 1998 and 2001, Nestlé outperformed its peer group on revenue growth, and net income grew almost 20 percent per year. And just as important, Nestlé began recapturing its reputation for innovation and industry leadership.

PRACTICE MAKES PERFECT

Contrast Nestlé's story to the recent course of deal-making history, especially as captured in the headlines, where it appears that most frequent acquirers have been some combination of inept, dishonest, greedy, or soaked in hubris. It is almost a morality tale. The fallen angels of these headlines—the Vivendis, MCIs, and Enrons—first served as the poster children for growth by acquisition. Their success was inextricably linked to their voracious appetite for deals. Then came the fall, and—as the morality-tale logic goes—their failures discredit the use of mergers and acquisitions to achieve growth.

This is simply human nature: A rash of spectacular failures in deal making tends to overshadow the quiet successes of, for example, a Nestlé. When enough companies suffer dire consequences as a result of their bad deals, decision makers become skittish about doing any deals. The meltdown in shareholder value at these and other high-profile deal makers has caused many a board and management team to muzzle aggressive M&A strategies and pull back from acquisitions—either because they have lost faith in these tools for growth, or simply because they don't want to incur the wrath of a public already angry at the Enrons of the world.

Our advice is, don't be taken in—either by the headlines or by this morality-tale logic. There is a huge difference between the way Peter Brabeck approached the Matterhorn and the way the doomed mountaineers described in Jon Krakauer's *Into Thin Air* approached Mount Everest. The difference lies in discipline.

Wretched excess in the M&A field tends to happen in waves. It happened in the go-go 1960s. It happened again during the junk-bond-lubricated deal frenzy of the 1980s, and again in the dot-com bubble of the new millennium. In each of these waves, management teams (and the investors who stood behind them) chased opportunity recklessly, then beat a hasty retreat from the M&A arena when their bad deals started to come undone. Many of these companies, moreover, have tended to use deal making as a scapegoat when conducting postmortems on their failed transactions. In fact, the true culprits should have been accounting improprieties, bad strategies, faulty due diligence, or an inability to integrate—all manifestations of a lack of discipline.

Meanwhile, the Nestlés of the world understand that acquisitions have to be an integral element of their growth strategy. They understand that it is very difficult to meet investor expectations for growth organically; they need acquisitions to meet their targets. They understand that acquisitions are critical to building scale and adding new competencies.

Experienced acquirers, as we have seen throughout this book, consistently discipline four key decisions. Drawing upon an intimate understanding of their true basis of competition, they draw up an investment thesis for each prospect. Having used due diligence to test the elements of each proposed deal against its investment thesis, they then make tough calls as to which deals to close. They decide early where they really need to integrate—based on the investment thesis involved. They exert discipline to limit their integration efforts to the essential, thereby keeping the vast majority of their employees focused on the base business. Finally, they carefully anticipate what could go wrong, and decide quickly when and how to change course.

Deal making is a tool that should be wielded by experienced hands. So acquirers are advised to start with small, lower-risk deals, build an organizational capability to do deals, institutionalize processes, and create a feedback loop to enable learning from mistakes. Over time, as companies refine their organization and processes, they can graduate to larger deals and move into adjacencies to the core business.

In other words, there is a learning curve associated with deal making, as with virtually every other complex activity. Companies that do deals on a regular basis have an advantage over those that enter the M&A arena infrequently. They build capabilities that become core competencies, and they continuously exercise and refine those capabilities over time. In that respect, committing the time and talent needed to organize for opportunities allows companies to dispassionately discipline their deal decisions.

Unfortunately, only a minority of companies have successfully built their M&A experience into a core competency. In a survey of fifty-three companies by The Conference Board in 2000, 55 percent of respondents said their company had not been able to transform their M&A experiences into a core competency, which would enable them to think about mergers as a planned process.[7]

This statistic, then, begs the question: How do the winners do it? Our answer, as already noted, is that they have figured out

- who should make deals happen,
- who should evaluate opportunities, and
- how to walk away from a deal that fails to measure up.

Let's look at each of these three decision points in turn.

WHO MAKES DEALS HAPPEN?

Like Nestlé, successful acquirers nearly always have a core M&A team that is heavy on transactional experience. These are the internal experts who recommend deals, supervise the process, and analyze the financials. Whether this team is 100 percent dedicated to M&A or assumes other responsibilities in addition to M&A depends on the level and complexity of deal activity, the size and nature of the parent organization, and the team structure. Some companies prefer to have one central deal team that resides at headquarters; others want their deal teams out in the field, where the action is.

Whichever approach a company takes, the team is a constant across every deal. That way, deal teams become the firm's walking, talking institutional memory, drawing lessons from each acquisition to inform new ones.

In the case of most successful acquirers, the deal team is in charge of the purchase, from screening through to due diligence. It perpetually reviews targets and maintains at the ready a list of companies it will attempt to buy when the owners decide to sell. As we saw in chapter 2, working the pipeline can be the critical edge if and when a target company decides to sell.

In the evaluation and due-diligence phase, the core deal team is responsible for the economic assessment of the deal, including valuation and financial structuring. In addition, it is responsible for gathering input from relevant experts. The team often relies on separate in-house legal and tax teams to scrutinize the structure of the purchase.

As we saw in chapter 3, the best private equity firms have exceptionally disciplined deal teams, and this discipline comes to the fore when it comes time to evaluate a target company. We asked Joe Trustey, a managing partner of top-tier investor Summit Partners, why he thinks private equity buyers have an edge in due diligence. "All we do is buy and sell companies," he told us. "If you look at the corporate M&A departments at the *Fortune* 500, very rarely do you have an organization that stays together for twenty years. People shuffle in and out. I'm 100 percent focused on what I do. I won't be going off to run a plastics division."[8] Good due diligence, we believe, requires a focused and cohesive deal team.

In many cases, members of the core deal team stay involved during the integration phase. They keep the integration team focused on the investment thesis; they steer the integration team back to the priorities set during the due-diligence phase, if they have wandered off course; they make sure that the terms of the deal are followed, resolving issues if they arise. They also deal with adjustments to the purchase price after closing. In all of this, they make sure that everybody is on the same page.

Consider the approach of Fidelity National Financial, Inc., which has grown from a small local title insurer to a national market leader with a 30 percent share across the United States, mainly through acquisitions. It has expanded both geographically and in scope as it has moved into additional services for the real estate industry. In the fifteen-year period we studied, Fidelity National's extensive acquisitions program helped to boost revenue growth by 30 percent and expanded the firm's market cap by 40 percent. It's been good for shareholders, too: The firm's average annual total shareholder return was 29 percent—13 percent above its cost of equity.

At first, acquisitions were handled on an ad hoc basis by the company's chief executive, William Foley, who led a $21 million leveraged buyout of Fidelity National back in 1984. That structure was satisfactory at that point, because most of the deals were small and fell within Fidelity National's core title insurance business. Then, in the late 1990s, Foley hired a veteran investment banker, Brent Bickett. Now the company's executive vice president of M&A, Bickett set out to structure the buying process. He set up a dedicated M&A team with plenty of transactional experience that works directly with Foley and the board.

Fidelity National's M&A team is in charge of the purchase, from screening through due diligence. First, it generates and screens prospects thoroughly. Apart from prospects brought in by advisors, bankers, lawyers, and private equity shops, Bickett and his team monitor a list of some one hundred potential targets.

In the evaluation and due-diligence phase, the core team is responsible for the economic assessment of the deal, including valuation and financial structuring, while a separate legal in-house team examines the structure of the purchase. Due diligence is driven by the M&A team, with plenty of help from the business units that will have to integrate the new companies, if they are brought on board. Foley himself checks out the key people at the target early on—"he has a great feel," said Bickett—and ultimately approves or disapproves all deals.

Fidelity National learned to instill discipline in its due-diligence process the hard way, when the purchase of a leasing company failed. "It broke down in due diligence," said Bickett. "The desire to get into the industry overrode the attractiveness of the company."[9] Since then, Fidelity National's due diligence has been disciplined enough to lead the firm to walk away from the altar repeatedly—in fact, several times within one recent eighteen-month period. One of the biggest reasons for walking away, Bickett reports, is what his team has learned from standard interviews with customers.

Nestlé and Fidelity National have chosen to maintain their core deal teams at headquarters; other successful acquirers have taken a more decentralized approach. Clear Channel, discussed at length in chapter 2, splits the difference: It maintains a central M&A team at company headquarters, but also has local M&A teams based in each of its three major divisions—radio, outdoor billboards, and entertainment.

As noted, the deal team is typically responsible for structuring the deal process, with clear guidelines for the purchase and integration of acquisitions. It carefully defines the rules of what a good acquisition looks like and maps the process steps—that is, how an acquisition and its integration will take place. Although the deal team generally works from a set of checklists, it tends not to set guidelines in stone, since it wants those guidelines to allow for customization in each specific situation.

In order to keep such guidelines effective, the deal team must update them at the end of each major deal through a postmortem. Many successful acquirers have opted to make the postmerger process a more formal one—a sort of audit—to make sure the company absorbs the knowledge gained from each deal and avoids making the same mistake twice. As Benoît Bassi, the private equity specialist whom we met back in chapter 3, tells us, "It's always failures that teach you the most."[10]

But the sobering reality, according to a study by KPMG, is that fewer than 45 percent of companies carry out a formal postdeal review process.[11] The study found this lack of postdeal assessment particularly troubling in light of the fact that (1) none of the companies involved were new to M&A, and (2) most of the firms studied appeared likely to participate in more deals in the future.

Let us restate those findings in somewhat starker firms: Fewer than half of the companies that seem likely to do deals in the future have a formal way of learning from their past successes—or failures. Our advice to you is, make sure your organization positions itself in the wise minority.

Successful acquirers not only define and update their guidelines; they also preserve their hard-won wisdom. Some burn it into the memories of those involved in the process. Others write everything down. Our sense is that certain complex due-diligence and integration issues absolutely demand to be written down. We described earlier the challenge of "making things stick," which is made far more difficult by unexpected departures of key leaders. This, too, argues for writing things down.

Before moving on to the next key question, let's look sideways at two acquirers who have learned to deploy merger teams effectively: Washington Mutual and Cintas. They have institutionalized the process with clear guidelines for the purchase and integration of acquisitions.

Washington Mutual rose to sector leadership by organizing for opportunity. "WaMu," as it is known, grew from a small Seattle thrift to become one of the nation's top consumer banks, with nearly $270 billion in assets. It is now the number-one national player in mortgage servicing, and a close number two to Wells Fargo in mortgage originations. From 1986 to 2001, a quiet but aggressive buying pattern helped boost revenues by 31 percent annually. The expansion has been good for shareholders: The company's average annual shareholder return was 24 percent—or 9 percent over its cost of equity. WaMu's success is particularly striking in light of the fact that many banks and brokers have a terrible time making acquisitions work.

According to WaMu's vice chair of corporate development, Craig Tall, his company is guided by four acquisition criteria as they analyze prospects:

1. They must match the parent company's business strategy.
2. They cannot present undue operating risk.
3. They cannot jeopardize capital ratios or impair asset quality.
4. They must be accretive to earnings within a reasonable period of time.

By consistently following these criteria, says Tall, the company has become very disciplined in how it looks at things. He elaborates: "I like to say we haven't really overpaid for an acquisition. We haven't taken on anything that held us up from an asset quality or from a capital perspective. We haven't taken on anything that caused us to blow up operationally."[12]

The other "winner" that deserves spotlighting in this section on deal teams is Cintas, the Cincinnati, Ohio–based supplier of uniforms, which we first introduced in chapter 2. Cintas started buying in the 1960s, supplementing its own organic growth with a steady diet of acquisitions. Since then, Cintas has bought hundreds of companies, in boom times and bust. From 1996 to 2002 alone, Cintas spent $3 billion on more than two hundred fifty acquisitions, driving 40 percent of its revenue growth. Cintas began by cutting its teeth on smaller deals—most for less than $10 million, with some as small as

$100,000. Over time, the company slowly graduated to larger deals, such as the $656 million acquisition of Omni Services, the industry's number-five player, in the spring of 2002. With the experience developed and honed through many transactions in its core business, Cintas next bought its way into the world of highly specialized business services—including sanitation supplies, first-aid and safety products, and clean-room supplies. These moves bumped Cintas to leadership in its sector, boosting revenues by 21 percent a year—from $124 million in 1986 to $2.3 billion in 2002. Cintas shareholders who hung on for the ride have been rewarded with an average annual return of 21 percent—or 5 percent more than the company's cost of equity.

At Cintas, vice chairman and former CEO Robert Kohlhepp runs through a checklist of critical stars that must align for a deal to consummate. As he told us: "We have carefully defined rules on what a good acquisition looks like."[13]

Cintas, which has acquired primarily to build scale, writes out its checklists with a particular focus on the integration phase, where so many deals tend to stray off track. Cintas's checklist covering operations integration alone—"who's going to take care of the customer," for instance—is a hundred pages long. This list is tailored for each different business unit to an amazing level of detail (including, for example, making sure that the rented uniforms from the acquired company get their new Cintas labels). There's a separate and equally detailed checklist for administrative issues, such as payroll. The operating officer in charge of the integration keeps the lists up to date, and they are reviewed on a regular basis to ensure that mistakes or omissions are not repeated. "If something comes up, a 'gotcha' that wasn't on the checklist, they'll add it," Kohlhepp said.

Washington Mutual similarly has documented its due-diligence and valuation approaches for its front-end deal team, and also has formalized protocols for its integration team. The protocols have been codified by the integration team and are modified at the end of each deal, when the deal team and the integration team hold a postmortem on the acquisition. This postmortem process is more formal than it used to be, Craig Tall says—mainly to make sure the knowledge gained from each deal is captured and absorbed by the company, and will be put to use in the next deal.

WHO EVALUATES OPPORTUNITIES?

The second of the three key questions that successful acquirers must answer correctly is, Who evaluates opportunities?

Regardless of the deal-team structure, successful acquirers always involve line management in the buying decision at an early stage. Input from operators is crucial. In fact, the best acquirers don't make a deal without the support of the operators.

To gain buy-in and get an early start, it is critical during the due-diligence process to involve the operators who will be responsible for integrating and running the acquired company if and when the deal is closed. Operators who get involved in the evaluation of the target become much more committed to making the deal work. This is a good thing, because the handoff of an acquired business to an operating team carries a high risk factor. Ultimately, the operators are the ones who have the most influence over making the deal a success. Conversely, failure to get sign-off from the operators has a snowball effect: It can trigger many of the problems that tend to be encountered down the road, either during integration or during the fix-the-broken-deal phase.

Fidelity National, for example, asks its business unit managers to participate in due diligence and sign off on profit-improvement opportunities. They're the ones, after all, who have to integrate the acquired company, and they have to be ready to act the instant the deal is done. "The first thirty to sixty days of a deal," says Brent Bickett, "are the most important."[14]

Similarly, at Cintas, the small M&A team does all the financial analysis and oversees the deal process, but the company pulls operations people into the process when it's time to evaluate a target. Although operators are not involved in assessing the detailed economics of the deal, they do immerse themselves in due diligence. Ultimately, the officers operating the business unit that will inherit the acquisition have to sign off on the deal. "They're the ones who have to wrestle that half-skinned bear if we buy it," says Cintas's Kohlhepp. "They need to buy into the final decision."

At Washington Mutual, vice chair Tall ensures that line management gets involved early and often, long before the deal is done. Tall leads a six-member core deal team—"the quarterbacks of the transaction," as he calls them—to pick and analyze acquisition prospects. This team supervises due diligence, determines the deal price and structure, negotiates the transaction, and develops tactical plans for the acquisition. But the deal team does not act alone. It seeks advice and help from the business-unit leaders who know the operations best. These leaders join the core deal team early on in analyzing and evaluating the target. This help from the front lines during the due-diligence process helps ensure that the deal team makes the right decisions at the right price. "You're asking the people who are going to inherit what you're buying to help assess what they're going to get, and make value judgments on whether [the target] fits the strategy, operational problems, and so on," says Tall.

Early help from the front lines also allows Washington Mutual to gain buy-in and get an early start on integration. As Tall explains:

> We get early understanding and early buy-in from business units and the corporate people on who the targets are, why it makes sense, what kind of benefits we'll get, and what kinds of hiccups they might be having. When an acquisition is consummated, they're already fully engaged. They've bought in, and they know what they're going to get. They have been asked to think about what they'd do with it if they were to get it.

At WaMu, the business units are as intimately involved in planning the integration as they are in due diligence. That's because Washington Mutual believes integration is the name of the M&A game: "You can pay the right price, but if it's not integrated properly, you won't have accomplished much," says Tall.

To help with integration, Washington Mutual has set up what it calls an "A team"—the acquisition team in charge of integration. It takes over from the deal team once a deal closes, although members of the deal team remain involved and business-unit people continue to participate in the process.

The A team fluctuates between twenty-five and thirty-five full-time equivalents, and is made up largely of people from within Washington Mutual who have extensive project-management experience. The A team is supplemented by senior managers who are subject-matter experts and act as liaisons with the business units and corporate functions. Finally, a good number of people from the business segments and corporate functions are also involved—either as part of the Executive Management Oversight Committee or the Program Management Office, or simply as integration team leaders and team members.

To summarize: The best acquirers involve a broad spectrum of people in both due diligence and integration. Among these people are the line operators who will be expected to deliver on the potential of the acquisition—and to do so within a relatively short time period.

HOW DO YOU PREPARE TO WALK AWAY?

The third of our three key questions, outlined at the outset of this chapter, is, How do you prepare to walk away?

It warrants repeating that one of the findings of the Bain M&A survey of two hundred fifty executives was that many respondents found that the most challenging due-diligence issue was "allowing politics or emotions to interfere with decision making." In chapter 3, we described how the private equity masters ensure that their decision-making process is clear-eyed and objective. Here, we will simply reiterate that successful corporate buyers excel at walking away from risky deals. They all have found ways to kill deal fever.

How do they do this? In most cases, they create an objective veto function. They tend to insist on high-level approval for deals, and—when it comes to the big deals—they seek the approval of the parent's board.

Cintas's Robert Kohlhepp believes that any deal, even a small one, needs scrutiny from a cool, dispassionate executive who has not been involved in the heat of negotiating the deal and conducting due diligence. Once Cintas's combined M&A and operations team signs off on a deal, therefore, top management needs to approve it. Every deal, no matter how small, needs approval from one of three senior executives (one of them being Kohlhepp) who has remained apart from the day-to-day acquisition process. In the case of large mergers, such as the Omni deal, the board must give its blessing and set a price limit based on realistic synergy valuation. If negotiations yield a price above that amount, the deal team must walk away. If the acquisition is a new business, the CEO himself has to approve the deal. "We don't want people going off the beaten path without the top people in the company knowing what we're doing, and why," says Kohlhepp.[15]

This process came about because, as Kohlhepp explains, "There were a few companies that we bought that in retrospect I said we should not have bought. When I looked at why we bought those companies, a lot of little things . . . were wrong." None of these problems alone would have killed the deal, he adds. "But in aggregate, they should have caused us not to make the deal. That's why it's important at the end to have somebody who's objective who wasn't involved in the due diligence to hear all the pros and all the cons and bless the final decision."

In earlier chapters, we have described how bankers, lawyers, and other outsiders may have a personal interest in making sure you do a deal—in the worst cases, any deal. But the desire to close the deal can also characterize people inside your company. As Kohlhepp warns:

> The thing you have to guard against the most is that the M&A group and the operating people want to make deals. The M&A group gets their papers graded on how many deals they make. The operating people want to grow. The more they grow, the more they're responsible for, and the more their potential income. Therefore you need discipline at a high level. You need somebody who's not right in the middle of the deal, who has an objective viewpoint, making sure [you're] not going ahead to make a deal just to make a deal.

Successful acquirers often use their compensation system to kill deal fever. In order to keep people from pushing dubious deals, these companies decline to tie the compensation of any of the people involved in the acquisition to the completion of the deal. Instead, they usually pay the M&A teams and the other participants in the deal process according to the financial performance of the combined firm. That simple compensation structure is a powerful remedy against the temptation to buy expensive companies in the heat of the deal. Explains Washington Mutual's Tall: "Sometimes the best deals are deals you never do."[16]

In order to effectively dedicate a deal team, commit line expertise, and make the call to walk away, decision-making roles and responsibilities need to be crystal clear. An organizational design tool we frequently use to achieve such clarity is called RAID (which stands for "Recommend, Agree, Input, Decide"). RAID codifies individuals' roles in contributing to or making decisions. RAID makes sure that only one person is on the hook for any given decision, but that the right parties have a voice at the right time in making recommendations (recommend), providing the input to vet a decision (input), and ensuring the final sign-offs occur (agree) before the decision (decide) is made.

In the context of deal making, the core deal team and line management typically recommend a move, and work in input from the line and their internal and external advisors. Senior management must agree with the move for a proposal to advance to a final decision. And the CEO must make the ultimate decision and stand by it in the boardroom. (See figure 6-1.)

FIGURE 6-1

RAID Framework for Decision Making

Example: Who decides to invest in a tuck-in acquisition?

Stakeholders	Recommend (Make the Case)	Agree (Present the Case)	Input (Set Standards)	Decide (Take Responsibility)
Core Deal Team	✓		✓	
Line Management	✓		✓	
Senior Management		✓		
CEO				✓

PUTTING YOUR COMPANY IN A POSITION TO WIN

In the world of sports, coaches tell players that preparation and training create their own luck.

Star forward Mia Hamm of the U.S. women's soccer team is renowned for working hard to achieve maximum fitness—in the off-season. Tiger Woods, the world's top golfer, routinely hits buckets of balls on the practice range to work on small details of his game—after having won a tournament.

A CEO can put his team in a position to win by applying the same relentless discipline. Working with and studying companies with winning deal records, we have found that they treat M&A as a core competency and consistently acquire businesses, through good times and bad. They recognize that a core competency requires training and regular application. They understand that the activities of evaluating an acquisition, structuring and negotiating a transaction, and then integrating people and assets are complex processes that take time to master. Consequently, they hire people with appropriately specialized skills—or train people internally to develop those skills—and take steps to ensure that they will improve over time as experience builds.

Executives who are winning deal makers also understand the critical role played by line managers. These leaders harmonize the specialized work of the deal teams with the ongoing imperatives of the line in order to realize their companies' overall objectives. And yet these leaders—the ones who rely the most on deal making—are the very ones best at cutting their company loose when a deal fails to meet their requirements. At the most successful deal-making companies, executives seek input on acquisitions from the front-line leaders, and these leaders in turn offer assessments—based not on what will benefit them personally, but on what will benefit the company as a whole.

Taken together, these are the ingredients of discipline.

Infrequent acquirers, on the other hand, make rookie mistakes. Because they tend to be opportunistic, they buy businesses simply because they are available, rather than because they represent a good strategic fit. Infrequent acquirers are less likely to have the necessary organization and processes to spot a deal's black holes or to measure synergies realistically. They do much of their work without consulting the operators—that is, the people who will have to integrate the acquisition and make it a success. Without adequate internal checks and balances in place, deal fever grips these players, making even a weak acquisition unstoppable.

Throughout this book, we have recited a single sobering statistic: Approximately 70 percent of all major mergers and acquisitions fail to create meaningful shareholder value. But such knowledge needn't paralyze. Even if the majority of deal makers are playing a loser's game of chance, the successful minority know the simple truth about M&A: Deal making is about developing the core competencies within your organization so that you can get it right again and again and again.

If you organize strategically for deal making, you'll move quickly down the learning curve and master the decisions that make or break deals. Your standing deal team will hone the science of acquisition through the development and use of an investment thesis, and by asking the big questions in due diligence. Your organization will embrace the art of integrating quickly where it really matters. It will plan for contingencies and correct course quickly when a deal strays.

By adopting this kind of discipline and applying it to our four critical decisions, over time you will master the merger. And you will accomplish more that that. By bringing this kind of rigor to a handful of key decision points, you wield one of the most powerful of corporate tools, and gain control of your organization's fortunes. And that is the true promise and potential of mastering the merger.

Appendix

The Empirical Evidence

LEARNING CURVE STUDY

Scope and Parameters of Study

Bain studied firms with revenues over $500 million in 2000 that also were in business as public entities as of 1986, and examined the acquisitions those firms made in the fifteen-year period from 1986 to 2001.

Region	Number of Firms	Number of Transactions (1986–2001)
United States	724	7,476
Europe (United Kingdom, France, Germany, Italy)	293	2,879
Japan	676	694
	1,693	11,049

In all three segments of the study (United States, Europe, and Japan), we compared the firms' acquisition behavior with the excess return delivered to shareholders. Here, we defined excess return as the total return to shareholders, including cash and stock dividends, minus the cost of equity. The cost of equity was computed using the Capital Asset Pricing Model, taking into account each company's beta and the movement in the broad nationwide stock market index over the fifteen-year period. We used excess return to reveal how companies measure up to investors' expectations, given the companies' risk profiles and the performance of the broader nationwide stock market index.

Study Findings

Frequent shoppers outperform. The first significant research finding is that frequent buyers posted a far superior performance over the fifteen-year period than the less-frequent buyers and the firms abstaining from deals (nonbuyers).

In the United States, 110 firms (15 percent of the 724 firms in our sample) in our frequent-buyer group did 20 or more deals over 15 years and outperformed the 94 nonbuyers by a factor of almost two to one. (See figure A-1.) They outperformed the 228 infrequent buyers,

FIGURE A-1

Frequent Acquirers Outperform (1986–2001)

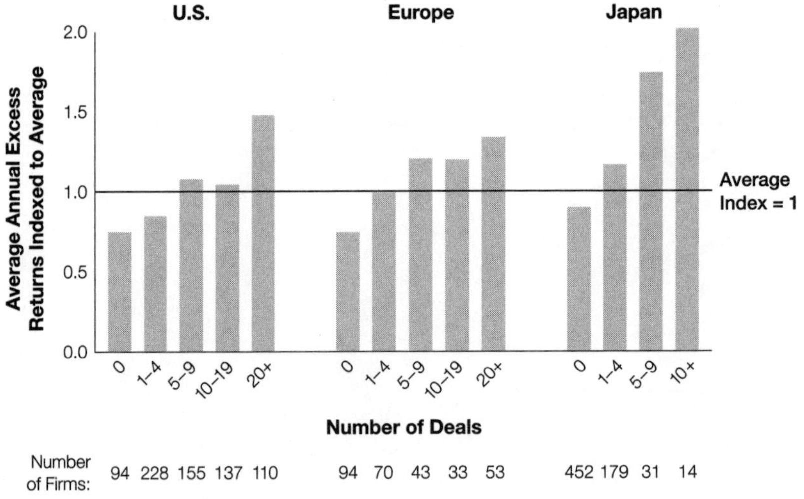

Source: Bain & Company Global Learning Curve Study.

those doing 1 to 4 deals, by a factor of 1.7. Similarly, in Europe, the 53 frequent buyers outperformed the 94 nonbuyers by a factor of 1.8 and outperformed the 70 infrequent buyers by a factor of 1.3. Even in Japan, where only a third of the companies in our sample made one or more acquisitions in the 1986–2001 time frame, the 45 buyers averaging 5 or more deals outperformed the 452 nonbuyers by a factor of 2 and the 179 infrequent buyers by a factor of 1.6.

This means that the more deals a company made, the more value it delivered to shareholders. Naturally, excess returns varied a lot, and the outcome of acquisitions was only one factor at play. But tellingly, we found that the performance of the nonbuyers and infrequent buyers varied a lot more than the performance of the frequent buyers. The frequent buyers had more-consistent results, and they were more likely to achieve success.

Studies by academics and other consulting firms corroborate the notion. McKinsey's 2001 Trading the Corporate Portfolio study, although more narrow in scope, also concluded that companies with active, balanced programs of acquisitions create more shareholder value than those with passive M&A strategies, hence fewer transactions.[1]

There are two clear messages. First, avoiding M&A altogether makes it difficult to grow shareholder value. This is intuitive given that the market rewards growth and that most industries are fairly low growth. Second, there clearly are advantages to being a frequent, as opposed to episodic, buyer. The greater the deal-making activity, the more likely companies are to achieve higher returns.

Examples of successful frequent acquirers in the long term in the United States include Clear Channel, Medtronic, Fidelity National, Cardinal Health, Fiserv, Danaher, Fifth Third Bancorp, Philip Morris, Washington Mutual, Johnson & Johnson, Citigroup, Intel, Wells Fargo, ADP, Cintas, and Coca-Cola. In Europe, successful frequent acquirers include the Royal Bank of Scotland, Rentokil Initial, Lloyd's, Bodycote, Carrefour, Pineault, Unilever, RWE, Danone, E.ON, Pernod Ricard, Publicis, BASF, and Heidelberger Zement.

Buy in good times and bad. The second significant research finding is that not only is frequency important, but consistency through economic cycles also appears to make a difference for frequent buyers. The most successful acquirers buy during both weak and strong economic periods. They treat acquisitions a bit like dollar-cost averagers treat mutual funds. They buy low; they buy high. They buy systematically—winning both as a rising tide lifts stock prices and by picking up assets in recessionary times at fire-sale prices. Effectively, they have a plan and stick with it.

In our research, we observed that frequent buyers (defined here as those firms that did twenty or more deals disclosed over fifteen years) are not all alike. To examine them more closely, we split U.S. frequent buyers into four groups:

1. Constant buyers, which bought consistently through economic cycles

2. Recession buyers, which increased their buying in recessionary times

3. Growth buyers, which bought principally in growth periods

4. Doldrums buyers, which tended to buy in stable or slightly uncertain periods between recession and growth

The 19 constant buyers were by far the most successful, outperforming the 40 growth buyers by a factor of 2.3 and the 24 doldrums buyers by a factor of 1.8. The 27 recession buyers came in second, outperforming the growth buyers by a factor of 1.4. (See figure A-2.)

In Europe, we took a slightly different approach. Given that the economic cycle was less pronounced there than in the United States, we analyzed how constant each frequent buyer's deal flow was over the 1986–2001 time frame. The results were similar. The 14 continuous buyers (those that bought continuously throughout the period) outperformed the 19 late buyers (those that bought predominantly in the latter part of the 1986–2001 period) by a factor of 1.7. They also outperformed the early buyers by a factor of 1.2. (See figure A-3.)

These numbers suggest that the least successful acquirers fall prey to the feeding frenzy of a growth economy. The success stories, on the other hand, suppress deal fever. They have the discipline to say no to expensive deals in good times and to store cash in times of plenty. That allows them to stay in the market during down times. No matter what the economic cycle, they remain proactive and rigorous;

FIGURE A-2

Constant Acquirers Outperform (1986–2001)

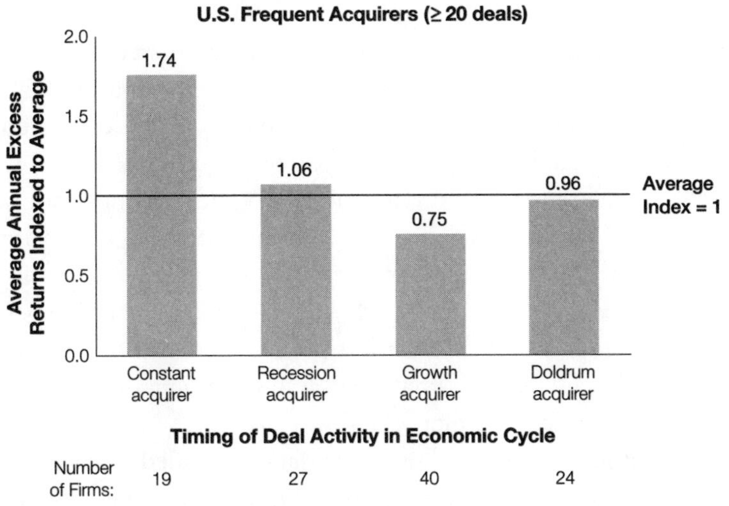

Source: Bain & Company Global Learning Curve Study.

FIGURE A-3

Continuous Acquirers Outperform (1986–2001)

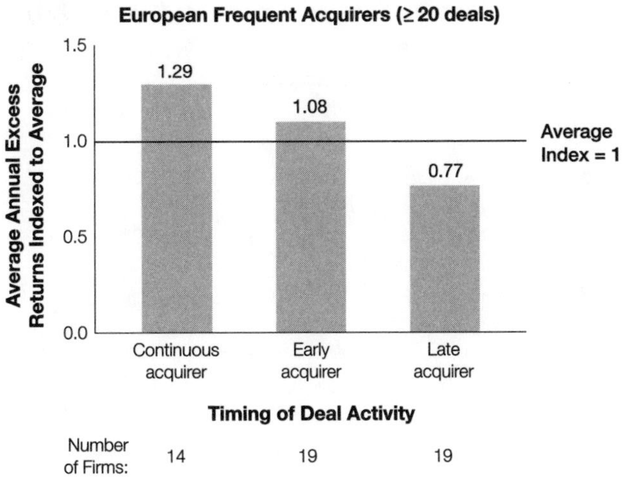

Source: Bain & Company Global Learning Curve Study.

their shareholders enjoy far richer returns than those of companies doing most of their buying in a growth economy.

Start small, then ramp up. Our research showed another revealing difference between the successful acquirers and the unsuccessful ones: the nature of the deal making. The companies that enjoyed the highest returns were ones that systematically bought companies a small fraction of their size. (See figure A-4.)

U.S. firms that focused on small deals—acquisitions that were less than 15 percent of their own size on average—outperformed those firms acquiring companies 35 percent or more their own size by a factor of almost 6. The worst performers tended to make big bets.

We observed a similar, albeit less pronounced, pattern in Europe, with firms that focused on small deals outperforming those acquiring companies 35 percent or more their own size by a factor of 1.8. Japan follows a similar pattern, although the data is clouded by a very small number of acquirers that did more than three deals in the 1986–2001 time frame.

Integrating these two findings, deal frequency and deal size, yields some interesting insights. (See figure A-5.)

FIGURE A-4

Acquirers Making Smaller Deals Outperform (1986–2001)

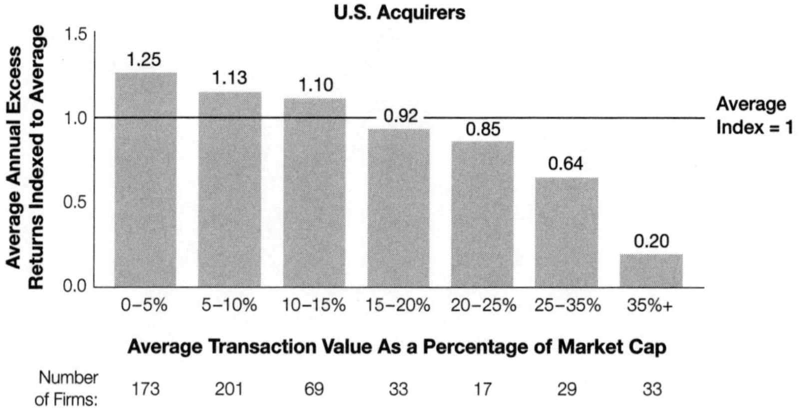

Source: Bain & Company Global Learning Curve Study.

FIGURE A-5

The Penalty Is Greatest for Rolling the Dice or Sitting on the Sidelines (1986–2001)

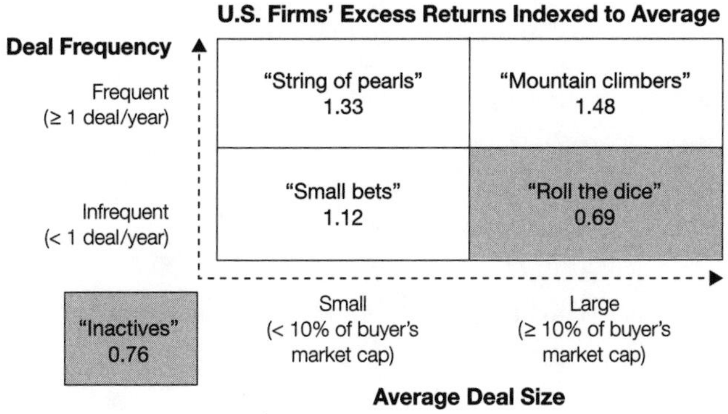

Source: Bain & Company Global Learning Curve Study.

The worst strategy a company can employ is to make one or a few big bets. Without experience, these companies are rolling the dice. Even if the acquisition supports a strong strategy, the odds are higher that the acquirer will overpay, fail to do an effective job on due diligence, and fall short on integration. Adding to the risk is the exponential difficulty of integrating a large company. The larger the target, the more likely a management team is to lose focus on both businesses, with attendant declines in share price and/or profitability.

Almost as bad are the returns for those who avoided deals altogether. Interestingly, frequent acquirers appear to do well with a succession of small deals or by ramping up to larger deals.

ACCRETION/DILUTION STUDY

Scope and Parameters of Study

In this study, we analyzed the relationship between deals' EPS accretion/dilution and deal success in terms of excess shareholder returns.

We examined 98 U.S. acquisitions announced between 1996 and 2000 with price tags over $1 billion. All the acquisitions in our study involved public companies, closed within one year of announcement, and had a purchase price greater than 10 percent of the acquiring company's market capitalization (to ensure the acquisitions were material to the acquirers).

We split the acquisitions into three groups:

- Accretive—deals that instantly boost earnings per share (in other words, the target's price-earnings ratio divided by the acquirer's price-earnings ratio was greater than one).
- Dilutive—deals that instantly slash earnings per share.
- Neutral—deals that do not have a significant impact on earnings per share.

We compared each acquisition's earnings-per-share impact with the excess returns delivered to shareholders in the year following the announcement. In this study, excess return was defined as the total return to shareholders, including cash and stock dividends, minus the average total shareholder return for the acquirer's relevant sector index. Effectively, we compared an acquirer's stock performance with that of its peers, one month before the announcement of a deal through to twelve months after the announcement.

Study Findings

We found that first-year accretion and dilution has no measurable correlation to subsequent deal success. In other words, accretive deals do not necessarily generate superior shareholder returns and dilutive deals do not necessarily depress shareholder returns.

Of the 98 deals that were done between 1996 and 2000, 30 of them were dilutive, in some cases significantly dilutive. Yet, in 47 percent of the cases, the dilutive deals surpassed their peers' average shareholder returns by more than 10 percent. Conversely, out of the 38 accretive deals in the sample, 34 percent succeeded in outperforming their peers by 10 percent. (See figure A-6.)

What might explain why accretive deals do not outperform dilutive deals? We can speculate on a host of reasons, but there are at least three logical answers:

FIGURE A-6

No Correlation Found Between Dilution and Failure or Between Accretion and Success

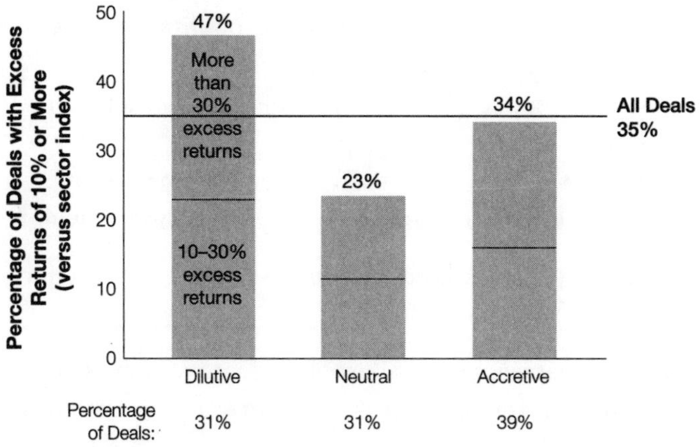

Source: Bain & Company Accretion/Dilution Study.

1. Dilutive deals tend to involve buying growth, and the market rewards growth.
2. Accretive deals tend to be about cost reduction, and companies invariably overestimate the amount and underestimate the degree of difficulty involved in cutting costs.
3. Finally, the market's suspicion of dilutive deals places significant pressure on management to be rigorous in both analyzing and executing transactions—in effect, instilling more discipline due to the higher hurdle.

CULTURAL INTEGRATION STUDY

Scope and Parameters of Study

In this study, we measured the impact of culture on deal success. We examined 125 acquisitions announced between 1996 and 2000. Those acquisitions were made by U.S.-based public companies and involved both domestic and cross-border targets. All the acquisitions in our study closed within one year of announcement, had a purchase price over $1 billion, and had a purchase price greater than 10 percent of the acquiring company's market capitalization (to ensure the acquisitions were material to the acquirers).

The study grouped the deals by objective—whether they were made to grow scale or to build scope.

The study then categorized each deal according to the type and significance of cultural issues, assigning weights to the following factors:

- Geography—cross-border or domestic, language barriers, and so forth.
- General management philosophy—factors such as cultural alignment, leadership styles, company values, customer orientation.
- Organization—large versus small, matrix versus silo, and so on.
- Compensation and incentive systems—for example, compensation policies, benefits packages and perks, performance appraisal processes.
- Workplace environment—technology use, overall age, dress code, and so forth.

Finally, the study categorized each deal according to whether management had taken a proactive approach to dealing with cultural integration and whether that approach meant consciously adopting a hands-on or hands-off approach.

We compared each deal's cultural issues and integration approach with the excess returns delivered to shareholders in the year following the merger announcement. In this study, as in the Accretion/Dilution Study, excess return was defined as the total return to shareholders, including cash and stock dividends, minus the average total shareholder return for an acquirer's relevant sector index. Effectively, we compared an acquirer's stock performance with that of its peers, one month before the announcement of a deal through to twelve months after the announcement.

Study Findings

Cultural issues do not significantly impact deal success. We found little difference in relative performance between deals with significant cultural issues and those with insignificant cultural issues. The acquirers devoid of cultural issues outperformed their peers by 1 percent, while the acquirers facing cultural issues underperformed their peers by only –0.5 percent. (See figure A-7.)

It is worth noting that U.S. acquirers in domestic transactions significantly outperformed U.S. acquirers involved in cross-border transactions, which inherently contain greater cultural issues (+2 percent versus –5.3 percent shareholder return compared with sector indices).

Proactively addressing cultural issues has a huge impact. We found a huge difference between deals that proactively identified cultural issues in due diligence and addressed them in integration and those deals that did not, regardless of the complexity of cultural

FIGURE A-7

Deals Marked by Important Cultural Issues Do Not Fare Much Worse

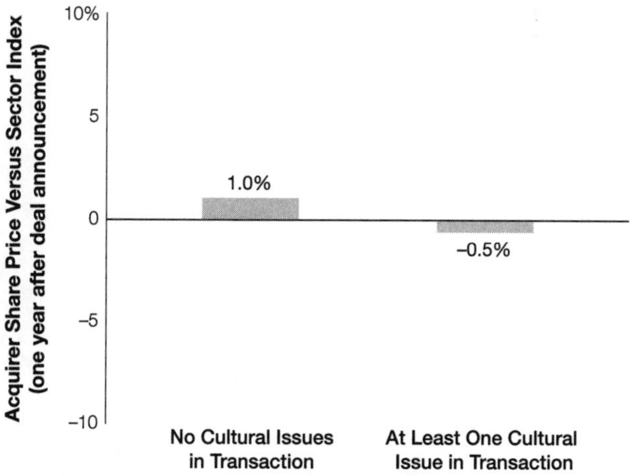

Source: Bain & Company Cultural Integration Study.

issues. A proactive approach to culture—whether or not there were cultural issues—netted a 5.1 percent higher shareholder return compared with sector indices versus –2.4 percent underperformance in deals that failed to identify and negotiate cultural hurdles. (See figure A-8.)

It is worth noting a couple more findings here:

- An even more important difference in excess shareholder return was evident when the acquirer's management team was proactive and actual cultural issues were identified in the transaction (5.3 percent versus –8.6 percent).
- Even in transactions where the acquirer's management team was proactive in screening for culture but no defined cultural issues were identified in the transaction, the average acquirer's excess return was greater than the average acquirer's excess return for all domestic targets in the sample (4.4 percent versus 2 percent).

FIGURE A-8

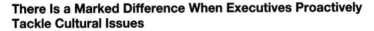

There Is a Marked Difference When Executives Proactively Tackle Cultural Issues

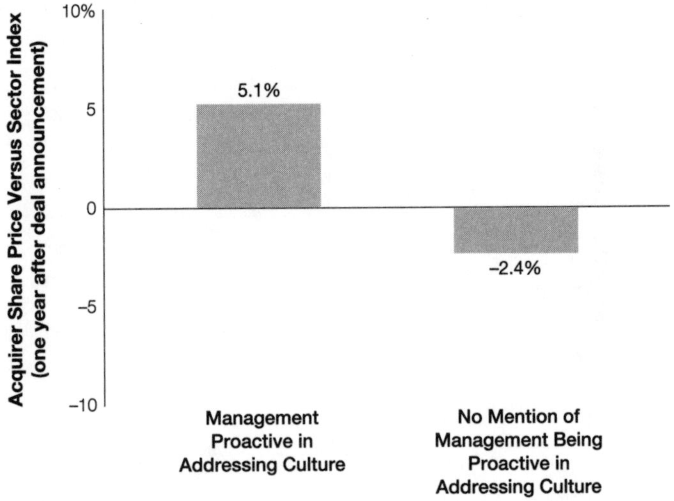

Source: Bain & Company Cultural Integration Study.

Proactively addressing cultural issues has an even greater impact for scale deals, where assimilation matters most. We found that cultural integration matters more in some types of deals than others, and it matters more in some functions than others, depending on the deal's objective. Perhaps not surprisingly, addressing culture proactively in scale deals has a very high payoff. Scale-driven deals in which the acquiring company took a proactive approach to cultural integration outperformed their relevant sector indices by 5.1 percent. Those ignoring culture underperformed their relevant sector indices by 7.9 percent. (See figure A-9.) The reason: Total integration of productive assets, processes, and people is necessary to achieve the desired scale. So in successful scale-driven deals, the acquirers not only take proactive steps to achieve cultural integration, but they also tend to do so by imposing their culture on the target company; if they adjust their own culture to accommodate that of the acquired company, it is only to a very limited degree.

Deals designed to expand scope also had much to gain from grappling early with cultural issues: Those with a proactive approach

FIGURE A-9

Difference Is More Marked for Scale Deals, Where Assimilation Matters Most

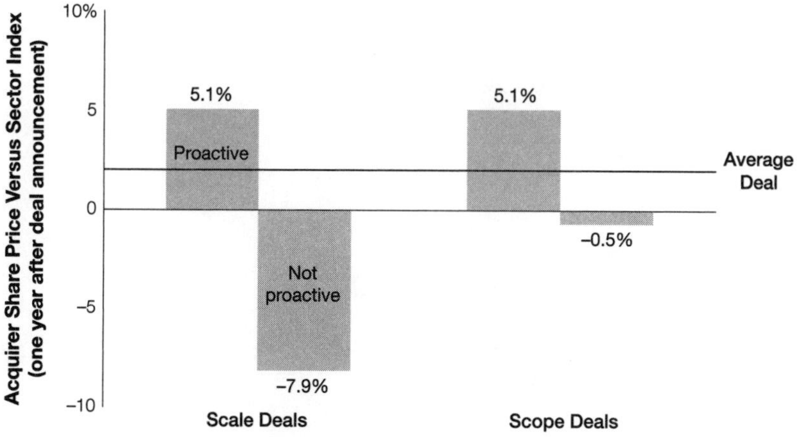

Source: Bain & Company Cultural Integration Study.

outperformed their relevant sector indices by 5.1 percent, whereas scope deals that didn't plan for cultural differences underperformed by 0.5 percent. But the best way to handle cultural issues in scope deals differs markedly from the scale-deal context. The best-performing scope deals, we discovered, gained ground in one of two ways: either by intentionally keeping the merged companies' culture separate or by creating an altogether new culture. The key was the degree of overlap in the businesses. When there was significant but not complete overlap, building a new culture was critical to achieving an organizational sum that was greater than its component parts. But when there was a very limited overlap, it made more sense to keep culture separate.

Notes

Introduction

1. Mark L. Sirower, *The Synergy Trap: How Companies Lose the Acquisition Game* (New York: Free Press, 1997), 9.

2. We refer here to a survey conducted in December 2002 on behalf of Bain & Company by the Economist Intelligence Unit, "M&A: Improving the Odds in Corporate Transactions," to which 250 senior and line executives from around the world responded about their M&A experiences.

Chapter 1

1. Carlos Gutierrez, telephone interview by David Harding, Bain & Company, Boston, 15 May 2003. Subsequent comments by Gutierrez are also from this interview.

2. A 2004 Bain & Company study of 790 deals made by U.S.-based companies from 1995 to 2001 corroborates the findings of the academic research.

3. All companies in our database had revenues exceeding $500 million. In other words, these were companies long forced to look beyond organic growth for expansion.

4. KPMG, "Unlocking Shareholder Value: The Keys to Success," KPMG M&A Global Research Report, November 1999.

5. David Henry, "Mergers: Why Most Big Deals Don't Pay Off," *BusinessWeek,* 14 October 2002.

6. Data from *Mergerstat Review 2004* (Los Angeles: Mergerstat, 2004).

7. Jay P. Brandimarte, William C. Fallon, and Robert S. McNish, "Trading the Corporate Portfolio," *McKinsey on Finance,* autumn 2001.

8. Bruno E. Mathieu and Collin Brown III, "Making M&A Pay: Lessons from the World's Most Successful Acquirers," *Marakon Commentary,* spring 2003.

9. We are indebted to Bain manager Catherine Lemire for her contributions to this discussion of deal success measures.

10. John Connaughton, telephone interview by David Harding, Bain & Company, Boston, 6 June 2003.

11. Blair Effron, speaking on "Strategic M&A in an Opportunistic Environment" (presentation at Bain's Getting Back to Offense conference, New York City, 20 June 2002).

12. Based on Kellogg's 1997 operating results reported in its Annual Report, 31 March 1998.

13. A 2002 RoperASW survey entitled "How America Eats" found that 62 percent of consumers want food that can be packaged for portability and easy consumption, up a full ten points from five years earlier.

14. A December 2002 Datamonitor report ("Bakery & Cereals in the USA to 2006") found that from 1996 to 2001, sales of handheld breakfast bars increased by 8.1 percent while sales of ready-to-eat cereal declined by about 5 percent.

15. Stephanie Thompson and Jack Neff, "P&G, Coke Could Face Distribution Challenge," *Advertising Age,* 26 February 2001, 3.

16. David Harding and Phyllis Yale, "Discipline and the Dilutive Deal," *Harvard Business Review,* July 2002.

17. Credit Suisse First Boston, "Kellogg Co.," Credit Suisse First Boston Report, 20 March 2001, 4.

18. Initiated as a dilutive deal under the accounting rules in place by the fall of 2001, the Kellogg–Keebler deal was slightly cash accretive.

19. Share price, as reported on Bloomberg, compared with S&P food index from 26 October 2000 to 26 October 2001.

20. Merrill Lynch, "Morning Meeting Note," Merrill Lynch Report, 26 October 2000.

21. Gutierrez, telephone interview.

22. Merrill Lynch, "Keebler Acquisition: Reducing Estimates," Merrill Lynch Global Research, 26 October 2000, 1.

23. Merrill Lynch, "Morning Meeting Note."

24. Eric R. Katzman, "Kellogg Company: Initial Opinion," Deutsche Bank Alex. Brown Equity Research, 30 November 2000, 2.

25. Anonymous, telephone interview by Ted Rouse, Bain & Company, Chicago, 21 February 2003.

26. Gutierrez, telephone interview. In May 2004, Keebler announced it was closing the Elmhurst facility.

27. Rahul Jacob, "Corporate Reputations: The Winners Chart a Course of Constant Renewal and Work to Sustain Cultures That Produce the Very Best Products and People," *Fortune,* 6 March 1995.

28. Joseph N. Fry, "Newell Company: The Rubbermaid Opportunity," Case study (Richard Ivey School of Business, University of Western Ontario, January 2001).

29. David J. Collis and Cynthia A. Montgomery, "Creating Corporate Advantage," *Harvard Business Review,* May–June 1998.

30. Ibid.

31. Daniel Ferguson, telephone interview by David Harding, Bain & Company, Boston, 11 March 2003. Subsequent comments by Ferguson are also from this interview.

32. "Newell Rubbermaid: Why It'll Bounce Back," *BusinessWeek,* 20 October 2003, 164.

33. Constance Maneaty and Parinaz Pahlavi, "Newell Rubbermaid," Bear Stearns Report, 24 March 1999, 3.

34. Carol Warner Wilke, "CNNfn: Capital Ideas," 21 October 1998.

35. Newell purchased Rubbermaid for $5.8 billion. Newell's biggest disclosed prior acquisition was Sanford Corp., a stand-alone producer of household products purchased in 1992 for $600 million.

36. Our thanks to baseball expert and author Bill James for this insight.

Chapter 2

1. Christine Y. Chen, "Not the Bad Boys of Radio," *Fortune,* 3 March 2003.

2. Ibid.

3. Chris Zook and James Allen, *Profit from the Core: Growth Strategy in an Era of Turbulence* (Boston: Harvard Business School Press, 2001). See also Chris Zook, *Beyond the Core: Expand Your Market Without Abandoning Your Roots* (Boston: Harvard Business School Press, 2004).

4. In this context, we are not presuming to pass judgment on the wisdom of deregulation, but simply to map a shifting competitive landscape. In fact, some industry observers fault CCC for abandoning local markets. See, for example, Eric Boehlert, "Fighting Pay-for-Play," 3 April 2001, <http://www.salon.com> (accessed December 2003).

5. For more on this distinction, see Vijay Vishwanath and Jonathan Mark, "Your Brand's Best Strategy," *Harvard Business Review,* May–June 1997.

6. Frederick F. Reichheld with Thomas Teal, *The Loyalty Effect: The Hidden Force Behind Growth, Profits, and Lasting Value* (Boston: Harvard Business School Press, 1996).

7. Bain analysis based on data from Bloomberg.

8. Bain analysis based on data from Thomson Financial.

9. Randall Mays, telephone interview by Sam Rovit, Bain & Company, Chicago, 27 September 2002. Subsequent comments by Mays are also from this interview.

10. Joe Trustey, telephone interview by David Harding, Bain & Company, Boston, 13 May 2003. Subsequent comments by Trustey are also from this interview.

11. Accenture, "Accenture Survey Shows Executives Are Cautiously Optimistic Regarding Future Mergers and Acquisitions," Accenture Press Release, 30 May 2002.

12. John R. Harbison, Albert J. Viscio, and Amy T. Asin, "Making Acquisitions Work: Capturing Value After the Deal," Booz Allen & Hamilton Series of Viewpoints on Alliances, 1999.

13. Craig Tall, telephone interview by Catherine Lemire, Bain & Company, Toronto, 1 October 2002.

14. Rolf Börjesson, interview by Tom Shannon, Bain & Company, London, spring 2001.

15. Hans Bieshaar, Jeremy Knight, and Alexander van Wassenaer, "Deals That Create Value," *McKinsey Quarterly* 1 (2001).

16. Todd Thomson, speaking on "Strategic M&A in an Opportunistic Environment" (presentation at Bain & Company's Getting Back to Offense conference, New York City, 20 June 2002).

17. Mike Bertasso, correspondence with David Harding, 15 December 2003.

Chapter 3

1. Benoît Bassi, telephone interview by Jean-Marc Leroux, Bain & Company, Paris, 26 February 2003. Subsequent comments by Bassi are also from this interview.

2. Connaughton, telephone interview by David Harding, Bain & Company, Boston, 6 June 2003. Subsequent comments by Connaughton are also from this interview.

3. Robert Kohlhepp, telephone interview by Catherine Lemire, Bain & Company, Toronto, 4 October 2002.

4. Orit Gadiesh and James L. Gilbert, "Profit Pools: A Fresh Look at Strategy," *Harvard Business Review,* May–June 1998.

5. Joe Trustey, telephone interview by David Harding, Bain & Company, Boston, 13 May 2003. Subsequent comments by Trustey are also from this interview.

6. Bassi, telephone interview.

7. "Newell Rubbermaid, Inc.," *Chase H&Q,* 22 November 2000.

8. Philippa Moreton, "Rank Wraps Up Odeon Sale to Cinven," Reuters News, 21 February 2000.

9. "Cinven Acquires Odeon for £280m," *Leisure Week,* 24 February 2000.

10. Ibid.

11. Graham Keniston-Cooper, Cinven, correspondence with Roger Siddle, Bain & Company, 13 January 2003.

12. Paul Rogers, Tom Holland, and Dan Haas, "Value Acceleration: Lessons from Private-Equity Masters," *Harvard Business Review,* June 2002.

13. Tom Hirsch, telephone interview by Aaron Good, Bain & Company, Toronto, 2 October 2002.

14. Gutierrez, telephone interview.

15. Jules Stewart, "Lack of Methodology in the Madness," *The Banker,* 1 April 2001.

16. Royal Bank of Scotland 2002 Annual Report. The initial plan was for £1.7 billion in annual benefits (including revenue benefits and cost savings). This target was later raised to £2 billion. By February 2003, the benefits had been fully implemented, although their full impact will not show as profits until 2004. In recognition of this outstanding achievement, RBS paid an integration bonus amounting to 5 percent of salary to all employees whose business units were involved in integration.

17. Jad Mouawad, "Ex-Vivendi CEO Admits Buying Too Much, Too Fast," *Ottawa Citizen,* 16 November 2002.

18. Jean-Marie Messier and Yves Messarovitch, *Mon vrai journal* (Paris: Balland, 2002), 189–208.

19. Bloomberg News Report, published in the Montreal *Gazette,* 30 March 2002.

20. Ibid.

21. Trustey, telephone interview.

22. Bassi, telephone interview.

Chapter 4

1. Sam Johnson, interview by David Harding, Bain & Company, Racine, Wisconsin, 24 May 2002.

2. "Announcement—O&Y Properties Corporation–Bentall Capital Limited Partnership," Canada News Wire, 18 February 2003.

3. Carlos Gutierrez, telephone interview by David Harding, Bain & Company, Boston, 15 May 2003.

4. "Kellogg Puts Keebler Integration on Fast Track," PR Newswire, 19 March 2001.

5. Benoît Bassi, telephone interview by Jean-Marc Leroux, Bain & Company, Paris, 26 February 2003.

6. Till Vestring, Brian King, and Ted Rouse, "Merger Integration: Why the 'Soft' Issues Matter Most," *European Business Forum,* spring 2003.

7. Henry Goldblatt, "Cisco's Secrets: Forty-two Acquisitions and Counting," *Fortune,* 8 November 1999.

8. Greg Lawton, telephone interview by Katie Smith Milway, Bain & Company, Boston, 8 October 2002. Subsequent comments by Lawton are also from this interview.

9. Merger closed on 18 November 1998 and capacity restructuring was announced on 24 November 1998. The specific plants (four in the United States, one in Canada) were announced on 1 December 1998.

10. Daniel Holland, correspondence with Ted Rouse, 9 October 2002.

11. Richard Gibson, "Flying Solo: The Autocratic Style of Northwest's CEO Complicates Defense," *Wall Street Journal,* 30 March 1989.

12. Todd Thomson, telephone interview by David Harding, Bain & Company, Boston, 29 May 2003.

13. Leah Nathans Spiro, "Class Meets Mass on Wall Street," *BusinessWeek,* 17 February 1997.

14. Leah Nathans Spiro, "They Said It Would Never Work—But After a Year, Morgan Stanley Dean Witter Is Meshing," *BusinessWeek,* 29 June 1998.

15. Tracy Corrigan, "One-Sided Marriage: The Merger of Morgan Stanley and Dean Witter Adds More to the Retail Arm Than to the Investment Bank," *Financial Times,* 15 July 1997.

16. Lehman Brothers, "Philips: Lighting-up Medical and Lighting," Lehman Brothers Global Equity Research, 2 July 2003.

17. William Curran, telephone interview by Ted Rouse, Bain & Company, Chicago, 7 March 2003. Subsequent comments by Curran are also from this interview.

18. Report on the Performance of the Philips Group, a quarterly report, 10 February 2004, available at <http://www.philips.com/InformationCenter/Global/FArticleSummary.asp?lNodeId=757&channel=757&channelId=N757A2031#> (accessed 15 April 2004).

19. Ronald N. Ashkenas, Lawrence J. DeMonaco, and Suzanne C. Francis, "Making the Deal Real: How GE Capital Integrates Acquisitions," *Harvard Business Review,* January–February 1998.

20. Transcript by Katie Smith Milway of Jack Welch's Q&A at the Fortune Leadership Conference, Chicago, 9 April 2002.

21. Curran, telephone interview.

22. Lawton, telephone interview.

23. Office of John Browne, correspondence with Robin Buchanan, Bain & Company, London, April 2001.

24. BP share price compared to FTSE oil-and-gas index, based on data from Bloomberg.

25. Matthias M. Beiker, Anna J. Bogardus, and Tim Oldham, "Why Mergers Fail," *McKinsey Quarterly* 4 (2001).

26. Choo Chiau Beng, interview by Till Vestring, Bain & Company, Singapore, 21 May 2003. Subsequent comments by Choo are also from this interview.

27. Ibid.

28. Lawton, telephone interview.

Chapter 5

1. John M. Gottman and Nan Silver, *The Seven Principles for Making Marriage Work* (New York: Three Rivers Press, 1999).

2. Joseph Galli, telephone interview by David Harding, Bain & Company, Boston, 21 May 2003. Subsequent comments by Galli are from this interview.

3. In December 2002, H. J. Heinz spun off $1.1 billion of its corporate portfolio to Del Monte Foods. The spun-off businesses included StarKist Tuna, Heinz Pet Products, Heinz Infant Feeding in the United States, and Heinz's private-label soup business. The transaction was a reverse Morris Trust and resulted in Heinz shareholders owning 74 percent of Del Monte.

4. Rick Wolford, interview by David Harding, Bain & Company, San Francisco, 14 July 2003. Subsequent comments by Wolford are from this interview.

5. James Daly, "John Chambers: The Art of the Deal," *Business 2.0,* October 1999.

6. Todd Thomson, telephone interview by David Harding, Bain & Company, Boston, 29 May 2002.

7. Gary Silverman and Leah Nathans Spiro, "Is This Marriage Working?" *BusinessWeek,* 7 June 1999.

8. Carlos Gutierrez, telephone interview by David Harding, Bain & Company, Boston, 15 May 2003.

9. Jon Birger and Nick Pachetti, "Leader of the Pack," *Money,* June 2002.

10. Harold M. Cody and Gregory Rudder, "Smurfit-Stone Container's Blueprint for Success Setting the Standard," *Pulp & Paper,* 1 January 2000.

11. William Curran, telephone interview by Ted Rouse, Bain & Company, Chicago, 7 March 2003.

12. Bryan Burrough and John Helyar, *Barbarians at the Gate: The Fall of RJR Nabisco* (New York: Harper & Row, 1990).

13. Vivian Imerman, telephone interview by Alistair Corbett, Bain & Company, Toronto, 12 February 2003. Subsequent comments by Imerman are from this interview.

14. Galli, telephone interview.

15. Newell Investor Relations, e-mail correspondence, 18 February 2004.

16. Blair Effron, speaking on "Strategic M&A in an Opportunistic Environment" (presentation at Bain's Getting Back to Offense conference, New York City, 20 June 2002).

17. Chris Brady and Andrew Lorenz, *The End of the Road: BMW and Rover—A Brand Too Far* (London: Financial Times Prentice Hall, 2000).

18. Prince Philipp of Liechtenstein, correspondence with Paul Wilson, January 2003.

19. Ibid.

20. Galli, telephone interview.

Chapter 6

1. Peter Gumbel, "Nestlé's Quick," *Time,* 27 January 2003.

2. In December 2000, Kraft's parent Philip Morris purchased Nabisco for $14.9 billion and then folded it into its Kraft divisions.

3. Nigel Cope, "Nestlé—Sweet Dreams Are Made of This," *The Independent-London,* 13 December 2000.

4. Morgan Stanley, "Nestlé," Morgan Stanley Equity Research Report, 12 March 2003.

5. James Singh, telephone interview by Sam Rovit, Bain & Company, Chicago, 3 June 2003.

6. James Singh, telephone interview by Sam Rovit, Bain & Company, Chicago, 20 February 2003. Subsequent comments by Singh are from this interview.

7. Stephen Gates, "Performance Measures During Merger & Acquisition Integration," The Conference Board, #1274, July 2000.

8. Joe Trustey, telephone interview by David Harding, Bain & Company, Boston, 13 May 2003.

9. Brent Bickett, telephone interview with Sam Rovit, Bain & Company, 20 September 2002. Subsequent comments by Bickett are also from this interview.

10. Benoît Bassi, telephone interview by Jean-Marc Leroux, Bain & Company, Paris, 26 February 2003.

11. KPMG, "Unlocking Shareholder Value: The Keys to Success," KPMG M&A Global Research Report, November 1999.

12. Craig Tall, telephone interview by Catherine Lemire, Bain & Company, Toronto, 1 October 2002. Subsequent comments by Tall are from this interview.

13. Robert Kohlhepp, telephone interview by Catherine Lemire, Bain & Company, Toronto, 4 October 2002. Subsequent comments by Kohlhepp are from this interview.

14. Bickett, telephone interview.

15. Kohlhepp, telephone interview.

16. Tall, telephone interview.

Appendix

1. Jay P. Brandimarte, William C. Fallon, and Robert S. McNish, "Trading the Corporate Portfolio," *McKinsey on Finance,* autumn 2001.

Bibliography

Books

Aiello, Robert J., et al., *Harvard Business Review on Mergers and Acquisitions* (Boston: Harvard Business School Press, 2001).

Arzac, Enrique, *Valuation: Mergers, Acquisitions and Buyouts* (New York: John Wiley & Sons, 2002).

Bendaniel, David, Arthur Rosenbloom, and James Hanks, *International M&A Joint Ventures and Beyond: Doing the Deal* (New York: John Wiley & Sons, 2002).

Borghese, Robert J., and Paul F. Borgese, *M&A from Planning to Integration: Executing Acquisitions and Increasing Shareholder Value* (New York: McGraw-Hill Trade, 2001).

Brady, Chris, and Andrew Lorenz, *The End of the Road: BMW and Rover—A Brand Too Far* (London: Financial Times Prentice Hall, 2000).

Briones, Juan, Jaimie Folguera, Andres Font, and Edume Navarro, *Merger Control in the EU* (New York: Oxford University Press, 2002).

Brown, Meredith M., Ralph C. Ferrar, Paul S. Bird, and Gary W. Kubek, *Takeovers: A Strategic Guide to Mergers and Acquisitions* (New York: Aspen Publishers, 2001).

Burrough, Bryan, and John Helyar, *Barbarians at the Gate: The Fall of RJR Nabisco* (New York: HarperCollins, 1990).

Child, John, David Faulkner, and Robert Pitkethyly, *The Management of International Acquisitions: Realizing Their Potential Value* (New York: Oxford University Press, 2001).

Coffey, John, Valerie Garrow, and Linda Holbeche, *Reaping the Benefits of Mergers and Acquisitions: In Search of the Golden Fleece* (Boston: Butterworth-Heinemann, 2002).

Copeland, Tom, Tim Koller, and Jack Murrin, *Valuation: Measuring and Managing the Value of Companies* (New York: John Wiley & Sons, 2000).

Daniel, Teresa A., and Gary S. Metcalf, *The Management of People in Mergers and Acquisitions* (Westport, CT: Quorum Books, 2001).

Deans, Graeme K., Fritz Kroger, and Stefan Zeisel, *Winning the Merger Endgame: A Playbook for Profiting from Industry Consolidation* (New York: McGraw-Hill, 2003).

DePamphilis, Donald, *Mergers, Acquisitions and Other Restructuring Activities: An Integrated Approach to Process, Tools, Cases and Solutions* (San Diego: Academic Press, 2001).

Evans, Frank C., and David M. Bishop, *Valuation for M&A: Building Value in Private Companies* (New York: John Wiley & Sons, 2001).

Ferris, Kenneth R., and Barbara S. Pecherot Petitt, *Valuation: Avoiding the Winner's Curse* (London: Financial Times Prentice Hall, 2002).

Galpin, Timothy J., and Mark Herndon, *The Complete Guide to Mergers & Acquisitions: Process Tools to Support M&A Integration at Every Level* (San Francisco: Jossey-Bass, 2000).

Gaughan, Patrick, *Mergers, Acquisitions and Corporate Restructurings* (New York: John Wiley & Sons, 2001).

Gilson, Stuart C., *Creating Value Through Corporate Restructuring: Case Studies in Bankruptcies, Buyouts, and Breakups* (New York: John Wiley & Sons, 2001).

Gottman, John M., and Nan Silver, *The Seven Principles for Making Marriage Work* (New York: Three Rivers Press, 1999).

Gun, Benton E., ed., *Megamergers in a Global Economy: Causes and Consequences* (Westport, CT: Quorum Books, 2001).

Habek, Max, Fritz Kroger, and Michael R. Tram, *After the Merger: Seven Strategies for Successful Post-Merger Integration* (Englewood Cliffs, NJ: Prentice Hall, 2000).

Hanson, Patti, *The M&A Transition Guide: A 10-Step Roadmap for Workforce Integration* (New York: John Wiley & Sons, 2001).

Harbison, John R., and Peter Pekar Jr., *Smart Alliances: A Practical Guide to Repeatable Success* (San Francisco: Jossey-Bass, 1998).

Hitt, Michael A., Jeffrey S. Harrison, and R. Duane Ireland, *Mergers and Acquisitions: A Guide to Creating Value for Stakeholders* (New York: Oxford University Press, 2001).

Hubbard, Nancy, *Acquisition: Strategy and Implementation* (New York: Palgrave Macmillan, 2001).

Krakauer, Jon, *Into Thin Air* (New York: Anchor, 1998).

Marks, Mitchell, *Charging Back Up the Hill: Workplace Recovery After Mergers, Acquisitions and Downsizings* (New York: John Wiley & Sons, 2003).

Mergerstat, *Mergerstat Review 2004* (Los Angeles: Mergerstat, 2004).

Messier, Jean-Marie, and Yves Messarovitch, *Mon vrai journal* (Paris: Balland, 2002).

Paulson, Ed, *Inside Cisco: The Real Story of Sustained M&A Growth* (New York: John Wiley & Sons, 2001).

Rankine, Denzil, *Why Acquisitions Fail* (London: Financial Times, 2001).

Reed, Stanley Foster, *The M&A Deskbook* (New York: McGraw-Hill Trade, 2001).

Reichheld, Frederick F. with Thomas Teal, *The Loyalty Effect: The Hidden Force Behind Growth, Profits, and Lasting Value* (Boston: Harvard Business School Press, 1996).

Reichheld, Frederick F., *Loyalty Rules! How Leaders Build Lasting Relationships* (Boston: Harvard Business School Press, 2001).

Rezae, Zabibollah, *Financial Institutions, Valuations, Mergers and Acquisitions: The Fair Value Approach* (New York: John Wiley & Sons, 2001).

Romenek, Broc, *Mergers and Acquisitions* (New York: John Wiley & Sons, 2002).

Rosenbloom, Arthur H., ed., *Due Diligence in Global Deal Making: The Definitive Guide to Cross-Border Mergers and Acquisitions, Joint Ventures, Financings and Strategic Alliances* (Princeton, NJ: Bloomberg Press, 2002).

Roster, Richard, and Sarah Kaplan, *Creative Destruction: Why Companies That Are Built to Last Underperform the Market—and How to Successfully Transform Them* (New York: Doubleday, 2001).

Sadtler, David, Richard Koch, and Andrew Campbell, *Breakup! How Companies Use Spin-Offs to Gain Focus and Grow Strong* (New York: Free Press, 1997).

Schmidt, Jeffrey A., ed., *Making Mergers Work: The Strategic Importance of People* (Alexandria, VA: Towers Perrin and The Society for Human Resource Management Foundation, 2002).

Schweiger, David M., *M&A Integration: A Framework for Executives and Managers* (New York: McGraw-Hill Trade, 2002).

Sirower, Mark L., *The Synergy Trap: How Companies Lose the Acquisition Game* (New York: Free Press, 1997).

Tauli, Tom, *The Complete M&A Handbook: The Ultimate Guide to Buying, Selling, Merging, or Valuing a Business for Maximum Return* (Rocklin, CA: Prima Publishing, 2002).

Temple, Paul, and Simon Peck, eds., *Mergers and Acquisitions: Critical Perspectives on Business and Management, Four Volume Set* (London: Routledge, 2002).

Wasserstein, Bruce, *Big Deal: The Battle for Control of America's Leading Corporations* (New York: Warner Books, 1998).

Weston, J. Fred, and Samuel C. Weaver, *Mergers and Acquisitions* (New York: McGraw-Hill Trade, 2001).

Weston, J. Fred, *Cases in Dynamic Finance: Mergers and Restructuring* (Englewood Cliffs, NJ: Prentice Hall, 2002).

Zhan, James Xiaoning, and Terutomo Ozawa, *Business Restructuring in Asia: Cross-Border M&As in the Crisis Period* (Copenhagen: Copenhagen Business School Press, 2001).

Zook, Chris, and James Allen, *Profit from the Core: Growth Strategy in an Era of Turbulence* (Boston: Harvard Business School Press, 2001).

Zook, Chris, *Beyond the Core: Expand Your Market Without Abandoning Your Roots* (Boston: Harvard Business School Press, 2004).

Research Reports and Articles

Accenture, "Accenture Survey Shows Executives Are Cautiously Optimistic Regarding Future Mergers and Acquisitions," Accenture Omnibus Executive Survey, Accenture Press Release, 30 May 2002.

Adolph, Gary, Ian Buchanan, Jennifer Hornery, Bill Jackson, John Jones, Torbjorn Kihlstedt, Gary Neilson, and Harry Quarls, "Merger Integration: Delivering on the Promise," Booz Allen & Hamilton Series of Viewpoints on Mergers, Acquisitions and Integration, July 2001.

Aiello, Robert J., and Michael D. Watkins, "The Fine Art of Friendly Acquisition," *Harvard Business Review,* November–December 2000.

Ainspan, Nathan D., and David Dell, "Employee Communications During Mergers," The Conference Board Research Report, 2000.

Anand, Jaideep, and Harbir Singh, "Asset Redeployment, Acquisitions and Corporate Strategy in Declining Industries," *Strategic Management Journal* 18 (1997).

Andrew, James P., and Michael Knapp, "Maximizing Post-Merger Savings from Purchasing," unpublished report, 30 April 2001.

Annema, Andre, William C. Fallon, and Marc H. Goedhart, "When Carve-Outs Make Sense," *McKinsey Quarterly* 2 (2002).

Anslinger, Patricia L., and Thomas E. Copeland, "Growth Through Acquisitions: A Fresh Look," *Harvard Business Review,* January–February 1996.

Anslinger, Patricia, Justin Jenk, and Ravi Chanmugam, "The Art of Strategic Divestment," Accenture's *Outlook Journal* 1 (January 2003).

Armour, Eric, "How Boards Can Improve the Odds of M&A Success," *Strategy & Leadership,* March–April 2002.

Ashkenas, Ronald N., Lawrence J. DeMonaco, and Suzanne C. Francis, "Making the Deal Real: How GE Capital Integrates Acquisitions," *Harvard Business Review,* January–February 1998.

Ashkenas, Ronald N., and Suzanne C. Francis, "Integration Managers: Special Leaders for Special Times," *Harvard Business Review,* November–December 2000.

Becher, David A., "The Valuation Effects of Bank Mergers," *Journal of Corporate Finance* 6 (2000).

Beiker, Matthias M., Anna J. Bogardus, and Tim Oldham, "Mastering Revenue Growth in M&A," *McKinsey on Finance,* summer 2001.

Beiker, Matthias M., Anna J. Bogardus, and Tim Oldham, "Why Mergers Fail," *McKinsey Quarterly* 4 (2001).

Beiker, Matthias M., and Michael J. Shelton, "Keeping Your Sales Force After the Merger," *McKinsey Quarterly* 4 (2002).

Beiker, Matthias M., and Michael J. Shelton, "Merging? Watch Your Sales Force," *McKinsey on Finance,* winter 2003.

Bieshaar, Hans, Jeremy Knight, and Alexander van Wassenaer, "Deals That Create Value," *McKinsey Quarterly* 1 (2001).

Bild, Magnus, "Valuation of Takeovers," Ph.D. diss., Stockholm School of Economics, 1998.

Birger, Jon, and Nick Pachetti, "Leader of the Pack," *Money,* June 2002.

Boehlert, Eric, "Fighting Pay-for-Play," *Salon.com,* 3 April 2001.

Boston Consulting Group, "Crossing Borders: European Mergers and Acquisitions," The Boston Consulting Group Report, September 2000.

Bower, Joseph L., "Not All M&As Are Alike—and That Matters," *Harvard Business Review,* March 2001.

Brandimarte, Jay P., William C. Fallon, and Robert S. McNish, "Trading the Corporate Portfolio," *McKinsey on Finance,* autumn 2001.

Campbell, Andrew, and David Sadtler, "Corporate Breakups," *Booz Allen & Hamilton Strategy & Business,* Third Quarter 1998.

Capron, Laurence, "The Long-Term Performance of Horizontal Acquisitions," *Strategic Management Journal* 20 (1999).

Carey, Dennis, "Lessons from Master Acquirers: A CEO Roundtable on Making Mergers Succeed," *Harvard Business Review,* May–June 2000.

Carreyrou, John, and Martin Peers, "How Messier Led Vivendi to the Brink," *Wall Street Journal Europe,* 31 October 2002.

Chen, Christine, "The Bad Boys of Radio," *Fortune,* 3 March 2003.

"Cinven Acquires Odeon for £280m," *Leisure Week,* 24 February 2000.

Cody, Harold M., and Gregory Rudder, "Smurfit-Stone Container's Blueprint for Success Setting the Standard," *Pulp & Paper,* 1 January 2000.

Collis, David J., and Cynthia A. Montgomery, "Creating Corporate Advantage," *Harvard Business Review,* May–June 1998.

Cope, Nigel, "Nestlé—Sweet Dreams Are Made of This," *The Independent-London,* 13 December 2000.

Corrigan, Tracy, "One-Sided Marriage: The Merger of Morgan Stanley and Dean Witter Adds More to the Retail Arm Than to the Investment Bank," *Financial Times,* 15 July 1997.

Credit Suisse First Boston, "Kellogg Co.," Credit Suisse First Boston Report, 20 March 2001.

Daly, James, "John Chambers: The Art of the Deal," *Business 2.0,* October 1999.

Deloitte Consulting, "Solving the Merger Mystery," Deloitte Consulting White Paper, date unknown.

Dobbs, Richard F., Tomas Karakolev, and Francis Malige, "Learning to Love Recessions," *McKinsey Quarterly,* 2002 Special Edition: Risk and Resilience.

Donahue, Kristen B., "How to Ruin a Merger: Five People-Management Pitfalls to Avoid," *Harvard Management Update,* September 2001.

Dranikoff, Lee, Timothy M. Koller, and Antoon Schneider, "Divestiture: Strategy's Missing Link," *Harvard Business Review,* May 2002.

Dranikoff, Lee, Timothy M. Koller, and Antoon Schneider, "Divesting Proactively," *McKinsey on Finance,* summer 2002.

Eccles, Robert G., Kersten L. Lanes, and Thomas C. Wilson, "Are You Paying Too Much for That Acquisition?" *Harvard Business Review,* July–August 1999.

Ernst, David, and Tammy Halevy, "When to Think Alliance," *McKinsey Quarterly* 4 (2000).

Feldman, Mark R. "The Seven Deadly Sins of Mergers: The Pros and Cons of Corporate Marriage," *San Francisco Examiner,* 5 October 1998.

Fisher, Lawrence M., "Post-Merger Integration: How Novartis Became No. 1," *Booz Allen & Hamilton Strategy & Business,* Second Quarter 1998.

Fisher, Lawrence M., "How Elan Grew by Staying Small," *Booz Allen & Hamilton Strategy & Business,* Third Quarter 1999.

Frank, Robert, and Robin Sidel, "Firms That Lived by the Deal Are Now Sinking by the Dozens," *Wall Street Journal,* 6 June 2002.

Frick, Kevin A., and Alberto Torres, "Learning from High-Tech Deals," *McKinsey Quarterly* 1 (2002).

Fritzon, Art, Robert Lukefahr, Amy Asin, Sanjay Bhatia, and Viren Doshi, "Making Mergers E-Merge: Using the Internet to Jump-Start Integration," *Booz Allen & Hamilton Strategy & Business,* Fourth Quarter 2000.

Fry, Joseph N., "Newell Company: The Rubbermaid Opportunity," Case study (Richard Ivey School of Business, University of Western Ontario, January 2001).

Fubini, David, "After the Merger," *McKinsey Quarterly* 4 (2000).

Fuller, Kathleen, Jeffry Netter, and Mike Stegemoller, "What Do Returns to Acquiring Firms Tell Us? Evidence from Firms That Make Many Acquisitions," *Journal of Finance,* August 2002.

Gadiesh, Orit, and James L. Gilbert, "Profit Pools: A Fresh Look at Strategy," *Harvard Business Review,* May–June 1998.

Gadiesh, Orit, Robin Buchanan, Mark Daniell, and Charles Ormiston, "The Leadership Testing Ground—Mergers May Be the Truest Test of Great Leaders," *Journal of Business Strategy,* March–April 2002.

Gadiesh, Orit, Robin Buchanan, Mark Daniell, and Charles Ormiston, "A CEO's Guide to the New Challenges of M&A Leadership," *Strategy & Leadership,* May 2002.

Gadiesh, Orit, and Charles Ormiston, "Six Rationales to Guide Merger Success," *Strategy & Leadership,* July 2002.

Gadiesh, Orit, Charles Ormiston, and Sam Rovit, "Achieving M&A's Strategic Goals at Maximum Speed for Maximum Value," *Strategy & Leadership,* May 2003.

Gates, Stephen, "Performance Measures During Mergers & Acquisitions," The Conference Board Research Report, July 2000.

Gibson, Richard, "Flying Solo: The Autocratic Style of Northwest's CEO Complicates Defense," *Wall Street Journal,* 30 March 1989.

Goldblatt, Henry, "Cisco's Secrets: Forty-two Acquisitions and Counting," *Fortune,* 8 November 1999.

Griffith, Victoria, "The People Factor in Post-Merger Integration," *Booz Allen & Hamilton Strategy & Business Case Study,* Third Quarter 2000.

Gumbel, Peter, "Nestlé's Quick," *Time,* 27 January 2003.

Harbison, John R., Albert J. Viscio, and Amy T. Asin, "Making Acquisitions Work: Capturing Value After the Deal," *Booz Allen & Hamilton Series of Viewpoints on Alliances,* 1999.

Harding, David, and Phyllis Yale, "Discipline and the Dilutive Deal," *Harvard Business Review,* July 2002.

Hart, Jeffery R., and Vince P. Apilado, "Inexperienced Banks and Interstate Mergers," *Journal of Economics and Business* 5207 (2002).

Henry, David, "Mergers—Why Most Big Deals Don't Pay Off," *BusinessWeek,* 14 October 2002.

Hopkins, H. Donald, "Cross-Border Mergers and Acquisitions: Global and Regional Perspectives," *Journal of International Management* 5 (1999).

Houston, Joel F., Christopher M. James, and Michael D. Ryngaert, "Where Do Merger Gains Come From?" *Journal of Financial Economics* 60 (2001).

Jacob, Rahul, "Corporate Reputations: The Winners Chart a Course of Constant Renewal and Work to Sustain Cultures That Produce the Very Best Products and People," *Fortune,* 6 March 1995.

Katzman, Eric R., "Kellogg Company: Initial Opinion," Deutsche Bank Alex. Brown Equity Research, 30 November 2000.

Kay, Ira, and Mike Shelton, "The People Problem in Mergers," *McKinsey Quarterly* 4 (2000).

Kleinert, Jorn, and Henning Klodt, "Causes and Consequences of Merger Waves" (paper presented at European M&As, Corporate Restructuring and Consolidation Issues, Barcelona, 16 March 2002).

Kotzen, Jeffrey, Chris Neenan, Alexander Roos, and Daniel Stelter, "Winning Through Mergers in Lean Times" The Boston Consulting Group Report, July 2003.

KPMG, "Unlocking Shareholder Value: The Keys to Success," KPMG M&A Global Research Report, November 1999.

KPMG, "World Class Transactions: Insights into Creating Shareholder Value Through Mergers and Acquisitions," KPMG Transactions Services, 2001.

Kramer, Robert J., "Post-Merger Organization Handbook," The Conference Board Research Report, 2001.

Lehman Brothers, "Philips: Lighting-up Medical and Lighting," Lehman Brothers Global Equity Research, 2 July 2003.

Lipin, Steven, and Nikhil Deogun, "Big Mergers of 90s Prove Disappointing to Shareholders," *Wall Street Journal,* 30 October 2000.

Lucenko, Kristina, "Implementing a Post-Merger Integration," The Conference Board Research Report, January 2000.

Maneaty, Constance, and Parinaz Pahlavi, Bear Stearns, "Newell Rubbermaid," Bear Stearns Report, 24 March 1999.

Mathieu, Bruno E., and Collin Brown III, "Making M&A Pay: Lessons from the World's Most Successful Acquirers," *Marakon Commentary,* spring 2003.

May, Michael, Patricia Anslinger, and Justin Jenk, "Avoiding the Perils of Traditional Due Diligence," Accenture's *Outlook Journal,* no. 2 (July 2002).

Merrill Lynch, "Keebler Acquisition: Reducing Estimates," Merrill Lynch Global Research, 26 October 2000.

Merrill Lynch, "Morning Meeting Note," Merrill Lynch Report, 26 October 2000.

Moreen, Bob, "People Issues and Mergers & Acquisitions," William M. Mercer White Paper, August 2001.

Moreton, Philippa, "Rank Wraps Up Odeon Sale to Cinven," Reuters News, 21 February 2000.

Morgan Stanley, "Nestlé," Morgan Stanley Equity Research Report, 12 March 2003.

Mouawad, Jad, "Ex-Vivendi CEO Admits Buying Too Much, Too Fast," *Ottawa Citizen,* 16 November 2002.

"Newell Rubbermaid, Inc.," *Chase H&Q,* 22 November 2000.

"Newell Rubbermaid: Why It'll Bounce Back," *BusinessWeek,* 20 October 2003.

Ormerod, John, and John Nendick, "Beyond the Headlines: A Survey of Lessons Learned from Merger and Acquisition Activity," Arthur Andersen White Paper, date unknown.

Pablo, Amy, and Manour Javidan, "Thinking of a Merger . . . Do You Know Their Risk Propensity Profile," *Organizational Dynamics* vol. 30, issue 3 (spring 2002).

Rad, Alireza Tourani, and Luuk van Beek, "Market Valuation of European Bank Mergers," *European Management Journal* 17 (1999).

Rappaport, Alfred, and Mark L. Sirower, "Stock or Cash: The Trade-Offs for Buyers and Sellers in Mergers and Acquisitions," *Harvard Business Review,* November–December 1999.

Rau, P. Raghavendra, "Investment Bank Market Share, Contingent Fee Payments, and the Performance of Acquiring Firms," *Journal of Financial Economics* 56 (2000).

Rhodes, David, Didier Ribadeau Dumas, Nick Viner, and Svilen Ivanov, "Making Mergers Work: Turning a Big Deal into a Good Deal," Boston Consulting Group: Opportunities for Action in Financial Services, 1 January 2000.

Rifkin, Glenn, "Growth by Acquisition: The Case of Cisco Systems," *Strategy & Business,* Second Quarter 1997.

Rifkin, Glenn, "Post-Merger Integration: How IBM and Lotus Work Together," *McKinsey Quarterly* 12 (1998).

Rogers, Paul, Tom Holland, and Dan Haas, "Value Acceleration: Lessons from Private Equity Masters," *Harvard Business Review,* June 2002.

Rovit, Sam, and Catherine Lemire, "Your Best M&A Strategy," *Harvard Business Review,* March 2003.

Rovit, Sam, David Harding, and Catherine Lemire, "Turning Deal Smarts into M&A Payoffs," *Mergers & Acquisitions: The Dealmakers Journal,* September 2003.

Schein, Lawrence, "Managing Culture in Mergers and Acquisitions," The Conference Board Research Report, November 2001.

Shelton, Michael J., "Managing Your Integration Manager?" *McKinsey Quarterly,* 2003 Special Edition: The Value in Organization.

Shpilberg, David, Steve Berez, and Sam Israelit, "Merger Integration Blueprint," *CIO Insight,* 19 July 2002.

Silverman, Gary, and Leah Nathans Spiro, "Is This Marriage Working?" *BusinessWeek,* 7 June 1999.

Skarzynski, Peter, "When Mega-Mergers Don't Make Sense," *Chief Executive,* June 2000.

Slywotzky, Adrian J., and Richard Wise, "The Growth Crisis—and How to Escape It," *Harvard Business Review,* July 2002.

Smith, Randall, "Dean Witter Holds Its Own at Morgan," *Wall Street Journal,* 10 March 1999.

Spiro, Leah Nathans, "Class Meets Mass on Wall Street," *BusinessWeek,* 17 February 1997.

Spiro, Leah Nathans, "They Said It Would Never Work—But After a Year, Morgan Stanley Dean Witter Is Meshing," *BusinessWeek,* 29 June 1998.

Stegemoller, Mike, "The Performance of Frequent Acquirers," Working paper, Terry College of Business, University of Georgia, Athens, December 2001.

Stevens, Tim, "Breaking Up Is Profitable to Do," *Industry Week,* 21 June 1999.

Stewart, Jules, "Lack of Methodology in the Madness," *The Banker,* 1 April 2001.

"Survey: Trans-Atlantic Deals Are Winners," CFO.com, 25 March 2002.

Thomas, Robert J., "Irreconcilable Differences," Accenture's *Outlook Journal,* no. 1 (2000).

Thompson, Stephanie, and Jack Neff, "P&G, Coke Could Face Distribution Challenge," *Advertising Age,* 26 February 2001.

Very, Philippe, and David Schweiger, "The Acquisition Process as a Learning Process: Evidence from a Study of Critical Problems and Solutions in Domestic and Cross-Border Deals," *Journal of World Business* 36 (1).

Vestring, Till, Brian King, and Ted Rouse, "Merger Integration: Why 'Soft Issues' Matter Most," *European Business Forum,* April 2003.

Vestring, Till, Brian King, and Ted Rouse, "Should You Merge Cultures?" *Harvard Management Update,* September 2003.

Vishwanath, Vijay, and Jonathan Mark, "Your Brand's Best Strategy," *Harvard Business Review,* May–June 1997.

Wetlaufer, Suzy, "The Business Case Against Revolution: An Interview with Nestlé's Peter Brabeck," *Harvard Business Review,* February 2001.

Wilke, Carol Warner, "Rubbermaid Deal Examined," *Capital Ideas,* CNNfn, 21 October 1998.

Zollo, Maurizio, and Dima Leshchinkskii, "Can Firms Learn to Acquire? Do Markets Notice?" Wharton School Financial Institutions Center Working Paper Series, Philadelphia, 2000.

Zollo, Maurizio, and Habir Singh, "The Impact of Knowledge Codification, Experience Trajectories and Integration Strategies on the Performance of Corporate Acquisitions," Wharton School Financial Institutions Center Working Paper Series, Philadelphia, 1998.

Acknowledgments

Writing a book is a labor of love. This book represents a lot of labor and a lot of love. We can scarcely do justice to the countless hours that our contributors, editors, and researchers committed to this project. But we shall try.

First, thanks to our partners at Bain & Company, who have encouraged us and contributed so much to the content. Each of the four critical decisions had several godfathers who helped mold our thinking. Special thanks go to Chris Zook (author of *Profit from the Core*) and Phil Schefter for pushing our thinking on the disciplines around the first critical decision: How should you pick your targets? Geoff Cullinan, Rolf-Magnus Weddigen, Jean-Marc Le Roux, Dan Haas, and Mike McKay, members of Bain's terrific private equity group, contributed mightily to thinking around the second critical decision: Which deals should you close? Our third decision—Where do you really need to integrate?—draws largely on the work of Ted Rouse, Till Vestring, and Brian King, all leaders at Bain in merger integration. Alistair Corbett and Mark Daniell provided much of the fodder and insight for explaining our fourth critical decision: What should you do when the deal goes off track?

Every answer we found seemed to beg another question. Catherine Lemire led our research on this project, a team that included James Pereira-Stubbs and Lorianne Pannozzo. Their diligence, energy, and rigor were evident throughout the thousands of hours they put into this work. And their work was buttressed by our corps of fact checkers, which included Lucy Richards, Andrea Ovans, Hilary McClellen, Brian Hershberg, Amy Mace Stackhouse, and Stephanie Thomas.

This effort would never have taken flight without the Harvard Business School Press editorial director, Hollis Heimbouch, and our editor at HBSP, Melinda Merino, who acquired the manuscript and developed it with us, moved it through peer review, and coached us to completion. Jeff Cruikshank stepped in as the ultimate manuscript doctor and made our chapters flow as a book. And executive assistant Heather Montgomery formatted and tamed all of our files for submission to HBSP.

Finally, our utmost thanks to the editorial director of this book, Katie Smith Milway. Katie also served as our project manager and agent. She led our chapter edit team, which included Zoe Brookes, Geoff Smith, Susan Donovan, and Nate Nickerson. Her combination of tough love, cajoling, and questioning led to the shape of our ideas and prose.

While many have contributed to this book, the responsibility for factual accuracy and insight is ours. If we have erred, we take responsibility and want to hear about it.

Index

About the Authors

David Harding is a director in Bain & Company's Boston office and is a leader in the areas of corporate strategy and organizational effectiveness. He has advised several of the world's leading consumer-products companies, retailers, manufacturers, and service providers on growth strategies and the role of deal making in creating and sustaining shareholder value.

David is a renowned expert in M&A, due diligence, and postmerger integration, and frequently shares his expertise through published articles and public speeches. His *Harvard Business Review* articles include "Brands Versus Private Label: Fighting to Win" (January–February 1996), "The Starbucks Effect" (March 2000), "Winning with the Big-Box Retailers" (October 2000), and "Discipline and the Dilutive Deal" (July 2002). He earned an M.B.A. from Harvard Business School and a Bachelor of Business Administration from the University of Cincinnati.

Sam Rovit is a director in the Chicago office and the leader of Bain & Company's Global Mergers & Acquisitions practice group. He also heads up Bain's Private Equity practice in the Midwest.

Over the last fifteen years, Sam has worked in Europe, Asia, and the United States on behalf of a wide array of clients, with a particular emphasis on retail, distribution, and industrial sectors. In addition to M&A, his experience includes merger integration, corporate strategy, operations improvement, and turnaround situations. He has published in *Harvard Business Review, Acquisitions Monthly,* and *Mergers & Acquisitions: The Dealmaker's Journal.*

Sam earned his M.B.A. from Harvard Business School, his Master of Arts in law and diplomacy from the Fletcher School of Law and Diplomacy, Tufts University, with majors in military strategy and international business, and his B.A. in public policy from Duke University.

He is a member of the board of directors of both McJunkin Corporation and Junior Achievement of Chicago.

About the Contributors

Alistair Corbett is a director in Bain & Company; he splits his time between Bain's Toronto and Chicago offices. He has worked extensively in the airline, industrial products, and forest products industries. His multiyear client relationships have involved a combination of corporate and business unit strategy, sales and marketing strategy, and operations improvement and merger integration. Alistair earned an M.B.A. with distinction from the European Institute of Business Administration, INSEAD, and is a graduate of Cambridge University, where he earned a first-class honors degree in Engineering and a master's degree in operational research.

Geoffrey Cullinan is a director in Bain & Company's London office and leads the Private Equity practice for Europe, with special responsibility for developing entrepreneurial companies and a focus on mergers and acquisitions and the creation of shareholder value. He has over thirty years of general management, strategy consulting, and investor experience in a wide range of industries, including consumer products, retail, automotive, chemicals, engineering, and financial services. Geoffrey is a graduate of the University of Essex, England and earned an M.B.A. with highest distinction from IMEDE, Lausanne.

Dan Haas is a director in Bain & Company's Boston office, where he has worked since 1988 on assignments in a variety of sectors for consumer, technology, retail, and industrial clients. His experience covers corporate strategy, mergers and acquisitions, merger integration, organizational effectiveness, supply chain optimization, and cost reduction. Dan currently works in Bain's Private Equity practice, helping investment funds with due diligence and portfolio company performance. He earned an M.B.A. from Harvard Business School and received Bachelor of Arts degrees in both economics and history from Brown University. Dan's writing has been featured in *Harvard Business Review* and *Worldlink*.

Brian King is a vice president in the Atlanta office of Bain & Company, which he joined in 1992. His experience covers corporate and business unit strategy, supply chain management, mergers and acquisitions, and operations integration. He has led assignments in a wide variety of industries, including the airline and automotive industries, distribution businesses, telecommunications, and trucking. Brian is a graduate of The Ohio State University, where he received a B.A. in accounting. He also holds an M.B.A. with a concentration in finance from the Wharton School of Business at the University of Pennsylvania.

Catherine Lemire is a manager at Bain & Company responsible for the development of intellectual capital in Bain's Global Mergers & Acquisitions practice. Her client work has focused on technology, media, financial services, retail, consumer products, transportation, and health care industries. She has worked on a variety of assignments in M&A, private equity, corporate and business unit strategy, growth strategy, and cost reduction. She has published in *Harvard Business Review* and *Mergers & Acquisitions: The Dealmaker's Journal*. Catherine graduated with an M.B.A. from INSEAD in 1993. She also holds a Bachelor of Commerce from McGill University.

Jean-Marc Le Roux is a vice president in the Paris office of Bain & Company. He currently leads the Private Equity group in the Paris office serving LBO clients on deal generation, due diligence, and postacquisition projects. Prior to joining the Private Equity group, Jean-Marc led several projects in the technology, finance, and service sectors, including growth strategy, performance, improvement, and postmerger integration in Europe and North America. Prior to Bain, he worked as a sales engineer for IBM in France and North America. He earned an M.B.A. from INSEAD and a B.S. from École Polytechnique.

Mike McKay, a director based in Boston, joined Bain in 1987 and today leads Bain's Private Equity group for the Northeast. He has led assignments in a variety of industries for both consumer and industrial clients. His experience covers merger and acquisition strategy, strategic due diligence, portfolio strategy, growth strategies, consumer marketing, and manufacturing cost reduction. Mike holds an M.B.A. from the University of Chicago Graduate School of Business, where he received the Mayer Prize as the top graduating student and the Brown Prize as the top marketing student. He holds a B.A. in economics from Harvard College.

Katie Smith Milway, based in Boston, is Bain & Company's global editorial director. She guides the transformation of Bain's intellectual capital into external and internal publications, collaborating closely with Bain's practice area directors. Katie joined Bain in 1994 as a consultant in Toronto, then Munich. She has served a variety of clients across multiple industries and markets on issues including business unit strategy, merger due diligence, change management, and operational improvement. Prior to business school, she edited and wrote for the *Wall Street Journal Europe,* Montreal *Gazette, Time,* and Harvard's Kennedy School of Government. Katie holds a B.A. in English from Stanford University, a master's in European studies from the Free University of Brussels, and an M.B.A. from INSEAD.

Ted Rouse is a company director and head of Bain's global industrial practice. He formerly led the firm's Global Mergers & Acquisitions practice and was managing director of Bain & Company's Chicago office for ten years. He has served major clients in the automotive, defense, technology, and telecommunications industries on a wide range of strategy and operational issues. These have included growth, business unit strategy, restructuring, manufacturing strategy, and operations improvement. He earned an M.B.A. from the Harvard Business School and a B.A. in economics, magna cum laude, from Williams College.

Phil Schefter is a director in Bain & Company' s Boston office. Over the last thirteen years, Phil has worked with leading firms in the industrial products, financial services, and automotive sectors to develop and implement active portfolio management and systematic growth strategies. He earned an M.B.A. from Harvard Business School and a B.S., summa cum laude, in industrial engineering and operations research from Syracuse University.

Till Vestring is a partner and director in Bain & Company's South East Asia practice based in Singapore. He heads Bain's Automotive and Industrial practice in Asia and is a leader in the Global Mergers & Acquisitions practice. He has worked on several of the most high profile acquisitions and integrations of Japanese companies by foreign entities as well as on several large intra-Asian deals. He has worked closely with senior executives on the full range of strategy, integration, and organization issues facing companies involved in M&A. Till earned a master's degree in economics from the University of Bonn in Germany and an M.B.A. from the Haas School of Business, University of California at Berkeley.

Rolf-Magnus Weddigen is a vice president in Bain & Company's Munich office. He is head of Bain's Private Equity practice for Germany. He serves financial investors and corporate clients in large European transactions and helps to create shareholder value in portfolio companies. His functional expertise is centered around private equity, venture capital, M&A, corporate and growth strategy development, sales and marketing optimization, and the development and implementation of full-potential programs. Rolf-Magnus is a graduate in mechanical engineering and business of the Technical University of Karlsruhe and earned an M.B.A. from INSEAD, Fontainebleau.